HEALTH
PROBLEMS
in the Classroom PreK-6

Advisory Board

HEALTH PROBLEMS
in the Classroom PreK-6

An A-Z Reference Guide for Educators

Dolores M. Huffman, RN, PhD
Karen Lee Fontaine, RN, MSN
Bernadette K. Price, RN, MSN, CMM

CORWIN PRESS, INC.
A Sage Publications Company
Thousand Oaks, California

For information:

Corwin Press, Inc.
A Sage Publications Company
2455 Teller Road
Thousand Oaks, California 91320
www.corwinpress.com

Sage Publications Ltd.
6 Bonhill Street
London EC2A 4PU
United Kingdom

Sage Publications India Pvt. Ltd.
B-42 Panchsheel Enclave
New Delhi 110 017 India

Printed in the United States of America

Library of Congress Cataloging-in-Publication Data

Huffman, Dolores M.
Health problems in the classroom PreK-6: An A-Z reference guide for
educators / Dolores M. Huffman, Karen Lee Fontaine, Bernadette K. Price.
    p. cm.
Includes bibliographical references and index.
    ISBN 0-7619-4577-6 (Cloth) — ISBN 0-7619-4578-4 (Paper) 1. School children—Health
and hygiene—United States—Handbooks, manuals, etc. 2. School health services—United
States—Handbooks, manuals, etc. 3. Health education (Elementary)—United
States—Handbooks, manuals, etc. I. Fontaine, Karen Lee, 1943- II. Price,
Bernadette K. III. Title.
LB3409.U5H84 2003
371.7'1—dc21

                                                2003002477

This book is printed on acid-free paper.

03   04   05   06   10   9   8   7   6   5   4   3   2   1

Acquisitions Editor:	Faye Zucker
Consulting Editor:	Patti Cleary
Editorial Assistant:	Stacy Wagner
Production Editor:	Diane S. Foster
Copy Editor:	D. J. Peck
Typesetter:	C&M Digitals (P) Ltd.
Proofreader:	Taryn L. Bigelow
Indexer:	Molly Hall
Cover Designer:	Michael Dubowe

Contents

Preface   xi

Acknowledgments   xv

About the Authors   xvii

PART I: HEALTH ISSUES IN THE CLASSROOM   1

1. Illness, Injury, and Disability in the Inclusive Classroom   3
   Common Health Problems   4
   Accidental Injury   5
   Chronic Illness   6
   Disabilities and Individualized Education Plans   7
   Hospitalization   9

2. Family and Community Issues   11
   Anger and Conflict Within the Family System   11
   Divorce, Remarriage, and Blended Families   12
   Chronic Illness or Disability Within the Family System   14
   Death   15
   Neglect and Abuse   16
   Homelessness   18
   Community Violence   18

3. Stigma and Student Self-Esteem   20
   Stigma, Prejudice, and Discrimination   20
   Self-Esteem   22
   Peer Relationships   24
   Gender Identity Issues   26
   Sexual Identity Issues Affecting Students and Families   27

PART II: HEALTH PROBLEMS A–Z   31
   Adjustment Disorder   32

Alcohol Abuse	34
Allergy: Drugs	37
Allergy: Food	39
Allergy: Hay Fever	42
Allergy: Latex	44
Anaphylaxis	47
Anemia/Iron Deficiency Anemia	50
Anger	52
Animal Bites	55
Anxiety Disorder: Generalized	57
Anxiety Disorder: Separation	60
Appendicitis	62
Asperger's Disorder	64
Asthma	67
Attention Deficit/Hyperactivity Disorder	70
Autistic Disorder	73
Behavior Disorders: Conduct Disorder	76
Behavior Disorders: Oppositional Defiant Disorder	79
Bipolar Disorder	82
Bladder Control Problems	85
Body Piercing Infection/Reaction	87
Bowel Control Problems	89
Bronchitis	92
Burns	94
Cancer	97
Cellulitis	100
Cerebral Palsy	102
Chicken Pox	105
Cold Sores	107
Color Blindness	109
Common Cold	112
Cystic Fibrosis	114
Depression	116
Diabetes	119
Diarrhea	122
Down Syndrome	124
Dystonia	126
Ear Infection	128
Eating Disorder: Anorexia	130
Eczema	132
Epilepsy/Seizure Disorder	134
Eye Injury	137

Eye Splash   139
Eye Stye   141
Fetal Alcohol Syndrome   143
Fever   145
Fifth Disease   147
Fractures   149
Frostbite   152
Grief   154
Headache   157
Head Injury   159
Head Lice   161
Hearing Loss   164
Heart Disease   166
Heat Exhaustion   168
Heatstroke   170
Hemophilia   172
Hepatitis A   174
Hepatitis B   176
Hepatitis C   178
HIV/AIDS   180
Human Bites   183
Impetigo   185
Inflammatory Bowel Disease   187
Influenza   189
Inhalant Abuse   191
Insect Bites and Stings   193
Juvenile Rheumatoid Arthritis   196
Lead Poisoning   199
Legg-Calvé-Perthes Disease   201
Lupus   203
Lyme Disease   206
Measles (German Measles)   209
Measles (Rubeola)   211
Meningitis   214
Mononucleosis   217
Mumps   219
Muscular Dystrophy   221
Nosebleed   224
Obesity   226
Obesity: Prader-Willi Syndrome   228
Obsessive Compulsive Disorder   230
Organ Transplant   233

Panic Disorder   235
Pediatric Autoimmune Neuropsychiatric Disorder   237
Phobia: Social   240
Phobia: Specific   242
Pica   244
Pink Eye   246
Pneumonia   249
Poisoning   251
Poison: Oak, Ivy, and Sumac   254
Posttraumatic Stress Disorder   256
Psoriasis   258
Reye's Syndrome   260
Rheumatic Fever   262
Rocky Mountain Spotted Fever   265
Scabies   268
Scarlet Fever   270
Schizophrenia   272
Scoliosis   275
Sensory Integration Dysfunction   277
Sexual Acting Out   280
Sickle Cell Anemia   282
Skin Infections: Fungal   285
Sleep Disorders   287
Snakebites   289
Spider Bites   292
Spina Bifida   294
Spinal Cord Injury: Acute Care   297
Spinal Cord Injury: Long-Term Care   299
Splinters   302
Staph Infection   304
Stomachache   306
Strep Throat   308
Suicide   310
Swimmer's Ear/Foreign Object in Ear   312
Tattooing Infection/Reaction   314
Thyroid Disorder   316
Tooth Abscess   318
Toothache   320
Tooth Injuries   322
Tourette's Syndrome   324
Tuberculosis   326
Urinary Tract Infection   329

Vision Problems 331
Whooping Cough 333
Worms 335

PART III: HEALTH POLICIES AND PROCEDURES 339
Procedure A: Hand Washing 340
Procedure B: Care of Minor Cuts/
    Abrasions and Lacerations 343
Procedure C: Care of Casts 345
Procedure D: Care of Tracheostomy 347
Procedure E: Tube Feedings 350
Procedure F: Medical Emergencies 353
Procedure G: Pets in the Classroom 355
Procedure H: Immunizations 358
Procedure I: EpiPen 361

Bibliography 364
Index 367

Preface

School-age children with a variety of common health problems, chronic illnesses, and disabilities are present in virtually every school system across the United States. Because these children are now included in the regular classroom environment, it is important for teachers, classroom aides, school administrators, and day care providers to be familiar with their unique health care needs.

The classroom teacher is often at the forefront in responding to classroom emergencies, recognizing potential health problems, and providing support to children living with chronic illness or disability. This book is a valuable and easy-to-use resource for teachers, school staff, and others in learning about various health problems and the appropriate classroom management of these problems. The goal of this book is to provide concise and practical information about selected health problems that teachers are likely to encounter in their classrooms. It is not, however, within the scope of this book to address every health problem known to school-age children or to include every known situation that can occur in the classroom environment. The authors realize that every child is unique and that deviations from suggested guidelines sometimes must be considered.

How This Book Is Organized

Part I provides an overview. Chapter 1 covers common health problems, accidental injuries, chronic illness, disability, and the effects of hospitalization on children and their impact on the classroom milieu. Chapter 2 discusses family and community issues influencing school-age children and offers strategies for promoting positive development of children. The central focus of Chapter 3 is stigmatizing issues associated with children. This chapter specifically addresses the concerns of labeling children and the importance of promoting self-esteem in children. Relationships related to peers, gender identity issues, and sexual identity are also discussed.

Part II is an alphabetical reference guide to 130 health problems that affect preK–6 students. Arranged for covenient "at-a-glance" review, each topic identifies a common health problem, chronic disease, or disability and then offers the following coverage of the topic:

- Provides other names by which the same problem/illness is known or referred to
- Gives a brief description of the problem/illness written in language appropriate for laypersons
- Identifies primary groups affected by the health concern
- Offers associated signs and symptoms
- Presents suggested classroom guidelines with cross-references to appropriate health policies and procedures as well as other related health problems
- Recommends attendance guidelines
- Indicates medications that the child may be taking
- Suggests communication topics to be discussed with a parent or caregiver
- Lists authoritative resources such as national organizations associated with the health problem or illness and possible Web sites where teachers can obtain further information

Part III provides a variety of useful health policies and procedures. This section describes the appropriate method of hand washing as the most effective way in which to decrease the spread of infectious disease in school-age children. In addition, it provides a pictorial guide for administering epinephrine in emergency situations and offers procedures for providing for the needs of children with casts, tracheostomies, and tubes for feeding. Additional sections list medical emergencies that warrant immediate response, a schedule of immunizations, a table of infectious diseases related to pets and reptiles that may be found in the classroom, and guidelines for handling bleeding, cuts, and abrasions. It is the hope of the authors to adequately address the concerns of teachers regarding appropriate management of health issues in the classroom.

How to Use This Book

The intent of this book is to provide an easy reference for school personnel to access in the event of encountering students who are experiencing health problems or concerns in the classroom. Teachers who just want to increase their knowledge in assisting students with a myriad of health concerns may also find this book of value. In addition, this book provides suggested guidelines for managing specific health problems in the most effective and least disruptive manner. Teachers can refer to the alphabetical listing of each health problem.

Health problems are identified in this book by both their common names and medical nomenclature. A boldface **911** label is assigned to selected signs and symptoms. This **911** designation serves as an alert that this selected sign or symptom may be indicating a medical emergency or life-threatening situation so that the teacher may want to elicit immediate medical assistance for this child. Classroom guidelines are intended to suggest certain strategies or techniques in planning for the health needs of children present in the classroom. Teachers can refer to the communication section for identifying key questions to be addressed so that the child experiencing health problems can be successfully integrated into the classroom environment. Teachers who desire to further their knowledge beyond the scope of this book may find the selected resources valuable in enhancing their understanding of school-age children's health issues.

Acknowledgments

The authors gratefully acknowledge the comments and support we received from our Advisory Board and from the many individuals who offered us substantive textual contributions:

Judith Conedera, R.N., M.S.N., C.P.N.P., associate professor, School of Nursing, Purdue University Calumet, Hammond, IN

Dennis R. Cullen, D.D.S., Munster, IN

Renee Fife, R.N., M.S.N., assistant professor, School of Nursing, Purdue University Calumet, Hammond, IN

Ellen E. Moore, R.N., M.H.S.N., C.S.–F.N.P., associate professor, School of Nursing, Purdue University Calumet, Hammond, IN

Chris Reid, R.N., M.S.N., associate professor, School of Nursing, Purdue University Calumet, Hammond, IN

Susan Siwinski-Hebel, R.N., M.S.N., C.C.R.C., lecturer, Indiana University Northwest, Gary, IN

Joy Whitman, Ph.D., associate professor, School of Education, Purdue University Calumet, Hammond, IN

Nan Yancey, R.N., M.S.N., associate professor, College of Nursing and Health Professionals, Lewis University, Romeoville, IN

Corwin Press gratefully acknowledges the contributions of the following reviewers:

Michelle Barnea, educational consultant, early childhood consulting and training, Millburn, NJ

Dottie Bauer, assistant professor of education, Keene State College, Keene, NH

Anita Davis, Chair, Charles A. Dana professor of education and director of elementary education, Converse College, Spartanburg, SC

Neil Izenberg, M.D., director, KidsHealth.org; director, Nemours Foundation Center for Children's Health Media, Alfred I. duPont Hospital for Children, Wilmington, DE

Dianne Koontz Lowman, assistant professor of occupational therapy, Virginia Commonwealth University, Richmond, VA

About the Authors

Dolores M. Huffman, R.N., Ph.D., has been a nursing educator for more than 30 years. In her academic career, she has taught classroom health issues for elementary teachers. In addition, she has been employed as a community health nurse. In that capacity, she has worked with families of school-age children living with disability and has previously served as a camp nurse for special needs children. Her interests cover the health needs of persons across the life span. She is currently Associate Professor of Nursing at Purdue University Calumet in Hammond, Indiana, where she may be reached by e-mail at huffman@calumet.purdue.edu.

Karen Lee Fontaine, R.N., M.S.N., is Professor of Nursing at Purdue University Calumet, where she has been teaching for 20 years. She is also a certified sex therapist and maintains a private practice counseling individuals and couples. Her publishing awards include the American Journal of Nursing Book of the Year Award (2000) for *Healing Practices: Alternative Therapies for Nursing* and the Annual Nursing Book Review Sigma Theta Tau (2000) for *Mental Health Nursing* (4th edition). Her distinguishing academic honors include the Luther Christman Excellence in Published Writing Award, Gamma Phi Chapter, Sigma Theta Tau, Rush University (1997) and Distinguished Lecturer, Sigma Theta Tau International (1994–1995). She has also served on the Editorial Advisory Board of the *Journal of Couple and Relationship Therapy* since 2000.

Bernadette K. Price, R.N., M.S.N., C.M.M., is a nurse midwife in private practice. Previously, she was Associate Professor of Nursing at Purdue University Calumet for 15 years. During her years in education, she taught maternity and pediatrics courses as well as a course for elementary education students about health problems in the classroom. During her three decades in nursing, she has worked with infants, school-age children, and adolescents in many different settings, including staff nursing in maternity, clinic and office settings, home visits with new families, Healthy Start and Head Start programs, and many community education programs. She can be reached by e-mail at bprice@comnetcom.net.

PART I

Health Issues in the Classroom

1

Illness, Injury, and Disability in the Inclusive Classroom

Elementary education teachers, preschool teachers, and day care workers are confronted and challenged in their settings by the presence of students who have some types of health problems. These problems can range from common illnesses, such as colds and influenza, to more serious medical circumstances, such as injuries, chronic illnesses, and disabilities. Advances in medical science and technology have dramatically influenced the survival rates among children living with chronic and serious health problems. As a result of changing attitudes and legislation, many children previously excluded from school are now integrated into the classroom. With these changes, teachers have had to learn new skills to respond to the needs of this particular student population. In addition, budget constraints have decreased the number of school nurses, forcing teachers to recognize potential health problems, provide support for those with chronic conditions, and respond to classroom emergencies. This book is designed to assist teachers and day care workers in the promotion of safety and well-being of all their students.

This chapter provides a basic introduction to the health problems and accidental injuries seen most frequently in young and preteen children. The chapter also provides an overview of the impact of chronic illness and long-term disabilities on the developmental stages and educational needs of these children. Attention is given to the effects of hospitalization during these formative years.

Common Health Problems

Colds are one of the leading causes of school absences in children. Estimates indicate that school-age children have as many as four or five colds a year. Although medical science has not been able to eliminate this common health problem, teachers can intervene proactively to reduce the number of colds that children experience, which then reduces the number of days they are absent from school. This information is found in Part II (*see* Common Colds) and in Part III (*see* Procedure A: Hand Washing).

Another common health problem seen in the classroom is head lice (pediculosis) (*see* Head Lice). Current estimates from the Centers for Disease Control and Prevention (CDC) are that head lice affects 6 million people worldwide. The most common infestation in the United States is among schoolchildren between the ages of 5 and 12 years. Because many schools restrict attendance until the children are completely free of lice, school days are lost and academic performance is affected. Teachers must be vigilant to prevent children with lice from becoming victims of teasing and taunting from their classmates.

Allergy (*see* Allergy entries) is another common health problem in school-age children. It is estimated that approximately one in every five children suffers from some form of allergy. Numerous allergens (substances that cause allergic responses) can be the cause of an allergic response. For example, exposure to pollen, dust mites, animals, insect bites, and smelling or eating certain foods or medications may initiate a child's allergic response. Symptoms can range from a runny nose, watery eyes, and sneezing (*see* Allergy: Hay Fever) to life-threatening situations (*see* Anaphylaxis). The effects in the classroom can range from poorer academic performance of an individual child to complete disruption of the classroom environment. Teachers must be ever alert to the signs and symptoms of severe reactions because there are many items in the classroom that can trigger an allergic response (*see* Allergy: Latex). Teachers must be well informed on the procedure of administering an epinephrine injection to students with life-threatening allergic responses and whose health care providers have recommended this course of treatment (*see* Procedure I: EpiPen).

These are just a few examples of common health problems encountered by teachers in their day-to-day interactions with children. Each day, teachers must understand the health concerns of children and often must make independent decisions regarding the management of these problems. In some instances, teachers play a role in reducing occurrences of health problems through preventive measures. In other situations, teachers initiate or follow through on strategies to manage health problems and bolster learning and academic achievement.

Accidental Injury

Accidental or unintentional injuries of school-age children have been identified as the major health problem encountered by school personnel. Annually, approximately 4 million children between the ages of 5 and 18 years are injured on school property. Injury-related problems account for 80% of visits to the school nurse. A compilation of statistics from several national studies indicates the following characteristics of injuries to school-age children:

- Approximately 38% of injuries occur in elementary schools.
- Most injuries occur on school playgrounds.
- The majority of injuries occur during the first 2 months of the school year.
- Morning hours and the lunch period are the most frequent times for injuries.
- Those in kindergarten have the least number of injuries, while first-graders have the greatest number of injuries.
- The head, arms, and legs are at highest risk for injury.
- Broken bones and injuries associated with falls account for the most serious accidents.
- Boys are at higher risk than girls, especially when boys are involved in organized sports or "pickup" athletic games.
- The rate of injury on asphalt surfaces is six times greater than that on sand or grass.

The CDC, in its 2001 report on *School Health Guidelines to Prevent Unintentional Injuries and Violence,* provides guidance for the prevention of accidental injuries in the school setting. Some of these guidelines are as follows:

- Establish a social environment that promotes safety and prevention of unintentional injuries.

- Implement health curricula and instruction that advocate health and safety. Through this provision, students develop the knowledge, attitudes, behavioral skills, and confidence necessary to adopt and maintain safe lifestyles.
- Provide safe physical education and extracurricular physical activity programs.
- Arrange for programs that teach and encourage all school personnel ways in which to promote safety and prevent accidents.

The rate of accidents can be decreased through preventive measures such as education and enforcement of safety rules and standards. These include the use of batting helmets for baseball; helmets, elbow, and knee pads for bicycling or skating; and mouth guards for contact sports. Following safety rules and using the right equipment makes for "smart and better players" and reduces children's vulnerability to injuries. Teachers who discuss and model healthy habits instill in their students a way of life that will serve them well throughout life.

Chronic Illness

Approximately 31% of children in the United States have some type of chronic illness with varying degrees of severity. Children living with chronic illness have a significantly greater number of obstacles to overcome. These hurdles may include alterations in normal growth and development, exclusion from certain classroom activities, a sense of being different from the other children, and excessive absences from school. Teachers who are knowledgeable about these unique health and educational challenges are able to respond sensitively and appropriately to students with chronic illness.

Not surprisingly, children who have excessive absences from school face more challenges in meeting academic standards and outcomes. The school environment not only provides opportunities for children to learn but also encourages children to interact, work together, resolve conflicts, and solve problems. With this process comes a feeling of accomplishment and a growing sense of autonomy. Children who miss school due to chronic illness are deprived of these invaluable experiences.

Asthma (*see* Asthma), one example of a chronic illness, is the most common long-term respiratory illness in children. It is the leading cause of health-related absenteeism, with more than 10 million school days missed each year. When children experience breathing difficulties, their attention is focused on their bodies and their anxiety levels increase. Inattention and anxiety interfere with the ability to learn. When this becomes a frequent or chronic situation, children with asthma may be at increased risk for learning problems. Not wanting to feel different from their peers, they may refrain from using their medications in front of other children or may avoid informing their teachers that they are in need of some assistance. Knowledgeable teachers are attuned to these problems and may be able to intervene before these situations worsen.

For children with chronic illness, having understanding teachers is critical for a positive school experience and academic success. For those schoolchildren who have no health problems, the sensitivity and role modeling by teachers often makes the difference between their acceptance and rejection of these vulnerable children. Teachers can gain knowledge regarding health problems from school health personnel, communications with parents/caregivers/children, this book, and resources available on the World Wide Web. Knowledgeable teachers are less likely to act on the basis of their acceptance or rejection of these biases and prejudices, and they are more likely to create a sensitive and caring school environment.

Disabilities and Individualized Education Plans

There are several labels that refer to the process of integrating children with disabilities in the regular classroom. This concept has been identified by some school systems as "mainstreaming," "regular education initiative," "full inclusion," "partial inclusion," or "inclusion." Regardless of the selected terminology, current federal laws, such as the Individuals with Disabilities Education Act (IDEA), mandate that a child with a disability has a right to attend free and appropriate public education in the least restrictive environment provided by his or her local school system. In response to these legislative directives and considerable commitment of some school districts, tremendous strides have been made in overcoming challenges in providing disabled children with access to education.

The U.S. Census Bureau indicates that 6.5 million children have some type of disability and that 96% of these students attend regular schools with their nondisabled classmates. Based on such statistical data, it is vital that all teachers have an understanding of these children's abilities and disabilities and of the unique needs inherent in being disabled. A knowledgeable and sensitive teacher, who understands a student's Individualized Educational Plan (IEP) and meets the student's needs, will do much in creating a classroom environment where "inclusion" is a positive experience for children with and without disabilities.

Common disabilities seen in children include impairments of speech, hearing, and sight as well as learning problems. In addition, some students have activity limitations and restrictions such as being confined to a wheelchair and requiring the use of a cane or walker. Regardless of the source of the disability, the teacher working with such a school-age child can significantly affect his or her ability to achieve the developmental task of gaining a sense of accomplishment and diminish feelings of inferiority. A focus on the child's strengths or abilities rather than on the disability may give the child a new perspective of what he or she believes can be accomplished and may foster a sense of self-worth. The child who attends school has the advantages of learning and socializing with a diverse group of peers and has the disadvantage of confronting the fact that he or she is "different" and may be the focus of ridicule and exclusion by classmates. The teacher who is sensitive to what it means to live with a disability, plans activities in which all children can participate, and models acceptance of differences may have a significant impact on the child's sense of belonging while enhancing nondisabled students' understanding of disability.

The child with a disability brings to the classroom a vast array of concerns to be addressed by school systems. In addition to educational issues, these concerns include the following:

- Arranging for a safe exit from the classroom in case of an emergency situation
- Sensitizing nondisabled students to promote inclusion without embarrassing or breaching the confidentiality of the disabled child
- Developing learning strategies that take into consideration the disabled child's frequent absenteeism and energy level
- Planning a classroom schedule that meets the unique health needs of the child

The teacher will need to communicate with parents/caregivers, school health and educational personnel, and the child to better understand these concerns. Enhanced understanding will ensure appropriate planning for the disabled child's successful integration into the classroom.

In addition to educational and safety concerns, teachers have identified fears related to appropriately responding to medical emergencies associated with specific disabilities in children. Classroom emergencies such as seizures (*see* Epilepsy/Seizure Disorder), a sudden onset of flushed and sweating skin in a child with spinal cord injury (*see* Spinal Cord Injury: Long-Term Care), and difficulty with breathing in a child with cystic fibrosis (*see* Cystic Fibrosis) involve knowledgeable teachers who understand both the significance and the urgency of responding to these situations. Access to information, training, and identification of resource personnel are crucial in addressing these issues and in decreasing the worries of teachers.

The importance of school in the lives of all children is well known. For a child with a disability, being in school serves to afford him or her a sense of normalcy and acceptance. Therefore, teachers play a significant role in enhancing the disabled child's self-esteem and in assisting him or her to have a positive view in attaining an education.

Hospitalization

Hospitalization is a traumatic experience for all children. A school-age child who is hospitalized may experience a variety of feelings due to being absent from school and thrust into an unfamiliar environment over which he or she has little or no control. The child's reaction will depend on many factors, including age, developmental stage, reason for hospitalization, and support of family and friends. The younger school-age child is more susceptible to the stresses of hospitalization and appears to have more difficulty in adapting.

Psychosocial responses to hospitalization in children may include anxiety related to separation from family and friends, a sense of isolation, regression and withdrawal, anger (*see* Anger), panic attacks (*see* Panic Disorder), and fear of the unknown. Further sources of anxiety for the child who is hospitalized may include being confronted by a number of strangers in the hospital, experiences of pain, environmental changes, and special procedures. The child may even view the hospitalization as punishment for wrongdoing. For example, diabetic children (*see* Diabetes), who consistently select food items from the cafeteria that are not conducive to their health, may interpret the hospitalization as their fault for not adhering to diet restrictions. Unfortunately, long-lasting emotional problems can occur in children who have experienced very stressful hospitalizations.

Another common reaction among hospitalized children is a feeling of isolation. Children who are absent from school frequently worry about not being with their friends. Anticipating that friends develop new relationships and exclude them from school and social events troubles these children. In addition, these children may be concerned that teachers will treat them differently and that special tasks assigned to them will be delegated to other classmates. They also may be struggling with the feelings of being different from other children due to their hospitalizations. Teachers' and classmates' visits, notes, telephone calls, e-mails, and videotapings may help to alleviate some feelings of isolation for these children and may serve to decrease some of the stressors associated with hospitalization.

A sick child normally exhibits signs of regression and withdrawal. As a result, the child who is hospitalized frequently experiences a sense of helplessness and dependency on others. The teacher may observe that after hospitalization, when the child is back in the classroom environment, the child requests more assistance, feels unable to learn new skills, may resist involvement in classroom activities, or becomes uncharacteristically compliant. The child also may become easily frustrated and readily relinquish control of a task to peers. The support and encouragement of the teacher will enhance the child's ability to conquer feelings of inadequacy and regain his or her sense of independence.

Although hospitalization can be stressful for children, it is also important to realize that it can also be very beneficial. Recovery from an illness is the most apparent benefit, but hospitalization can also assist children in learning to deal with stress and to cope with new situations. Emphasizing these positive experiences can serve to increase children's sense of well-being and can negate some of the unpleasant effects associated with the hospital experience in school-age children.

2

Family and Community Issues

A number of family and community issues affect the physical, emotional, cognitive, and academic development of children. Because development occurs in the context of relationships, understanding children as a part of their families and communities provides a holistic perspective. This chapter is an overview of the impact on children's development of familial conflict and abuse as well as adjustment problems within the community.

For most of us, families are our earliest and most enduring social relationships. As the fabric of our day-to-day lives, families shape the quality of our lives by influencing our outlooks on life, our motivation and strategies for achievement, and our approaches to coping with adversity. Within our families, we develop our sense of self and our capacity for intimacy. Through family interactions, we learn about relationships and roles and about our expectations of others and ourselves. As individuals and family members, we are simultaneously independent of and part of our families.

Anger and Conflict Within the Family System

Anger and conflict are a normal part of living with others and are a dimension of family process. Conflict can be either constructive or destructive to individuals and to the family system as a whole. Constructive conflict is issue focused and involves strategies of negotiating and mutual problem solving. Destructive conflict escalates beyond the initial issue and involves threats and coercion as strategies.

Expression of anger within the family is not necessarily harmful. In fact, it is healthy for children to observe anger in adults when conflicts are expressed constructively and are perhaps resolved. It is through this family process that children find out how to work out disagreements and learn appropriate ways in which to handle interpersonal differences with friends, peers, and loved ones.

When anger is combined with criticism, contempt, defensiveness, or withdrawal, conflict becomes destructive to individuals and the family system. Children who witness unhealthy conflict show greater emotional and behavioral reactivity and often are inappropriately drawn into adult disputes. Adults who engage in repeated negative and hostile interactions are less able to parent their children effectively. Daily, intense adult-adult conflict makes family life unpleasant, may cause a breakdown in discipline, and decreases adults' sensitivity to children's needs. The spillover effect of adult-adult destructive conflict is the transfer of negative mood, affect, or behavior to the adult-child relationship. Children react not so much to the fact that adults are fighting as to the impact of conflict on their sense of security. Children worry about possible divorce and what will happen to everyone in the family. If the themes of the adult conflict are child related, such as fighting over discipline or spending money on toys, then children experience greater shame and self-blame than if the themes are adult related.

Exposure to destructive conflict increases children's vulnerability to disorders such as depression and anxiety. Destructive conflict also increases the probability that children themselves will become aggressive with others and will develop oppositional defiant disorder or conduct disorder. These disorders are presented in Part II (*see* Behavior Disorders entries).

Divorce, Remarriage, and Blended Families

Divorce is a transitional crisis that interrupts children's developmental tasks. Divorce forces major practical as well as emotional readjustments, and short-term distress is normal. As in other family crises—job loss, serious illness, death—the key that determines whether the crisis is temporary or results in permanent impairment is the family's response and coping abilities. Even divorces that are handled well both emotionally and financially may contribute to temporary maladjustment in children. Studies show that, after a period of time, children who have experienced divorce differ very little from those who have not experienced divorce.

The transitional crisis consists of two overlapping phases: (a) separation and legal divorce and (b) settling in to the new family structure. When adults work at the transition in healthy ways, it takes 2 to 3 years for a family to adjust to its new structure. When emotional issues are not resolved or there is an angry and vengeful divorce, a family can remain stuck for years, perhaps even for generations.

The new family structure, referred to as the binuclear family, consists of two households—those of both parents—and both extended family networks. Ground rules are established for living separately such as where the children will reside and how visitation is arranged.

When parents remarry or form a new family unit, the new structure is referred to as a blended family. The two expected peaks of emotional tension are at the time of a parent's serious commitment to a new relationship and again at the time of actual formation of a blended family. If both parents blend families at about the same time, children may feel as though they are on an emotional roller coaster. In addition, all children suffer when there is intense conflict between their biological parents, and they benefit when parents maintain civil, cooperative, co-parental relationships.

New relationships are harder to negotiate because they do not develop gradually (as intact families do) but rather begin midstream. Children cannot forget the relationships that existed before and that may still be more powerful than the new relationships. Children rarely surrender their attachments to their first parents, no matter how negative the relationships. Preschool children, given time and encouragement, adjust most easily to new blended families. Family integration is harder when members include adolescents. Both girls and boys in early adolescence, beginning at age 11 or 12 years, seem to have a particularly difficult time in adjusting to blended families. If they are concerned about being distanced and individuating from their families of origin, teens especially will often resist learning new roles and relating to new family members.

One of the greatest challenges for parents is to allow children to experience and express the full range of negative and positive feelings toward both sets of parents and stepparents. Often, parents will subtly or directly demand the children's complete allegiance. Children feel caught—afraid that if they do not express love for a new stepparent, they will anger one parent, but that if they do, they are being disloyal and will lose the love of the other parent. Some children attempt to resolve their divided loyalties by taking sides or by playing one side against the other.

Children's struggles with blended family issues may surface at school. If depressed or anxious, they may withdraw from teachers and peers. Or they may engage in acting out or antisocial behaviors. Suggestions for classroom management of these problems are provided in Part II.

Chronic Illness or Disability Within the Family System

Chronic illness or disability often places the family under significant levels of stress. The family must master the practical and emotional tasks of the immediate situation while trying to plan for the uncertainties of the future. Family burden is the overall level of distress experienced as a result of the illness or disability. This burden includes disruption in household functioning, restriction of social activities, and financial hardship due to medical bills and perhaps the loss of one income. Hospitalization for acute episodes leads to disruption of the family system as children suffer from repeated separations and an unpredictable environment.

When chronic illness or disability of a parent occurs during the child-rearing phase in the family life cycle, it usually serves to prolong this period. Appropriate reallocation of roles and high levels of adaptability and problem solving may make the difference between successful and dysfunctional coping and adaptation. The new structure of the family may resemble a single-parent family with an added "dependent"—the ill or disabled adult. It is likely that the well parent will have to turn to the children to share responsibilities. In some cases, children may have to sacrifice their own developmental needs.

In general, illness and disability tend to push individual and family developmental processes toward transition and increased cohesion. Symptoms, loss of function, demands of new roles, and fear of loss through death all require the family members to pull together. Relapsing illnesses alternate between periods of drawing the family inward and periods of release from the immediate demands of the disease.

Death

Coming to terms with death is the most difficult task a family must confront in life. The death of a family member radically disrupts the family system. The first priority in managing the crisis of grief is to reestablish a stable equilibrium that is necessary to support ongoing family development. The fewer the family resources—extended family, friends, financial supports—the more the family system will be stressed. Family members need to be able to talk with one another about their emotions concerning the death and its circumstances. A family's ability to communicate about death is partially determined by its members' previous patterns of communication. When individuals are unable to talk about the death, any misconceptions about the cause or circumstances cannot be corrected. For example, in some families the cause of death is never told to children, who then grow up with questions or distorted ideas.

Children experience the same emotions of grief as do adults but are less likely to show acute grief during the initial phase and are more likely to experience the process over a much longer period of time. At each developmental level, children rework the meaning of a family member's death from more mature levels of cognitive and emotional functioning. Preverbal children understand death as a separation, not as a finite end to life. They are often convinced that the deceased person could come back if she or he really wanted to come back. When children develop language skills at the age of 2 to 3 years, they can begin the process of comprehending death and its causes, although they still believe death to be reversible. School-age children tend to be more avoidant in speaking of their grief than do either preschoolers or teens, resulting in an appearance of unconcern. Because they equate death with abandonment, this age group is especially vulnerable to reacting with depression, self-blame, and low self-esteem for some months.

Children's reactions to the death of a parent depend in part on the degree of caretaking they have lost, the emotional state of the surviving parent, and the availability of other caretakers. It is important that adults do not underestimate the significance of the loss, especially for those children who verbalize few of their feelings.

When a child in a family dies, the needs of the surviving siblings are too often neglected. If the child who dies was ill for an extended period, the siblings may have had less attention to their needs for some time. Normal sibling rivalry may contribute to intense survival guilt that can block normal growth and development. Complicating the loss is a sense of also losing the parents, who may be preoccupied with their own grief. Parents may also become overprotective of the surviving children, leading to difficulties with autonomy and separation.

All family members play roles both within and outside the family. Realignment of roles is a necessary function of grieving. Roles may be reassigned on the basis of achievement and interest or on the basis of gender and age. Individuals must adapt and adjust to the new roles and the absence of the deceased member. The more flexible family will typically be more successful. Like individuals, families are unique in their mourning processes. What is effective for one family might not be effective for another.

Neglect and Abuse

Abuse refers to a pattern of behavior that dominates, controls, lowers self-esteem, and/or takes away freedom of choice. It is systematic persecution of another individual, ranging from subtle words or actions to violent battering—acts of commission. Abuse also includes various types of neglect—acts of omission. In all 50 states, teachers are required by law to report suspected incidents of child abuse, and there is a penalty—civil, criminal, or both—for failure to report child abuse.

Each year, approximately 2.8 million American children experience at least one act of physical violence, and 1.4 million are otherwise abused or neglected. Children who live in homes in which a parent is being abused are 1,500 times more likely to be abused than the national average. Physical abuse is often disguised as discipline. For many, hitting begins when they are infants and does not end until they leave home. Younger children are spanked, punched, grabbed, slapped, kicked, bitten, and hit with fists or objects. Boys are at a higher risk for serious or even fatal injuries. Adolescents are more likely to be beaten up and to have a knife or gun used against them.

Emotional abuse is often equally as damaging as physical abuse. Words can hit as hard as a fist, and the damage to self-esteem can last a lifetime. Emotional abuse involves one person shaming, embarrassing, ridiculing, or insulting another person either in private or in public. It may include the destruction of personal property or the killing of pets in an effort to frighten or control the victim. Statements such as "You can't do anything right," "You're ugly and stupid—no one else would want you," and "I wish you had never been born" are devastating to self-esteem.

Neglect is the most frequently reported type of child maltreatment. It includes lack of adequate physical care, nutrition, and shelter. It also includes unsanitary conditions that often contribute to health and developmental problems. Lack of human contact and nurturance is considered to be emotional neglect.

In the United States, homicide is one of the five leading causes of death before the age of 18 years. Fully 60% of children who are killed by their parents/caretakers are under the age of 4 years, and 40% are less than 1 year old. Most of these deaths are from battering in response to colic in the infant, to toilet training difficulties in the toddler, and to special needs children.

Victims develop low self-esteem as they begin to believe that the abuse they endure is evidence of personal worthlessness. The effect of living in a climate of fear and uncertainty contributes to an increased risk for several mental disorders, including depression, substance abuse, self-mutilation, and eating disorders. Fully 60% to 85% of abused children are at risk for posttraumatic stress disorder. Family violence has the worst mental health outcomes of any form of inter-personal violence because there is no safe and supportive place for retreat.

Childhood sexual abuse is a process, not just an event. Not all children become symptomatic following sexual abuse; some might not encounter difficulties until adulthood, and some might never experience symptoms. A single traumatic experience does not usually lead to mental disorders. To the extent that other life experiences are positive, children are likely to have no or few long-term effects. To the extent that other life experiences are also negative, the effects of the sexual abuse are amplified.

There is no identified "sexual abuse syndrome," and reactions vary greatly from one child to another. The effects of sex abuse are most severe when the incidents are frequent and occur over a long period of time, the activities are wide ranging and extensive, there is more than one perpetrator, the relationship to the perpetrator is close, and sex abuse is combined with physical and emotional abuse. In these situations, behavioral, cognitive, and physical problems emerge, as do difficulties with emotional stability and interpersonal relationships, during childhood, adolescence, and adulthood.

Abuse disrupts the smooth progression of development in several ways. For some, there is an intensification and fixation of the current developmental stage. Others regress to an earlier stage. And some prematurely accelerate and develop a pseudo-maturity. The general rule of thumb is that the earlier the abuse, the more profound the damage.

Homelessness

For the past 25 years, more than a half million Americans have been left homeless, living on city streets, and (if they are lucky) sleeping in emergency shelters each night. The homeless include people of every race, ethnic background, and educational level. Families now constitute 37% of the homeless population. Many homeless families are headed by women who take their children and flee from abusive husbands or partners. One of the most profound effects of homelessness is that families may lose their sense of identity as a family, parents may lose their sense of competence, and children may lose their concept of home.

Many adolescents find themselves living on their own as a consequence of running away or being thrown out of their homes by their families. Some leave to escape physical or sexual abuse. In other situations, parents of acting-out adolescents may force the teens out of their homes as a way of gaining control in their own lives. Adolescents also become homeless because of family conflict, chaotic family systems, and unsuccessful foster care situations.

Homelessness has a significant impact on the education of children. The inability to prove residency for local school systems becomes an enrollment problem. Live-in shelters often have a time limit for residency, after which the family must seek a different shelter. This situation disrupts the educational process by forcing school changes every few months. Multiple new curricula, new teachers, and new peers make for poor educational outcomes.

Community Violence

Violence in the United States has reached epidemic proportions in urban, suburban, and rural areas. Although urban youth may experience higher levels of exposure than do others, children in general are exposed to a startling amount of violence. Those who are not direct victims or witnesses hear stories of violence told by family members, peers, and neighbors. The media also present many models of violence to which children are exposed. Some movies and television shows demonstrate that "good" people use force to achieve "good" ends. Many story lines make no attempt to justify the use of force for "good" ends; they simply portray endless senseless acts of cruelty by one human on another. With these types of community and media examples, children develop values that tolerate, and even accept as normal, everyday violence between people.

A child dies from a gunshot wound every 2 hours, and many more are seriously wounded. Armed assailants are becoming significantly younger, with nearly half between the ages of 11 and 20 years. Males, the chief perpetrators and also the chief victims of violent acts, are twice as likely as females to be victimized by other males. Males also hurt themselves at a much higher rate, with a suicide rate four times that of teen girls.

Affective violence is the verbal expression of intense anger and emotions. It is the bullying, ugly taunts, disrespect, alienation, scapegoating, and physical threats that many children experience every day. Victims of affective violence are more likely to experience distress and depression than are children who are not subjected to it. More research is needed on how exposure to violence affects growth and development, intellectual growth, school performance, decision making ability, and hope for the future.

Children who are at risk for becoming violent often are unable or unwilling to accept responsibility for their choices and behaviors. When things go wrong, they blame others. As a teacher, you may hear, "She started it" or "I couldn't help it, he made me do it." Some violence-prone children alienate their peers by interrupting, intruding in particular situations, invading personal space, and treating the property of others as if it were their own. When there is conflict with peers or adults, they often refuse to back down, even on little points.

Even young children can be taught the concept of good choices versus bad choices. As a teacher, you need to establish reasonable and meaningful consequences for both good and bad decisions. Excuses are not accepted for bad choices, and the focus returns to the children's personal decisions regarding behavior.

Victims, victimizers (bullies), and bystanders (observers) all need to be involved in antiviolence intervention. Schools should have zero tolerance for bullying, victimization, and standing by during violent acts. The Centers for Disease Control and Prevention has developed a program called *Best Practices for Youth Violence* to assist schools and communities in formulating and implementing appropriate interventions. Call (888) 252–7751 to obtain a free copy.

3

Stigma
and Student
Self-Esteem

A number of stigmatizing issues affect the emotional, cognitive, and academic development of children. Because development occurs in the context of relationships, understanding how children are marginalized provides a holistic perspective. This chapter provides an overview of stereotypes, discrimination, gender identity issues, and sexual identity issues and their impact on children's dignity and belief in their selves. It also provides suggestions to assist students in developing positive self-esteem.

Stigma, Prejudice, and Discrimination

Stigmas are created when individuals possess personal attributes and belong to social categories that make them different from others in such a way that they are perceived as tainted, discounted, and/or discredited. The effect of being seen as having a stigma, then, leads people to being stigmatized and assigned labels according to their differences from the norm, the norm depending on the environment or culture in which these individuals are immersed. These labels bring with them negative connotations, which lead to disrespecting those individuals being stigmatized, creating barriers between people, and interrupting communication. At its worst, labeling results in fear and mistrust of others, prejudice, discrimination, and even violence.

When stigmas are being assigned to individuals, stereotypes are being used. Stereotypes are assessments and beliefs we create about groups of people based on characteristics of those groups. They limit us in that we look for those characteristics that agree with our preconceived ideas about a group and disregard the evidence that does not fit with our beliefs. When we use stereotypes to form opinions of individuals, we ignore the unique characteristics of the individuals in front of us and assign them characteristics we believe to be true of the group to which these individuals may belong. For example, we may have a stereotype of gay men as effeminate, Asian Americans as smart, Jewish Americans as thrifty, or lesbians as masculine. When meeting a lesbian, we may expect her to like to do "manly" things or to look like a man when in fact she does not. Engaging in these kinds of stereotyping behavior allows us to easily move to stigmatizing individuals, holding prejudices about them, and then discriminating against them.

Prejudice is similar to stigmatizing and stereotyping in that it is maintaining a negative feeling about people who are different from us. Prejudicial attitudes are based on limited knowledge, early learning, limited contact, and emotional responses rather than on careful observation and thoughts. They are beliefs, opinions, or points of view that are formed before the facts are known—or in spite of them. They often operate as if they were the "truth," which makes them difficult to change unless they are actively counteracted.

Discrimination is prejudice that is expressed behaviorally. When people discriminate against others, they are using prejudice, stereotypes, and stigma to justify their actions. These actions often include behaviors such as denial of access to resources (e.g., education, a job), power (e.g., advancement in a career), and respect (e.g., assuming women are not good at math and so expecting less of female students).

In addition, acts of racism, heterosexism, ageism, ethnocentrism, sexism, classism, and ableism are examples of discrimination. Each of these "isms" involves a tendency to judge others according to similarity to or dissimilarity from a standard considered ideal or normal and is shaped by personal or group judgments. In a society composed of multiple groups, we must counteract such biases, or isms, to prevent discrimination and injustice. Discrimination might not always be obvious in the classroom, but it exists and it hurts.

Self-Esteem

The price of discrimination and stigma is high when it comes to the self-esteem of children. It undermines their belief in themselves and their dignity. Often, children are confused about why they are being labeled and/or treated unfairly. Without the cognitive capacity to understand that the discriminatory behavior is not about them as unique individuals but rather about the group to which they belong, children eventually integrate the stigma into their self-concepts. This ultimately affects their self-esteem.

Self-esteem consists of two major components. It is how we realistically perceive ourselves and the value—both cognitive and emotional—that we put on that perception. For example, if a child is smart, sees himself or herself as smart, and values being smart, the child's self-esteem will be enhanced. When this process encompasses many core characteristics of the child, self-esteem will be high. Maintaining positive self-esteem includes having many of these kinds of experiences and being able to manage negative appraisal from others without significantly damaging our positive perceptions of ourselves.

The development of self-esteem for young children—those under the age of 6 or 7 years—is based on the feelings they have of being loved, accepted, and valued by important adults in their lives. The more they have positive experiences of being valued for themselves without condition, the greater their self-esteem. In addition, because they do not yet have the capacity to evaluate themselves against external standards, they look to significant caregivers to provide that evaluation. For example, young children will say that they are very capable of doing nearly any activity you can name.

As children develop and move beyond the preschool years, they become more aware of their abilities and qualities as well as society's criteria by which they are evaluated. Their self-esteem now has conditions of worth, and children internalize the yardsticks imposed on them by outside influences. Repeated experiences of being valued by others for their behavior or characteristics lead children to value those themselves and to increase their self-esteem. Important in this process is that children see themselves as doing something to cause the positive evaluation and therefore reaching the expected standard by which they are judged. Children with high self-esteem have more positive evaluations of themselves and have a sense of competence. They also know their good points, can take care of themselves, are able to accept failures, and can learn from mistakes.

In contrast, when children experience consistent and persistent negative social, emotional, verbal, physical, and educational experiences, they begin to evaluate themselves negatively and to develop low self-esteem. Many times, emotional and verbal neglect and abuse of a child can be as damaging as, if not more damaging than, physical neglect or abuse. Being shamed, insulted, ridiculed, or embarrassed either privately or publicly is destructive and can have long-term effects. If children are told that they are not "good enough" because of their gender, nationality, or race, this too will negatively affect their self-esteem. What occurs as a result of these experiences is a process by which children begin to evaluate themselves negatively and then form damaging opinions about themselves. These experiences can result in feelings of social isolation, shame, and worthlessness, which can lead to feelings of hopelessness, helplessness, anxiety, and depression.

Although our self-esteem becomes fairly well established by middle childhood, it remains vulnerable throughout our lives and is particularly malleable during the early years of childhood development. During those school years, children are faced with many challenges to their self-esteem, and teachers can be instrumental in helping to build and solidify positive self-esteem in their students. Because criteria for building self-esteem differ between and within cultures, communities, and societies, teachers who are mindful that there exist varying criteria can support children in continuing to develop their self-esteem within those children's worldviews. Ways in which to do so include the following:

- *Providing compassion, caring, and patience.* This will give children a sense of acceptance, belonging, and security. They will remember the smile on your face when they failed and the softness of your voice when they were upset long after they will remember what you taught them about math and English.
- *Encouraging children to believe in themselves by helping them to develop confidence in their own judgment about their abilities.*
- *Helping children to develop a curiosity about themselves as wonderers, producers, initiators, problem solvers, explorers, and partners.* Encouraging children to investigate phenomena worthy of their attention will help them to see how their actions resulted in outcomes that were meaningful to them and others.
- *Teaching social skills and coach skills as needed.* This will promote successful coping as all students learn how to give and receive positive feedback and negative feedback.
- *Promoting cooperative learning strategies and helping to establish cooperative goals so that self-evaluations created through competition and comparison with others is diminished.* Children can learn how

their efforts individually affected the whole. This builds children's sense of self-efficacy and encourages feeling valued by the group.

- *Providing a variety of kinds of interpersonal situations for children, particularly those during early childhood.* Because children vary so greatly in terms of culture, background, abilities, and personalities, self-esteem can be enhanced when children can successfully manage differing relationships.

- *Creating a wide range of ways in which children can contribute to and take part in the classroom experience.* This can be done when a range of behaviors are seen as acceptable and rewarded and when children are exposed to a variety of social, intellectual, and artistic activities.

- *Teaching children positive self-talk.* Much of our self-esteem has to do with what we tell ourselves. Helping children to tell themselves, "I can do this—I am a worthwhile kid," will be useful for the times when they are frustrated with their own abilities.

- *Acknowledging and celebrating children's talents and achievements.* This will provide them with a sense of industry and competence.

- *Reframing failures as successful failures, where something can be learned by each attempt that children make at achievement.* This will communicate your support of their persistence, competence, and overall ability to deal effectively with life's problems, even when events do not go as planned.

- Finally, at the end of the school day, having children ask themselves the following questions:
  - What have I tried that was new today?
  - What have I done today better than before?
  - Who are the people I have helped today?
  - Who has helped me today?
  - What gave me the most pleasure today?

Peer Relationships

As children develop, they begin to enter into social relationships and create friendships. Through those friendships, children enhance their social skills (e.g., taking turns, helping others), interpersonal skills (e.g., empathy, listening), cognitive skills (e.g., using reason and negotiation in relationships, learning the concept of relativity given that relationships are not "black and white"), and understanding about themselves (e.g., "I'm liked because I can jump high," "My friends like me because I share"). These relationships provide social support that affects children's emotional, physical, and spiritual health. It gives them a sense of belonging and how to be responsible to others' feelings and needs. They also begin to value themselves according to how valued they perceive themselves to be by their friends and how they see themselves fitting in.

How children communicate and attempt to fit in with friends is influenced by many factors, one being their self-esteem. As has been discussed, discrimination and stigma can negatively affect children's feelings about themselves. When this occurs, it is difficult for children to know how to manage their feelings. Difficulty in modulating their feelings often translates into problematic behavior with others. Children who have inferior feelings about themselves may isolate, be impulsive, or act out in ways that signal to adults that they are angry, sad, or hurt. These feelings may be derivatives of poor self-esteem.

If, as a way in which to manage negative feelings about themselves, children isolate or become passive in their relationships with peers, they may fail to express their needs and feelings, allow others to direct their behavior and influence their decisions, and have their rights violated. They may be unable to defend themselves against comments or behaviors that are hurtful and stigmatizing, which then affects their already poor self-esteem and leads to feelings of helplessness and depression. These children may interpret behaviors of friends and adults as signs that they are not liked and, in turn, might not try new things or engage in play with others. The result is poor peer relationships and little opportunity to have positive experiences with friends.

Some children manage negative feelings about themselves through outward expressions of anger. These children may hear negative comments about themselves and, rather than hold those feelings in (as do the children who isolate), may become enraged and hostile. They direct their anger toward peers through aggressive actions and may be seen by others as children who are inconsiderate of people's feelings, who become easily frustrated when situations do not go their way, who easily get into verbal and physical fights, and who have little tolerance when attention is given to others. Their initial feelings of rejection that have negatively influenced their self-esteem become transformed into acting-out behavior. This brings about more rejection by peers and further decreased self-esteem.

Similar to children who become aggressive are those who have difficulty with impulse control. They may blurt out their thoughts without taking the time to think about the consequences of their statements, or they may push their way into interactions without planning for the impact of those actions on their relationships with others. These children might not have learned how to tolerate feelings or "hold" them rather than act on them indiscriminately. As this relates to self-esteem and stigma, these children may have experienced emotionally and psychologically overwhelming negative experiences without the guidance of adults to help them understand, manage, and then dissipate these feelings and thoughts. The result of these repeated incidents leaves children without the resources to internally tolerate their own feelings or thoughts. They therefore explode with them, needing to get their ideas or feelings out. Their peers, however, do not understand this and react by moving away or with their own anger. Over time, these children have less positive interactions with friends and fewer occasions on which to learn how to manage stigma and negative feelings about themselves.

In school, poor peer relationships can become disruptive to the socialization of children and can interfere with their learning. Children who have problems with relating to their peers may have difficulty in engaging in cooperative learning activities, behaving appropriately in classroom situations where they must interact with others, and feeling a part of the classroom environment. Their ability to concentrate can be impaired as they are internally grappling with a mix of feelings that they do not understand or know how to manage. These children often require additional attention from teachers that can alienate them from their peers. Implementing the suggestions offered previously can assuage some of these difficulties by targeting children's low self-esteem and vulnerability to stigma.

Gender Identity Issues

Gender is often thought of as a biologically determined, and therefore fixed, component of a person's being. How one conducts oneself as a boy or girl is thought to be influenced by one's gender or sex. However, one's gender and one's sex are different concepts, although they have often been used interchangeably. One's sex is the result of biology and chromosomal makeup. Gender has been defined as how one expresses or performs one's sex as prescribed by society. That is, how one acts as male or female is the result of the messages one receives about what it means to be male or female in the society into which one is born and how to express that femaleness or maleness through behaviors, attitudes, and desires. These messages are pervasive and are present even before a child is born, including the color of the child's clothing, expectations of how the child will behave, and beliefs about what the child will grow up to become. These gender role expectations influence the gender identity that the child is to adopt. Girls therefore are expected to wear pink, play with dolls, and show an interest in being helpers and to see themselves as female when they engage in these activities or ideas, while boys are expected to wear blue, play with trucks, and show an interest in leading others and to see themselves as male when they do so.

Gender identity, however, has great fluidity because it is a concept created by society. Unlike one's sex, it is not unalterable (although with recent advances in medicine, one's sex can be altered as well). Yet Western societies tend to cast children into categories of male and female, and they expect them to behave in ways that fit the societies' positions of those categories as if these classifications were unalterable. Children learn early in life what the expectations are and how to perform their gender so as to not become marginalized. The messages about how to be a boy or girl are given to them by their parents, teachers, media, and other children.

Nevertheless, not all girls and boys perform gender in the same way, agree with the impositions of societal messages, or feel that their biological sex fits their gender identity. As a result, a common route through which children become stigmatized is that of gender identity issues. When children blur the boundaries of traditional gender roles and engage in cross-gender identity behavior, they are often labeled, ostracized, and treated with suspicion by teachers and society; harassed, teased, and rejected by their peers; and misunderstood and embarrassed by their parents.

The effect on the self-esteem of children who claim gender identities that are unexpected of them is only now beginning to be understood. Because they do not have people to go to with whom they can talk and feel understood, they feel isolated and angry, experience anxiety and depression, and socially withdraw. They may be classified as having gender identity disorder, a mental disorder, and be treated for this through psychotherapy. This further stigmatizes and entrenches the shame they feel as a result of not fitting in and being treated as different by their parents, peers, and teachers.

Sexual Identity Issues Affecting Students and Families

Related to the stigma associated with gender identity issues is the stigma associated with gay, lesbian, and bisexual sexual identities. Often thought of as a person's sexual orientation and behavior, sexual identity is most commonly classified as either homosexual, bisexual, or heterosexual. As with gender identity, the expectation of society is that children will grow up to be heterosexual. We know that even though most children do grow up to be heterosexual, there are a percentage of children who will be gay, lesbian, or bisexual (GLB). And although sexual identity is not acknowledged until adolescence or young adulthood, GLB adults recalling childhood experiences often are able to remember feeling "different" when it came to their sexual orientation. They also remember the stigma they felt in feeling that way.

The stigma attached to GLB people is historic. In schools, children continue the process of stigmatizing GLB people even when they do not know that the language they are using is harmful. Jokes are often made; words such as "sissy," "fag," "gay," and "homo" are used freely; and boys' behavior that can be seen as "feminine" and girls' behavior that can be perceived as "masculine" are discouraged by peers and teachers for fear that these children will "become gay." All children exposed to these words and behaviors incorporate the idea that being homosexual is a bad thing. For the children feeling "different," these messages are internalized and then understood as a part of them being bad. This has damaging effects on their self-esteem.

The issue of GLB sexual identities is also relevant when discussing the sexual identity of parents and the impact this has on children in school. The number of families headed by same-sex parents is significant. Estimates currently are somewhere between 6 million and 14 million families with GLB parents. Some of these homes have been created after children had been raised with opposite-sex parents for a period of time and then transitioned into homes with parents of the same sex. These children will have multiple concerns as they adapt to homes that are different from their previous ones and to ones that are stigmatized by society. Depending on their age, they will have the typical questions about the separation of their same-sex parents but will also have questions about the union of their new parents and how their families are different from most of their friends' families and what is talked about in school.

Regardless of how GLB families were created, children of GLB parents will face certain challenges in school. When they hear jokes about GLB people, hear derogatory names being used, or watch discriminatory behavior being conducted, they will feel the same kind of shame, anger, and hurt that GLB people feel. Young children will not understand hurtful language or actions but will know that something bad is happening and that something hurtful is being said about their parents.

In the classroom, these children may feel that their families are invisible when reading or hearing stories that discuss families with moms and dads but not families with two moms or two dads. At school events, they may feel ashamed to have both parents attend or may feel protective of them if they do. They may encounter discrimination from parents of their friends when these parents do not understand what it means to be GLB and are afraid to allow their children to interact with the children of GLB parents. This is very confusing for the children of GLB parents when the children do not yet understand why their parents would be seen as frightening or bad.

All school personnel face the challenges of having children from GLB families in their schools and children who feel different from the rest because of their sexual identities. There are many things that teachers can do to help these children feel more included and manage the stigma they are experiencing as well as to create a safer environment for all students. Some ideas include the following:

- For children from GLB homes, invite the parents to school to talk about what they might need, how they have talked to their children about their families, and how they would like to be included in school activities. This is particularly important when there are multiple caregivers such as biological and non-biological parents.
- Read books to students where different kinds of families are represented. There are a variety of books that discuss children having two moms or dads that can be read and discussed in class. This helps these children to feel visible and included, and it educates the other students as well.
- Have pictures of different kinds of families displayed in the classroom. Doing so will mirror for those children with GLB parents that their families are important. When drawing pictures of their families, these children will feel less inhibited or ashamed. Be sure to talk about the different families so that all children can hear about them and learn how to be non-discriminatory.
- Use language that is inclusive. When describing relationships or families, use words that indicate that families and relationships can consist of same-gender partnering.
- When language that is derogatory is used, jokes that are offensive are told, or behavior that is discriminatory is observed, stop the interaction and talk about the harm that these behaviors cause.

- When you notice a child that talks about himself or herself as feeling "different" or "not fitting in" in some way, be aware that these may be indications that the child has same-sex attractions that he or she does not understand. Be sensitive to this language and talk to the child about his or her feelings in a way that normalizes the child.
- Be aware of your own language that communicates information that traditional gender roles are the norm. Many GLB children do not ascribe to traditional gender roles and will feel excluded. In addition, those children with GLB parents will be confused by your language given that their parents will most likely cross gender roles.
- If you know of an "outed" GLB teacher at your school, ask him or her if you can consult about these issues. That will decrease your own homophobia and lack of knowledge about these issues as well as help you to feel supported.
- Finally, use the ideas about how to increase self-esteem. Listening to GLB children and taking their concerns seriously will ultimately help them to feel that they too belong in your classroom.

PART II

Health Problems
A–Z

Adjustment Disorder

Also known as: stress response

Description

Adjustment disorder is a response to an identifiable stressor or stressors that results in significant emotional or behavioral symptoms. The associated distress is in excess of what would be the expected response to the stressor. If the symptoms last less than 6 months, the adjustment disorder is referred to as acute; if the symptoms last 6 months or longer, it is referred to as chronic.

Primary Group Affected

- Between 2% and 8% of children experience adjustment disorder.
- Children from disadvantaged life circumstances experience a high rate of stressors and may be at increased risk for disorder.
- Boys and girls are affected equally.

Signs and Symptoms

- Decreased performance at school
- Temporary changes in social relationships
- Somatic (physical) complaints
- Temper tantrums that are out of balance with the events that caused them
- Depressed mood, tearfulness, or feelings of hopelessness
- Nervousness, worry, or fears of separation from parents/caregivers
- Disturbed conduct such as violating age-appropriate social norms or engaging in truancy or vandalism

Classroom Guidelines

- Provide support and reassurance for child during times of stress.
- If child has difficulty in concentrating, present activities and lessons in short segments.
- Provide opportunities for success. Praise and reinforce behavior whenever possible, focusing on positive characteristics and behaviors.
- Plan for child to interact with one other child for short time segments.
- Discuss and model resolution of interpersonal conflict—compromising, negotiating, and dealing with frustration.
- Establish reasonable and meaningful consequences for both compliant and noncompliant behavior.

Attendance Guideline

- Exclusion from school is not required.

Medications

- Depending on symptoms, child may be on antidepressant or antianxiety medications.

Communication

- Ask parent/caregiver how family has tried to resolve problem.
- Discuss what has worked and what has not worked.
- Encourage parent/caregiver to help child use problem-solving skills at home.

Resource

- Center for Mental Health Services (800) 789-2647
  www.mentalhealth.org

Alcohol Abuse

Also known as: binge drinking, substance abuse

Description

Alcohol abuse is defined as the purposeful use of alcohol, for at least 1 month, that results in adverse effects to oneself or others. Alcohol dependence occurs when the use of alcohol is no longer under control and continues despite its adverse effects. Adults may take from 2 to several years from the first use to full dependency. Preteens and teens often make this progression in 6 to 18 months.

Primary Group Affected

- Ages 10 to 14 years is a time of special risk for beginning to experiment with alcohol.
- If a biological parent/caregiver is alcoholic, there may be a genetic influence as well as a modeling influence.

Signs and Symptoms

- Mood changes: flare-ups of temper, irritability, defensiveness, family conflict
- "Nothing matters" attitude, sloppy appearance, lack of involvement in former interests, general low energy, intolerance for delayed gratification
- School problems: poor attendance, low grades, recent disciplinary action
- Switching friends to peers also abusing alcohol, impaired social skills
- Memory lapses, poor concentration
- Smell of alcohol on breath, bloodshot eyes

- Mild impairment: euphoria, impaired thinking and judgment, slurred speech, staggering gait
- Severe impairment: confusion, stupor, decreased respirations, coma—**911**

Classroom Guidelines

- If you suspect alcohol abuse during school hours, confront the issue rather than ignor it.
- Be aware that if student is moderately or severely impaired, emergency treatment may be necessary.
- Help students to develop problem-solving skills given that they have avoided problems through the use of alcohol.
- Encourage child to improve fitness through regular exercise or by becoming involved in a sport.
- Check with administration to provide drug education classes for students.

Attendance Guideline

- Exclusion from school is required when child is under the influence of alcohol.

Medication

- None is required.

Communication

- Ask parent/caregiver whether family conflict has recently escalated.
- Ask whether there are signs that child is abusing alcohol.
- Suggest that family contact the National Institutes of Health regarding "Make a Difference: Talk to Your Child About Alcohol" program.

Resources

- National Institute on Alcohol Abuse and Alcoholism
  National Institutes of Health
  www.niaaa.nih.gov
- 12 Step programs (Alcoholics Anonymous) for children and teens (See local chapter)

- Children of Alcoholics Foundation
  164 W. 74th Street
  New York, NY 10023
  (212) 595–5810
  www.coaf.org

Allergy: Drugs

Also known as: drug reactions

Description

It is very difficult to distinguish among a drug allergy, a side effect of taking a particular drug, a bad reaction to a drug, and a reaction due to taking a combination of drugs that are incompatible. A health care provider's diagnosis is necessary to identify a true allergy. Any of these responses, however, can range from mild to a severe, life-threatening allergic response that may develop within a few minutes after taking a particular medication. In a true drug allergy, antibodies in the body mistake a drug as a harmful substance and attack it, causing an allergic response. It is not known exactly how prevalent drug allergies are among children. It is known that most drug allergy deaths from anaphylactic (an uh fi lak' tik) shock occur in persons with no medical histories of allergic reactions. Medications that have been found to have a higher incidence of initiating allergic reactions include antibiotics and some heart medications. Atypically, drug reactions can be delayed, occurring up to 7 days after the last ingestion of the drug.

Primary Group Affected

- Any child may experience a drug reaction; however, incidence increases with number and amount of drugs taken.

Signs and Symptoms

- Itching
- Stuffy nose
- Dizziness/headache/disorientation—**911**
- Anxiety/irritability/restlessness
- Red blotchy skin

- Puffiness around eyes
- Hives (red bumps)
- Swelling of face, neck, hands, and legs—**911**
- Wheezing—**911**
- Difficulty in breathing—**911**
- Increased heart rate with irregular rhythm—**911**
- Decreased blood pressure—**911**
- Abdominal cramping
- Loss of consciousness—**911**

Classroom Guidelines

- If child exhibits *any* **911** identified signs or symptoms, activate local emergency medical system.
- If child loses consciousness, establish an airway and prepare to start CPR if needed.
- Be aware that if child is in severe distress, he or she may need epinephrine (*see* Procedure I).
- Keep child warm and calm.
- Keep child flat unless breathing is too difficult in this position.
- If child shows any of the above signs and symptoms, observe carefully because reaction may progress from a mild reaction to a severe one in a very short period of time.

Attendance Guideline

- Exclusion from school is not required.

Medications

- EpiPen injectable may be necessary during a severe reaction.
- If EpiPen is used, activate local emergency medical system anyway. Secondary reactions do occur hours after initial allergic response.

Communication

- Notify parent/caregiver of any drug reactions immediately.
- Ask parent/caregiver to identify drug allergy history on school forms so that record can be tagged as a medical alert.
- Ask whether child has an identifying bracelet or card to be worn.

Resources

- www.allergic-reactions.com
- www.mayoclinic.org

Allergy: Food

Also known as: adverse reaction to food, food intolerance, food anaphylaxis (an uh fi lak' sis), food hypersensitivity

Description

Allergic or hypersensitivity reactions to specific foods are a result of eating or touching certain food items. In addition, some children may experience reactions to food from the odor of the food substance. Foods that most commonly cause a reaction are peanuts, milk, eggs (egg yolk is considered less allergenic than egg whites), seeds (e.g., sesame, caraway), soy, shellfish, fish, and wheat. Although rare, food-induced deaths do occur. In studies of children who died from food-induced allergies, most ingested the offending food at school.

Primary Group Affected

- Children of any age may be affected, and the reactions may become more severe each time children are exposed to the food.
- Children living with asthma tend to experience serious reactions if they are allergic to certain foods.

Signs and Symptoms

- Food reactions vary from child to child, from a relatively mild case of hives to life-threatening breathing problems.
- Most severe reactions to food occur within the first hour after ingestion.
- Never assume that just because child says a prior reaction was mild, the current reaction will be mild.
- Stomach reactions can include nausea, vomiting, gas, cramping, and diarrhea.

- Breathing (respiratory) reactions can include runny nose, stuffy nose, sneezing, coughing, change in voice, difficulty in swallowing, tightness of chest, shortness of breath, and itching or swelling of lips, tongue, or throat—**911.**
- Skin reactions can include hives, itching, and a red flat skin rash.
- Remove offending food and activate local emergency medical system if life-threatening reaction. Notify school health care provider or nurse.

Classroom Guidelines

- Take all reactions seriously and treat promptly.
- Make certain that child avoids offending food.
- Be alert for "treats" brought in for school celebrations.
- When in doubt concerning a food, do not allow child to eat it.
- Look for key words that warn of the presence of offending foods.
- Have parent/caregiver provide foods that child can eat.
- Send child to school nurse or activate local emergency medical system if symptoms occur after eating certain foods.
- Be aware that epinephrine might need to be administered at first indication of any lip, tongue, mouth, or throat allergies (*see* Procedure I).
- Send child to hospital after injection because reaction can occur again for 6 to 9 hours.

Attendance Guideline

- Exclusion from school varies depending on the severity of reaction.

Medication

- Epinephrine may be used in severe emergencies (*see* Procedure I).

Communication

- Ask parent/caregiver what happens to child when he or she is exposed to food that causes a allergic reaction.
- Ask whether the reaction occurs with eating or just smelling the scent of the offending food.
- Ask whether reaction seems to be getting worse with each exposure.

- Ask whether food allergy has been confirmed with testing.
- Ask whether child wears a medic alert band regarding allergy.
- Ask what ingredient words should be identified regarding items brought into classroom by other students/parents.
- Ask what child can eat as alternative snack or treat.

Resources

- American College of Allergy, Asthma, and Immunology
  85 West Algonquin Road, Suite 550
  Arlington, IL 60005
  www.acaai.org
- National Institutes of Health
  NIH Publication No. 91–2650
  Managing Allergy and Asthma at School: Tips for Schoolteachers and Staff
  (Free booklet)
  http://allergy.mcg.edu
- Food Allergy Network
  4744 Holly Avenue
  Fairfax, VA 22030
  (703) 691–3179
  (Has an informative newsletter and sends out regular warnings about commercial food products containing unwanted food proteins)

Allergy:
Hay Fever

Also known as: allergic rhinitis (ri ni' tis), summer cold

Description

Hay fever is the most common chronic condition of all allergic disorders. A child with hay fever reacts to one or more specific allergy-causing substances such as pollen, mold, dust mites, and pet dander. Inhaling one of these allergens causes child to release substances that inflame the linings of the nose, sinuses, eyelids, and eyes.

Primary Group Affected

- Teenagers are usually affected, but younger children are occasionally affected, especially children with family histories of hay fever.

Signs and Symptoms

- Congestion
- Runny nose
- Frequent sneezing
- Watery eyes
- Itchy eyes, nose, and roof of mouth or throat
- Cough
- Can trigger an asthma attack or cause wheezing or shortness of breath—**911**

Classroom Guidelines

- Adhere to medication regimen as ordered by health care provider and school policy.

- Remove offending substance from room if possible.
- Keep classroom windows and doors closed and use air-conditioning if available.
- Keep child indoors as much as possible during pollen season and especially when grass is being cut.
- Keep classroom as free of dust as possible during pollen season to reduce levels of pollen and mold. Do not let child be present during cleaning.
- Avoid chalk dust, room deodorizers, and cleaning solutions.
- Remind parent/caregiver to provide tissues for child and bag receptacle for disposal.
- Limit child's exposure to classroom pets.

Attendance Guideline

- Exclusion from school is not required.

Medications

- As ordered by health care provider, these may include oral medications, sprays, and eye drops.
- Antihistamines may cause drowsiness.
- Child receiving allergy shots might not get relief for 6 months to 2 years.

Communication

- Notify parent/caregiver if child complains of any symptoms.
- Ask for information regarding allergies and any medication management.

Resource

- www.mayoclinic.org

Allergy: Latex

Also known as: NRL, IgE reaction

Description

Latex allergy is allergic or hypersensitivity reactions to natural latex. Reactions are unique to each child and vary from skin reaction to severe breathing difficulties. The specific cause of reaction is unknown. Each exposure to latex may bring on a more serious reaction than the previous one. Latex can be found in numerous classroom items. Latex reactions may be in response to exposure to the following: erasers, rubber bands, carpet backings, rubber balls (e.g., Koosh balls, tennis balls, rubber basketballs), balloons, elastic in clothes, spandex swimwear, rubber sole shoes, insulation material, bicycle helmets, chewing gum, mouse pads for computers, sports equipment handles (e.g., table tennis paddles, golf clubs, baseball bats), raincoats, rubber boots, Silly Putty, socks with elastic, swimming goggles, caps, snorkels, bandages, and adhesive tape.

Primary Group Affected

- Any age group
- Children with spina bifida
- Children with bowel or bladder programs that require urinary catheters or latex instruments
- Children with cerebral palsy
- Children having multiple surgeries
- Children experiencing allergic reactions to bananas, kiwis, avocados, potatoes, tomatoes, and chestnuts

Signs and Symptoms

- Skin reaction (allergic contact dermatitis)
- Sneezing, itching, redness resulting from contact with latex

- Wheezing, chest tightness, difficulty in breathing—**911**
- Facial swelling, lip swelling, tongue swelling, swelling of any body part—**911**
- Decreased level of consciousness—**911**

Classroom Guidelines

- If child is experiencing difficulty in breathing, activate local emergency medical system.
- Modify latex exposure in the classroom.
- Keep low-protein, powder-free, nonlatex gloves in the classroom.
- Keep current list of latex-free items (may be obtained by contacting the Spina Bifida Association, (800) 621–3141).
- Notify parent/caregiver if child has local skin reaction after an exposure.
- Send child to school nurse if symptoms occur after exposure or activate local emergency medical system for severe reaction.
- Be aware that a child in severe distress may need epinephrine (*see* Procedure I) as ordered by the health care provider. Another dose may be needed in 20 minutes if child is not improving and local emergency medical system has not arrived.

Attendance Guideline

- Exclusion from school varies depending on the severity of the reaction.

Medication

- Epinephrine may be needed in severe emergencies (*see* Procedure I).

Communication

- If child has a known allergy to latex, ask parent/caregiver what a reaction looks like.
- Ask whether the reactions seem to be getting worse with each exposure.
- Ask whether child had latex antibody testing and results.
- Ask whether child wears a medic alert band regarding the allergy.
- Ask whether child uses epinephrine for any latex reactions.

Resources

- Spina Bifida Association
  (800) 621–3141
  sbaa@sbaa.org
  (Semiannual list of items that contain latex and alternatives)
- Latex Allergy Information Service
  (860) 482–6869
  www.latexallergyhelp.com
  (Monthly newsletter)

Anaphylaxis

Also known as: anapylactic (an 'uh fi lak' tik) shock

Description

Anaphylaxis (an' uh fi lak' sis) is an extremely serious form of an allergic response to a specific allergen (something that causes an allergic response) that is life threatening. It can affect breathing and significantly decrease blood pressure as a result of an allergic response to certain foods, medications, or immunizations; insect stings; or exposure to latex or other chemicals. Immediate action is needed to prevent death from occurring. It takes only 1 to 2 minutes for a mild reaction to go to anaphylaxis. In addition, the faster the onset of an anaphylactic reaction, the greater the chance that it will be severe. It should be noted that among children who have previously experienced only mild reactions to one of the triggers, many will experience more severe reactions with repeated episodes.

Primary Group Affected

- Any child may experience anaphylaxis.

Signs and Symptoms

- Anxiety/irritability/restlessness
- Generalized flushing or red blotchy skin
- Puffiness around eyes
- Hives (red bumps)
- Abdominal cramping, nausea, vomiting, diarrhea
- Itching (may include itching in mouth)
- Tingling sensation around mouth or face
- Sudden feeling of weakness

- Sweating
- Change in quality of voice
- Stuffy nose
- Swelling of face, throat, lips, tongue, neck, hands, or legs—**911**
- Wheezing—**911**
- Difficulty in breathing or swallowing—**911**
- Increased heart rate with irregular rhythm, weak rapid pulse—**911**
- Decreased blood pressure (and accompanying paleness)—**911**
- Collapse, loss of consciousness—**911**
- Dizziness/headache/disorientation—**911**

Classroom Guidelines

- If child exhibits identified signs/symptoms, activate local emergency medical system.
- If child loses consciousness, establish an airway and prepare to start CPR if needed.
- Be aware that a child in severe distress may need epinephrine (*see* Procedure I). Another dose may be needed in 20 minutes if child is not improving and emergency medical system has not arrived.
- Keep child warm and calm.
- Keep child flat unless breathing is too difficult in this position.
- If child shows any of the above signs and symptoms, observe carefully because reaction may progress from a mild reaction to a severe one in a very short period of time.
- Send child's health record and empty EpiPen(s) with the emergency medical system responders and write time when you gave medication.

Attendance Guideline

- Exclusion from school is not required.

Medications

- Epinephrine by injection may be needed for severe reaction; check expiration date (*see* Procedure I).
- If epinephrine is given, continue to activate local emergency medical system. Secondary reactions do occur hours after initial allergic response.
- Antihistamines, which may cause drowsiness, may be prescribed for child.

Communication

- If child has a known severe allergic response, discuss with parent/caregiver the necessity of having an EpiPen (check expiration date) and technique for administration.
- Notify parent/caregiver immediately.
- Ask parent/caregiver to identify allergy history on school forms so that record can be tagged as a medical alert.
- Ask whether child has an identifying bracelet or card to be worn.
- Discuss with parent/caregiver measures to avoid reoccurrence of exposure to triggers such as avoidance of certain foods and precautions to use outdoors with child who experiences insect allergies.
- Ask parent/caregiver to consult health care provider for information about allergies and circumstances under which medication should be used.

Resources

- www.allergic-reactions.com
- www.mayoclinic.org
- www.schoolnurse.com

Anemia/Iron Deficiency Anemia

Also known as: low energy, poor blood, low blood

Description

Iron deficiency anemia (ah ne' me ah) is a common type of anemia. As the name implies, the body does not have enough of the mineral iron. Iron is needed by the body to make hemoglobin in the red blood cells. The hemoglobin carries oxygen from the lungs to all the cells and tissue of the body and carries away all of the carbon dioxide. Iron deficiency anemia may be caused by poor iron intake in the diet, blood loss, or inadequate absorption of iron. Anemia can be diagnosed by a blood test (complete blood count) and can usually be treated by dietary improvements and iron supplements. If iron deficiency anemia is left untreated, it can lead to serious health problems such as delayed growth in children, irregular heartbeat, and even heart damage.

Primary Group Affected

- Children of any age, but most common under age 2 years
- Also seen in teenagers, especially girls

Signs and Symptoms

- Fatigue
- Pale skin color, nail beds
- Decreased pinkness of lips
- Brittle nails
- Cracks in sides of mouth

- Sores on tongue
- Cravings for non-nutritive substances such as ice, dirt, paint, clay, and starch
- Headaches
- Poor appetite
- Frequent infections
- Restless legs syndrome (uncomfortable tingling or "crawling" in legs that is relieved by walking)

Classroom Guidelines

- Dispense medications according to school regulations.
- Help child to make good food choices: iron-fortified grains, pasta, and cereals; red meats and egg yolks; green and yellow vegetables; raisins, dried fruits, and seeds.
- Be aware that coffee and tea inhibit absorption of iron.
- Understand that vitamin C (e.g., in citrus juices) increases absorption of iron.
- Be aware that iron supplements may cause constipation and will cause child's stools to become black in color.

Attendance Guideline

- Exclusion from school is not required.

Medications

- Vitamin, iron, and folic acid supplements may be prescribed (usually oral form but sometimes by injection).
- Iron supplements are usually best absorbed on an empty stomach; however, if they cause stomach upset, taking with food may help.

Communication

- Clarify with parent/caregiver acceptable and unacceptable foods to eat.
- Inquire about schedule of medications so as to support/monitor child's compliance with treatment plan.

Resource

- www.mayoclinic.org

Anger

Description

Anger serves a variety of adaptive functions. It signals that something is happening in the environment to which individuals must pay attention. Anger mobilizes and sustains energy at high levels of intensity so that individuals can respond to the situation. Individuals learn how to regulate their anger through socialization by parents/caregivers, peers, and the larger society.

Primary Group Affected

- First clear expressions of anger appear at about 4 months.
- By 7 months, anger is targeted to another individual.
- Anger remains a human emotion throughout life.

Signs and Symptoms

Infants

- Anger is associated with infants' attempts to master physical environment.
- Anger is a social signal to parent/caregiver.
- Anger may be in response to frustration.
- Infants show distress when witnessing others' angry interactions.

Preschool Children

- Language gives children a new way in which to express their anger.
- Preschool children still have relatively poor control over their displays of anger.
- By the age of 4 or 5 years, children are better able to regulate anger and express it in socially acceptable ways.

- Some 4- or 5-year-olds begin to show signs of difficulty in managing their anger, which is predictive of poorer social functioning and problem behaviors.

School-Age Children

- School-age children learn a great deal about appropriate expression of anger from their peers; being accepted by peers and having friends is of great importance.
- Children are more likely to express anger at family members than at peers, especially by middle childhood when the norm is to be "cool"—calm and under emotional control.

Classroom Guidelines

Infants and Preschool Children

- Respond calmly and with a cheerful expression.
- Use coaxing or diversion of attention.
- Do not reward children by giving attention for inappropriate displays of anger.
- Use puppets or dolls to act out feeling of anger appropriately.
- Reward and praise positive and neutral emotions.
- Teach and coach children about expression of anger.
- Look at how you handle your own anger, making sure to set a good example.

School-Age Children

- Listen to what children are saying about their feelings, letting them know that you care about their problems.
- Present children with hypothetical, anger-producing situations and discuss how they would feel and what they would do in these situations.
- Discuss consequences of nonhostile responses to provocation and acknowledge positive behavioral choices.

Attendance Guideline

- Exclusion from school is not required.

Medication

- None is required.

Communication

- Ask parent/caregiver how anger is managed at home by all family members.
- Develop school and home plan for consistent response to inappropriate expressions of anger.
- Child and family may benefit from therapy if child is being rejected by peers.

Resource

- Caring for Every Child's Mental Health Campaign
  Center for Mental Health Services
  U.S. Department of Health and Human Services
  (800) 789–2647
  www.mentalhealth.org/child

Animal Bites

Description

Young children are especially vulnerable to animal bites and need to be protected. Children may be the victims of animal bites from pets in the classroom or from animals encountered in play areas or on outdoor field trips. Dog bites are the most frequent source of animal bites. Cat bites, however, are more likely to cause infection in children. The incidence of rabies is more common in bites from raccoons, skunks, bats, and foxes. There are many instructional reasons for having animals in the classroom; however, it may be prudent to have all classroom pets examined by a veterinarian prior to boarding these animals in the school. Bites that break the skin have a greater likelihood of becoming infected. Serious injury, viral and bacterial infections, psychological trauma, and even death are complications that can be associated with animal bites (*see* Procedure G).

Primary Group Affected

- Boys more often than girls
- Any children in contact with animals

Signs and Symptoms

- Open area on the skin with surrounding teeth marks
- Significant crush injury—**911**

Classroom Guidelines

- Be aware that animal should be captured if this can be done safely.
- Call local animal warden/authority to capture animal.

- Speak calmly to child to decrease anxiety.
- Wash wound with soap and water; if antiseptic soap is available, use it. You may need to repeat this procedure three or four times to decrease animal's saliva in the bite site.
- For deeper bites, apply a sterile pressure bandage.
- Raise affected part to decrease bleeding.
- Apply ice to site if needed to decrease swelling.
- Notify parent/caregiver and encourage to see health care provider.
- Follow school guidelines in reporting bite to health department.
- Discuss with children how to protect themselves from animal bites (e.g., do not separate fighting animals, do not bother animals when they are eating, avoid strange and sick animals).

Attendance Guideline

- Exclusion from school is not required.

Medications

- Antibiotics may be ordered and need to be given on schedule.
- Tetanus toxoid is given if child is not sufficiently immunized. Tetanus shots are given every 10 years; if child's last tetanus shot was more than 5 years ago and the wound is dirty, a booster may be given. Boosters should be given within 48 hours of a bite injury.
- If animal is not found or shows evidence of rabies, child will undergo a series of rabies vaccines and antiserum injections.

Communication

- Notify parent/caregiver immediately and urge to see health care provider.
- Follow school policy in documenting incident.
- If child is receiving series of rabies vaccine and antiserum injections, ask parent/caregiver for information concerning reactions.

Resources

- www.r09.tdh.state.tx.us/zoonosis/rabies.html
- www.mayoclinic.org

Anxiety Disorder: Generalized

Also known as: overanxious, severe anxiety

Description

Generalized anxiety disorder is extreme unrealistic worry that is unrelated to any recent event. These children are so afraid or worried that they are unable to function normally and the routines of daily life are disrupted. They may also exhibit excessive conformity and a strong desire to please others. This disorder may be accompanied by panic attacks or social phobias (*see* Panic Disorder and Phobia entries).

Primary Group Affected

- Disorder tends to occur more commonly in small families, in the oldest children, and in upper socioeconomic-level families.
- High levels of anxiety in children ages 6 to 8 years may be a warning sign of a developing anxiety disorder.

Signs and Symptoms

- Worry about a broad range of situations, strong need for reassurance
- Physical symptoms: restless, on edge, easily fatigued, muscle tension, stomach complaints, shortness of breath, headaches, dizziness
- Decreased concentration
- Impaired relationships with peers

- Often perfectionist; may spend hours doing and redoing homework or other tasks that most peers do in a short time period
- May refuse to go to school (if severe)

Classroom Guidelines

- Encourage child to verbalize concerns. Assure him or her of safety.
- Draw on child's previous coping methods that have been successful.
- Help child to identify alternative outlets for a moderate level of anxiety such as running, climbing, sports, and group games.
- Guide child in identifying his or her own desires in specific situations so as to minimize need to please others.
- Frequently reassure child that mistakes are an important part of learning and are expected on homework and tests.

Attendance Guideline

- Exclusion from school is not required.

Medication

- Unlikely to be on any medication

Communication

- Ask parent/caregiver about usual symptoms that child exhibits at a moderate level of anxiety as well as at a panic level of anxiety.
- Discuss what measures child has developed to manage anxiety.
- Ask whether child has age-appropriate social relationships among family and other familiar people.
- Communicate clearly the amount of time assigned homework should take child and encourage parent/caregiver to set restrictions on child redoing homework in an attempt to achieve perfection.

Resources

- Anxiety Disorders Association of America
  11900 Parklawn Drive, Suite 100
  Rockville, MD 20852

(301) 231–9350
www.adaa.org
- National Mental Health Association
  1021 Prince Street
  Alexandria, VA 22314–2971
  (800) 969-NMHA
  www.nmha.org

Anxiety Disorder: Separation

Also known as: fear of strangers, intense homesickness

Description

From 7 months through the preschool years, healthy children may show anxiety at times of separation from parents/caregivers. Normal separation anxiety becomes a disorder when children experience excessive anxiety on routine separation from parents/caregivers, home, or other familiar situations. The severity of the anxiety interferes with daily life.

Primary Group Affected

- Usually occurs after 7 months and peaks at about 18 months
- May recur when school starts
- May also be seen in preteens and teens

Signs and Symptoms

- Reluctance to sleep alone, may have nightmares
- Physical symptoms: headaches, stomachaches, nausea, and vomiting that may occur even when child anticipates separation
- Morbid fears that injuries or illnesses will happen to loved ones or children themselves, fear that children will never see their families again, prevalent themes of death and dying
- Social withdrawal
- School refusal

Classroom Guidelines

- Introduce child to teacher and classroom slowly to keep anxiety to a minimum and to promote a positive school experience.
- Provide support and reassurance during times of stress, especially during separation from parent/caregiver.
- Introduce peer interactions slowly to keep anxiety to a minimum.
- Encourage child to interact with one other child in an activity.
- Support and reassure child as interactions with peers are attempted.

Attendance Guideline

- Exclusion from school is not required.

Medication

- May be on an antidepressant medication

Communication

- Ask parent/caregiver what family has tried to do to resolve the problem.
- Discuss effective strategies.
- Discuss how child gets along with other children in neighborhood.
- Ask how daily activities are interrupted by disorder

Resources

- Anxiety Disorders Association of America
  11900 Parklawn Drive, Suite 100
  Rockville, MD 20852
  (301) 231–9350
  www.adaa.org
- National Mental Health Association
  1021 Prince Street
  Alexandria, VA 22314–2971
  (800) 969-NMHA
  www.nmha.org

Appendicitis

Description

The appendix is a small wormlike pouch that extends out from the colon on the right-hand side of the body. It has no known purpose. Appendicitis (ah pendi site' is) occurs when the appendix becomes inflamed and filled with pus. It is the most common cause of abdominal pain requiring surgery in children. Treatment is removal of the appendix (appendectomy) within 24 to 48 hours of the first symptoms.

Primary Group Affected

- Anyone can develop appendicitis.
- The highest risk group is between ages 10 and 30 years.

Signs and Symptoms

Early Symptoms

- Child has aching pain over the belly button.
- Pain shifts to the lower right abdomen, halfway between the belly button and the hip bone.
- Pain often worsens if child coughs, walks, or makes other sharp movements.
- Pain may decrease if child lies on his or her side and bends the knees.
- Child suffers from nausea and sometimes vomiting.
- Child has a low-grade fever (99 to 102 degrees) that starts after the other symptoms appear.

Late Symptoms

- The most serious complication is rupture of the appendix, which is a medical emergency—**911.**

- The pus from the appendix and the contents of the small intestine are released into the abdominal cavity.
- There may be a sudden relief of pain immediately after the rupture, followed by intense pain throughout the abdomen—**911.**
- The abdomen becomes distended and rigid—**911.**
- The child has a rapid heart rate and rapid shallow breathing—**911.**

Classroom Guidelines

- Because children might not always have typical symptoms of appendicitis, do not take abdominal pain lightly.
- If child is in acute distress, have parent/caregiver notify primary health care provider.

Attendance Guideline

- Child will need to recover from surgery at home. The physician will determine when child may return to the classroom.

Medications

- Antibiotics to prevent complications from surgery

Communication

- Because appendicitis is not uncommon in children, all "stomachaches" should be reported to parent/caregiver.

Resource

- www.mayoclinic.org

Asperger's Disorder

Also known as: mild autism (aw' tizm)

Description

Asperger's is a disorder of the brain characterized by severe impairment in social interactions as well as repetitive patterns of behavior and activities. The child may have eccentric obsessional interests. The disorder may range from mild to severe.

Primary Group Affected

- Usually diagnosed after age 3 or 4 years
- Five times more frequent in males than in females
- Increased frequency of Asperger's disorder and autistic disorder among family members

Signs and Symptoms

- Continuous and lifelong disorder
- Normal IQ and may exhibit exceptional skill or talent in specific area
- Often obsessively preoccupied with particular subject
- Normal language development, but attempts at conversation often are one-sided lecturing
- Impaired nonverbal social behavior such as eye contact, facial expression, body postures, and gestures to regulate social interaction
- Failure to develop peer relationships appropriate to developmental level, may be rejected by peers and at risk for teasing

- Rigid adherence to routines or rituals
- Repetitive motor mannerisms such as hand or finger flapping and complex whole-body movements

Classroom Guidelines

- Be aware that early intervention services result in more positive outcomes. The LEAP (Learning Experiences: an Alternative Program for Preschoolers and Parents) intervention model is based on social learning theory and focuses on children's social development.
- Teach social skills through discussion, modeling, and practice.
- Because two thirds of communication is considered to be nonverbal, teach students how to observe, understand, and respond to nonverbal cues; teach body language of active listening using the OFFER mnemonic device:

  O = open posture

  F = face person

  F = lean forward

  E = make eye contact

  R = relax

- Teach students to recognize when they are talking too much. A vibrating watch set at 3 minutes at the beginning of interactions can be a silent reminder to stop talking and give the other person a chance.
- Be aware that TEACCH (Treatment and Education of Autistic and Related Communication-Handicapped Children) provides a lifelong continuum of services, including assessment, diagnosis, treatment, use of community resources, and supported employment and living situations.

Attendance Guideline

- Exclusion from school is not required.

Medications

- Mood stabilizers such as Catapres (clonidine) and Tenex (guanfacine) may reduce temper tantrums.

Communication

- Coordinate social modeling with parental/caregiver efforts.
- Ask parent/caregiver how family responds to need for rigid routines.

Resource

- National Alliance for Autism Research
  99 Wall Street
  Research Park
  Princeton, NJ 08540
  (888) 777-NAAR
  www.naar.org

Asthma

Description

Asthma is a disease in which airways in the lungs are narrowed and inflamed, causing episodes of wheezing, difficulty in breathing, tightness in the chest, and coughing (asthma attack). Triggers (e.g., exercise, cold air, allergens, other irritants) and some viral infections (e.g., a cold) cause the airways to get narrowed or blocked. If asthma attacks become severe, emergency treatment is needed.

Primary Group Affected

- Children of any age may be affected.
- Asthma is the most common respiratory chronic illness among children.
- Asthma is most common in African Americans, urban residents, and boys.
- Children with asthma usually show symptoms by 5 years of age.

Signs and Symptoms

- Wheezing noises
- Difficulty in breathing—**911**
- Tightness in the chest
- Feeling of fear and confusion
- Tingling or numbness in the fingers or toes
- Unable to talk without stopping for breath—**911**

Classroom Guidelines

- Identify and control triggers as much as possible (e.g., dust mites and mold, animal fur or feathers, pollen, smoke, air pollution, paint fumes, strong odors, cockroaches, cold air, exercise).

- Know signs and symptoms of an asthma attack.
- Keep copy of asthma action plan handy, and review it with child and parent/caregiver.
- Seat child's desk away from open windows if asthma attacks are brought on by pollen, grass, and the like.
- In case of an asthma attack, check child, activate local emergency medical system if breathing difficulty does not get better quickly, care for child by assisting to comfortable breathing position, give medication if ordered, and stay calm and reassure child—**911.**
- Understand that a child with asthma may feel drowsy or tired, different from other children, anxious about medications, or embarrassed about disruption to school activities.
- Know medication side effects such as increased heart rate after inhalers are used.
- Encourage child to participate in physical activities within the guidelines on the asthma action plan.
- Allow quiet activity if child is recovering from an asthma attack.
- Maintain confidentiality.
- Keep many copies of asthma action plan in classroom, and take them along on field trips and school outings.
- Develop clear procedure with child and parent for handling missed schoolwork.

Attendance Guideline

- Exclusion from school is not required. Follow asthma action plan for specific guideline. (Written asthma action management plan should include medications, peak flows, triggers, phone numbers, and when to go to emergency room.)

Medications

- Long term control medications include anti-inflammatory medications.
- "Quick relief" medications include bronchodilators.

Communication

- Ask parent/caregiver whether child has asthma. If yes, ask whether a copy of the asthma action plan is on file.

- Ask for information about and demonstration of medications such as inhaler and peak flow meter.
- Communicate often about triggers and asthma management.

Resources

- www.aafa.org
- www.mdnet.de/asthma
- www.mayoclinic.org

Attention Deficit/ Hyperactivity Disorder

Also known as: ADHD, ADD

Description

Attention deficit/hyperactivity disorder is a persistent pattern of inattention and/or hyperactivity/impulsivity. Those who are affected have significant problems with family and peer relationships as well as with educational functioning and achievement.

Primary Group Affected

- It is difficult to establish this diagnosis in children under age 4 or 5 years.
- Some symptoms usually present before age 7 years.
- Boys outnumber girls with this disorder by three to one.

Signs and Symptoms

- Inattention: appears as if not listening, makes careless mistakes in schoolwork, fails to give close attention to details, has difficulty in organizing work, shifts frequently from one uncompleted activity to another, fails to follow through on instructions, is reluctant to engage in activities that require sustained attention, is easily distracted by extraneous stimuli

- Hyperactivity: exhibits excessive movement in situations where inappropriate, is constantly "on the go" and into everything (preschoolers), has difficulty in remaining seated (school-age children), talks excessively, sings or talks to self, taps or drums with fingers on objects
- Impulsiveness: shows impatience, has difficulty in delaying responses; interrupts or intrudes on others to the point that it causes social difficulties, breaks educational rules

Classroom Guidelines

- Do not confuse with sensory integration dysfunction.
- Get child's attention by calling his or her name and moving physically closer to child or lightly touching his or her arm.
- If classroom is overstimulating, redirect child to a quieter area to facilitate self-control.
- Ask child to repeat what he or she heard of instructions before beginning task. If there is a time lag between instructions and activity, repeat instructions as necessary.
- Allow child to carry out one instruction before being given another, and provide positive feedback for completion of each step.
- Do not exempt child from curricular requirements and outcomes.
- Deal with disruptive behavior immediately, decisively, and as quietly as possible.
- Talk to child away from other children. Write comments/feedback in child's planner.
- Establish a behavioral contract using stickers or points as rewards for positive behavior, later exchanging for more concrete rewards such as a privilege and a favorite activity.

Attendance Guideline

- Exclusion from school is not required.

Medications

- Medications provide a "window of opportunity" to allow other strategies to be more effective.
- Stimulant medications increase activity in parts of brain that are underactive, improving attention and reducing impulsiveness and hyperactivity.

- Ritalin is rapidly metabolized and may need to be given as often as five times a day for children age 6 years or over.
- Cylert may be used for children age 6 years or over.
- Dexedrine and Adderall may be too stimulating for the hyperactive child. They may be given to children age 3 years or over.
- Side effects are minimal and transient. Symptoms may become worse (rebound effect) as medication wears off.

Communication

- Coordinate behavioral guidelines with parent/caregiver's established routine.
- Discuss meaningful rewards for appropriate behavior.
- Develop a system for informing parent/caregiver of academic assignments, expectations, and due dates using a daily planner that may become a valuable communication tool for student, teacher, and parent/caregiver.

Resource

- Children and Adults with Attention Deficit/Hyperactivity Disorder (CHADD)
  8181 Professional Place, Suite 201
  Landover, MD 20785
  (800) 233–4050
  www.chadd.org

Autistic Disorder

Also known as: autism (aw' tizm)

Description

Autistic disorder (aw tis' tik) is a disorder of the brain characterized by social isolation, communication impairment, and strange repetitive behaviors. This is the most severe form of pervasive developmental disorders.

Primary Group Affected

- Onset is prior to age 3 years.
- This disorder is four to five times more likely in males than in females.
- Females with this disorder are more likely to also be cognitively impaired.
- Siblings are at increased risk for the disorder.

Signs and Symptoms

- During infancy, symptoms may be subtle and nearly unnoticeable.
- The most striking feature is profound social isolation. Child experiences no pleasure in sharing experiences with others and is unable to anticipate thoughts and actions of others.
- Child dislikes being touched or looking people in eyes.
- Disturbed motor behavior may include whirling, lunging, darting, rocking, and toe walking.
- Child throws tantrums for no apparent reason.

- Child shows an obsessive interest in a single toy, activity, or person.
- Child resists changes in routines.
- Child shows abnormal language development. He or she may be mute, make unintelligible sounds or say words repeatedly, or be unable to use or understand abstract language.
- Odd responses to sensory stimuli may include oversensitivity to sounds or being touched and exaggerated reactions to light or odors.
- Child may exhibit self-injurious behaviors such as head banging and finger, hand, or wrist biting.
- Among these children, 5% to 10% will become independent as adults, 25% will require supervision as adults, and the remainder will continue to be severely impaired and in need of a high level of care.

Classroom Guidelines

- Be aware that early intervention services result in more positive outcomes. The LEAP (Learning Experiences: an Alternative Program for Preschoolers and Parents) intervention model is based on social learning theory and focuses on children's social development.
- Teach social skills through discussion, modeling, and practice.
- Because two thirds of communication is considered to be nonverbal, teach students how to observe, understand, and respond to nonverbal cues. Teach body language of active listening using the OFFER mnemonic device:

  O = open posture

  F = face person

  F = lean forward

  E = make eye contact

  R = relax

- Be aware that TEACCH (Treatment and Education of Autistic and Related Communication-Handicapped Children) provides a lifelong continuum of services, including assessment, diagnosis, treatment, use of community resources, and supported employment and living situations.

Attendance Guideline

- Exclusion from school is not required.

Medications

- Mood stabilizers such as Catapres (clonidine) and Tenex (guanfacine) may reduce temper tantrums.

Communication

- Coordinate social modeling with parental/caregiver efforts.
- Coordinate response to temper tantrums with parental/caregiver response.
- Ask parent/caregiver how family responds to need for rigid routines.
- Discuss the best way in which to communicate with child.

Resource

- National Alliance for Autism Research
  99 Wall Street
  Research Park
  Princeton, NJ 08540
  (888) 777-NAAR
  www.naar.org

Behavior Disorders: Conduct Disorder

Also known as: CD

Description

Conduct disorder is characterized by a persistent pattern of aggressive and destructive behavior with disregard for the rights of others and the norms of society. The problematic behavior is usually present at home, in school, and in the community.

Primary Group Affected

- Onset before age 10 years is more typical in boys than in girls.
- Children may have had oppositional defiant disorder during early childhood.
- Many children with this disorder also have attention deficit/hyperactivity disorder.
- Socioeconomically deprived children are at higher risk.

Signs and Symptoms

- Problems ranging from mild to severe
- Deliberate destruction or theft of property
- Often lies to obtain goods or favors or to avoid obligations ("cons" others)

- Before age 13 years, often stays out at night or runs away from home overnight despite parental prohibitions
- Before age 13 years, often is truant from school or often drops out of school
- May be physically cruel to people and animals
- Little concern for feelings and well-being of others
- Disturbed peer relationships
- At high risk for substance use disorders
- This disorder more likely to persist into adulthood when onset is during childhood

Classroom Guidelines

- Discuss and model resolution of interpersonal conflict: compromising, negotiating, and dealing with frustration.
- Teach and reteach problem-solving process.
- Discuss peer likability factors such as the following:
  - Trustworthiness: Do what they say they will do.
  - Responsibility: Acknowledge their contributions to situations in which they are involved.
  - Sense of humor: Laugh with others and do not ridicule others.
- Provide frequent, immediate, and consistent feedback on behaviors.
- Establish reasonable and meaningful consequences for both compliant and noncompliant behaviors.
- Use behavioral contract to establish expectations, how they will be achieved, and specific rewards such as a reward system, making certain that teacher, student, and parent/caregiver are familiar with specifics of behavioral contract.

Attendance Guideline

- Exclusion from school is not required unless child is expelled for antisocial behavior.

Medication

- None is required.

Communication

- Encourage parent/caregiver to help child use problem-solving skills at home.

- Use a daily planner for assignments and for daily teacher-parent/caregiver communication.
- Explain to parent/caregiver that this is considered a mental disorder and not just childhood rebellion; as such, it needs professional intervention.

Resource

- Center for Mental Health Services
  (800) 789–2647
  www.mentalhealth.org

Behavior Disorders: Oppositional Defiant Disorder

Also known as: ODD

Description

Oppositional defiant disorder is a recurrent pattern of disobedient and hostile behavior toward authority figures. Disruptive behavior occurs at a more frequent rate, at greater intensity, and for longer periods of time than do the usual behavioral problems of peers.

Primary Group Affected

- Transient oppositional behavior is very common in preschool children and does not warrant diagnosis of oppositional defiant disorder.
- The number of oppositional symptoms increases with age.
- This disorder is more prevalent in boys than in girls before puberty.

Signs and Symptoms

- Frequently disruptive, argumentative, hostile, and irritable; deliberately annoys other people

- Deliberately defies adult rules
- Tends to blame others for child's own mistakes and difficulties
- Spiteful and vindictive behavior, leading to social problems with peers and adults
- Behavior leading to impaired academic functioning

Classroom Guidelines

- Discuss and model resolution of interpersonal conflict: compromising, negotiating, and dealing with frustration.
- Use peer mediation if available. Model students who are trained in mediation to help students who have problems with others.
- Teach problem-solving process.
- Discuss peer likability factors such as the following:
  - Trustworthiness: Do what they say they will do.
  - Responsibility: Acknowledge their contributions to situations in which they are involved.
  - Sense of humor: Laugh with others and do not ridicule others.
- Provide frequent, immediate, and consistent feedback on behaviors. Praise appropriate behaviors.
- Establish reasonable and meaningful consequences for both compliant and noncompliant behaviors.
- Use behavioral contracts to establish expectations, how they will be achieved, and the specific rewards, making certain that teacher, student, and parent/caregiver are familiar with specifics of behavioral contract.

Attendance Guideline

- Exclusion from school is not required.

Medication

- None is required.

Communication

- Ask parent/caregiver whether problem behavior occurs outside school setting.
- Encourage parent/caregiver to help child use problem-solving skills at home.

- Explain that this is considered a mental disorder and not just childhood rebellion; as such, it needs professional intervention.

Resource

- Center for Mental Health Services
  (800) 789–2647
  www.mentalhealth.org

Bipolar Disorder

Also known as: manic depressive disorder

Description

Bipolar disorder is characterized by periods of normal mood alternating with periods of depression and periods of mania. Intense mood swings typically last only 1 to 2 hours. There is a tendency to remission and recurrence throughout the life span.

Primary Group Affected

- Onset may occur in children of any age, but incidence increases with age of children.
- 75% of children with bipolar disorder also have attention deficit/hyperactivity disorder.
- 42% of children with bipolar disorder also have conduct disorder.

Signs and Symptoms

- Eating and sleeping disturbances
- Academic difficulties

Depression

- Younger children: loss of interest in newly acquired skills
- Separation anxiety
- Unexplained physical complaints
- Suicidal thoughts
- Tendency to get sad (girls)
- Tendency to act out negative feelings (boys): irritable, aggressive

Mania

- Elation or irritability
- Over-talkativeness
- Increased physical activity
- Poor attention span/concentration

Classroom Guidelines

- Set firm limits on unacceptable behavior.
- If concentration is a problem, provide a quiet and nonstimulating environment and keep activities simple and short.
- Limit decision making until child is able to make appropriate decisions more easily.
- Work with child to "stop and think" before acting impulsively.
- Be aware that child might not be able to participate in vigorous physical or mental activities due to an inability to stay focused or to a lack of energy.
- Help child to engage in quiet activities with one peer.
- Make sure that child eats lunch. He or she may have no appetite or be "too busy" to eat.
- Be aware that child may find that drawing or painting his or her feelings is easier than verbalizing these feelings.
- Look for any cues that child may be suicidal such as giving favorite objects away, making references to hurting self, or asking whether others will miss him or her—**911.**

Attendance Guidelines

- Exclusion from school is required when behavior is out of control or when child is unable to participate in curriculum. Education may be provided in an alternative setting.
- Readmission is usually allowed only with permission of therapist.

Medications

- Child will likely be on antidepressant medication.
- Child may also be on mood-stabilizing medication.

Communication

- Ask parent/caregiver about usual signs and symptoms when relapse is impending.

- Discuss effective approaches that help child to concentrate.
- Ask about medications and associated side effects.
- Ask about any previous suicidal thoughts or behaviors.

Resources

- National Depressive and Manic Depressive Association
  730 N. Franklin, Suite 501
  Chicago, IL 60649
  www.ndmda.org
- Child and Adolescent Bipolar Foundation
  1187 Wilmette Avenue
  Wilmette, IL 60091
  www.bpkids.org

Bladder Control Problems

Also known as: enuresis, bed-wetting

Description

Bladder control problems are characterized by involuntary urination when the child would be developmentally expected to have control of urination. Of these cases, 50% occur at night, 10% occur during the day, and 40% occur during both day and night. Bladder control difficulties may be related to neurological problems, congenital abnormalities, illness, or emotional stress.

Primary Group Affected

- Daytime enuresis is more common in girls than in boys.
- Nighttime enuresis is much more common in boys than in girls.
- In children who have been reliably dry for 6 to 12 months, enuresis is often associated with stress, infections, and sleep disorders.
- Children with attention deficit/hyperactivity disorder are at higher risk for bed-wetting.

Signs and Symptoms

- Urgency: immediate urge to urinate, frequent complaints of discomfort
- Restlessness: inability to sit still, fidgeting behavior
- Frequency: need to urinate frequently
- Withdrawal from play, decreased desire to be at school or to interact with other children

Classroom Guidelines

- Provide child with privacy to avoid ridicule from peers.
- Look for any cues that child needs to urinate.
- Coordinate established treatment approaches into child's school day; for example, set times for bathroom visits every 2 hours.
- Coordinate with parent/caregiver to have a change of clothing: underwear, socks, slacks/pants, top, and shoes.

Attendance Guidelines

- Exclusion from school is not required.
- Be aware that school performance and attendance may be affected if peers are rejecting child.

Medications

- Child may be on an antidepressant medication.
- Oxybutynin (Ditropan) or hyoscyamine may be used for night-time bed-wetting.
- Desmopressin may be given as a nasal spray or pill for night-time bed-wetting. Because it is expensive, it is usually reserved for times when child is away from home such as sleepovers and camp. Avoid excessive fluids if child is on this medication.

Communication

- Discuss any new or chronic stressors present in child's life.
- Ask parent/caregiver what child says about his or her experience when episodes occur at school.
- Ask whether child talks about guilt, blame, shame, and/or embarrassment.
- Ask for description of the bladder training program, fluid or food restrictions (e.g., carbonated and caffeinated drinks, citrus and mild products, sweets, vitamin C, beverages containing artificial dyes), and behavioral or reward management approaches.

Resources

- National Kidney Foundation
  kidney.org/patients/bedwet.cfm
- www.drybed.com
- www.bedwet.com

Body Piercing Infection/ Reaction

Description

Body piercing infection is a reaction of the body due to a perforation of any human body part other than the ear lobe for the purpose of inserting jewelry or other decoration or for some other nonmedical purpose. Healing times for piercing are usually as follows: ear lobe, 6 to 8 weeks; ear cartilage, 4 months to 1 year; eyebrow, 6 to 8 weeks; nostril, 2 to 4 months; nasal septum, 6 to 8 months; nasal bridge, 8 to 10 weeks; tongue, 4 weeks; lip, 2 to 3 months; and navel, 4 months to 1 year.

Primary Group Affected

- Teenagers are the primary group affected, but children of any age may get their bodies pierced with parental consent.

Signs and Symptoms

- Reactions to body piercing may include swelling, clear yellow-green drainage, rash or bumps around the piercing, increased temperature (99 degrees or higher), redness, fatigue, nausea, and vomiting.
- In rare instances, hepatitis B or C may occur.

Classroom Guidelines

- Restrict child from participating in swimming or field trips at beaches or public pools until healing occurs.

- Urge child to avoid public pools and beaches until piercing is completely healed.

Attendance Guideline

- Exclusion from school is not required unless child has increased temperature.

Medications

- Antibiotics and mild pain relievers may be ordered for child, in which case a schedule needs to be followed.

Communication

- Ask whether child needs to clean piercing site with any special solutions.
- Notify parent/caregiver and school health provider if child complains of any of signs and symptoms listed above after having body part pierced.

Resource

- www.vh.org/patients/ihb/derm/tattoo

Bowel Control Problems

Also known as: encopresis, fecal incontinence

Description

Bowel control problems are characterized by a recurrent, abnormal elimination pattern of soiling of passage of feces at inappropriate times. Most cases result from chronic constipation that leads to overflow. The problem is called primary encopresis in children who never develop bowel control by age 4 years. Secondary encopresis occurs after children have established bowel control for at least several months.

Primary Group Affected

- Occurs in 1% of school-age children
- May be related to emotional problems and/or changes in family such as new baby, recent move, and stressful or violent environment
- May coexist with bed-wetting, but bowel control problems are less frequent
- More common in boys than in girls

Signs and Symptoms

- Feces may be passed at inappropriate times or settings, more frequently during the day than at night, in child who developmentally should have bowel control.
- Child may want to avoid using bathroom—a habit begun while having pain with bowel movements.

- Seepage of feces or leaking stools may be mistaken for diarrhea, which may be more likely to occur during times of high physical activity such as recess and gym class.
- Clothing may be soiled with stool, and child may have an offensive odor from leaking stool without his or her being aware.

Classroom Guidelines

- Avoid power struggles, punishment, and situations that expose child to ridicule from peers.
- Look for any cues that child needs to have a bowel movement.
- Provide regular trips to bathroom.
- Coordinate established treatment approaches into child's school day; for example, child may need to sit on toilet for 5 to 10 minutes after meals.
- Coordinate with parent/caregiver to have change of clothing: underwear, socks, slacks/pants, top, and shoes.
- Follow dietary suggestions, including high-fiber foods such as fruits, vegetables, and whole grains. Child may have dietary limitations of refined, highly processed foods and dairy products.

Attendance Guidelines

- Exclusion from school is not required.
- Be aware that school performance and attendance may be affected if peers are rejecting child.

Medications

- May be treated with mineral oil, bulk-forming laxatives, and/or stool softeners to temporarily relieve existing constipation and reestablish normal bowel habits

Communication

- Discuss with parent/caregiver any new or chronic stressors present in child's life.
- Discuss what child says about his or her experience when episodes occur at school.
- Ask parent/caregiver whether child talks about guilt, blame, shame, and/or embarrassment.

- Inquire regarding treatment approaches used to manage condition.
- Ask about medications that child is taking.

Resource

- www.medicine.uiowa.edu/uhs/enco.cfm

Bronchitis

Also known as: tracheobronchitis, chronic cough

Description

Bronchitis (brong ki' tis) is an inflammation of the large airways called the bronchial tubes (main air passageways) and trachea (windpipe). Typically, bronchitis is a viral infection (not bacterial) and often follows another infection such as a cold, influenza, or upper respiratory infection. Factors that predispose a child to bronchitis include exposure to the virus, chilling, fatigue, and malnutrition. Bronchitis can also be the result of exposure to cigarette smoke, dust, fumes, or other pollutants. Bronchitis can be classified as acute or chronic. Most people with acute bronchitis are ill for 3 or 4 days, although the cough may last 3 weeks or longer. Acute bronchitis is self-limiting and generally requires only symptomatic treatment. Chronic bronchitis is characterized by repeated or extended episodes of coughing, and other symptoms may be related to a more serious underlying respiratory problem such as asthma.

Primary Group Affected

- Infants
- Preschool and school-age children

Signs and Symptoms

- Shortness of breath
- Fast breathing
- Cough: initially dry, hacking, and painful; later with mucus expectoration
- Runny nose, nasal congestion

- Yellow or green sputum
- Wheezing
- Feeling of constriction in chest
- Chills and slight fever (101 degrees) with acute (not chronic) bronchitis
- Fatigue
- No appetite

Classroom Guidelines

- Ensure proper hand-washing technique (*see* Procedure A).
- Ensure proper disposal of child's tissues.
- Avoid sharing of personal articles such as drinking glasses and eating utensils.
- Be aware that child can become easily dehydrated. Provide opportunities to drink water.
- Advise any child or staff member with a persistent cough to seek care from a health care provider.

Attendance Guideline

- Exclusion from school is required until fever has resolved.

Medications

- Because it is usually a viral infection, no antibiotics are needed.
- Cough medicine may be ordered.
- If there is underlying asthma, an inhaler might be used (*see* Asthma).

Communication

- Ask parent/caregiver about schedule of medications to support/monitor child's compliance.

Resource

- www.mayoclinic.org

Burns

Description

A burn is an injury that results in cell/tissue death as a result of a thermal, chemical, or electrical source. The severity of the burn will depend on its initial cause and on the length of time it remained in contact with the tissue. Burns are classified as first, second, or third degree. If no infection occurs, minor burns generally heal without complications except for scarring. Serious burns require the constant wearing of special pressure garments after healing has occurred. These may include a jacket, tights, an arm sleeve, and/or a face mask.

Primary Group Affected

- Higher incidence in children under age 5 years and from lower socioeconomic families

Signs and Symptoms

- First-degree burns are red, warm, tender, and painful but usually do not blister (outer skin only).
- Second-degree burns have the same symptoms as well as blistering and swelling (through the outer skin and into the inner skin)—**911.**
- Because third-degree burns involve the destruction of nerve endings, pain may be reduced (through the inner skin [dermis] and into the underlying tissue)—**911.**

Classroom Guidelines

- Remove child from the source of the burn immediately and apply cool water to the affected area with towels or running water.

- Seek immediate assistance from the school health care provider.
- Call **911** if the burn appears large or deep, due to an electrical source or lightning strike, or involves smoke inhalation.
- Clean minor burns with soap and water, and cover them with a topical antibiotic and dressing.
- Evaluate the area of the burn and determine whether child will have difficulty with any activities.
- Adjust the assignments/expectations of child to accommodate his or her level of functioning.
- Ensure that the wound dressing does not become wet or soiled during school activities.
- Ask child whether he or she is experiencing pain if child's attitude or work quality changes.
- Prepare other students for the return of child if the burn has been significant, stressing how the burn may have affected child's outward appearance and ability to play/interact.

Attendance Guideline

- Exclusion from school is not required except for serious burns requiring hospitalization and rehabilitation. This may cause a significant lapse in school attendance.

Medications

- Acetaminophen is used to control pain, but a stronger prescription drug might be needed depending on the severity of the burn.

Communication

- Ask parent/caregiver whether the burn is over a joint surface or is causing difficulty with motion.
- Ask how much pain child is experiencing.
- Ask whether child requires pain medication at school and, if so, what the medication is.
- Ask what the side effects of any pain medication are and whether they will affect the child's ability to concentrate in class.
- Ask what should be done if there is excessive drainage or bleeding on the wound dressing.
- Ask for instructions if child is wearing a special pressure garment on burned area.

Resource

- American Burn Association
  625 N. Michigan Avenue, Suite 1530
  Chicago, IL 60613
  (312) 642–9260
  www.ameriburn.org

Cancer

Also known as: malignancy (ma lig'nan si), leukemia (lu key'me a), lymphoma (limf o' ma)

Description

Cancer involves the abnormal growth of cells in organs and tissue. Cancer affects only 14 of every 100,000 American children every year. The most common childhood cancers include leukemia, lymphoma, and brain cancer. Leukemia causes abnormalities of the white blood cells in the bone marrow. This type of cancer leads to anemia, infection, and bleeding problems. Lymphoma affects the lymph system, that is, the system that travels through the whole body and fights off infection. This type of cancer results when the cancerous lymphocytes (a type of white blood cells) multiply and crowd out normal cells. In most cases, cancer in children occurs as the result of mutations in the genes; therefore, there is no effective way in which to prevent it. Cancer treatments include medications to kill cancer cells (chemotherapy), radiation, and surgery. Chemotherapy involves the use of anti-cancer medicines given through intravenous feedings. Radiation uses energy rays like X rays to destroy or damage abnormal cancer cells. Surgery involves an operation to remove the cancer.

Primary Group Affected

- Any age group

Signs and Symptoms

- Fevers
- Frequent infections
- Weight loss

- Nausea
- Anemia
- Poor appetite
- Headaches
- Tire easily
- Bruise/bleed easily
- Frequent nosebleeds
- Pain in joints
- Swollen glands (lymph nodes)
- Seizures
- Poor coordination
- Weakness on one side of the body
- Headaches (particularly in the early morning) combined with nausea and vomiting
- Slurred speech
- Dizziness
- Sudden change in vision or sense of smell

Classroom Guidelines

- Assist child and classmates in understanding the side effects of cancer treatments.
  - Chemotherapy side effects:
    - Nausea
    - Very tired
    - Hair loss
    - Infection
  - Radiation side effects:
    - Very tired
    - Nausea and vomiting
    - Diarrhea
- Ensure proper hand-washing technique to minimize the spread of infection (*see* Procedure A).
- Develop a plan to assist child in learning during time absent from school.
- Schedule frequent rest periods to accommodate decreased energy levels.
- Provide opportunity for frequent small snacks to aid with nausea and vomiting.

Attendance Guideline

- Exclusion from school is not required except when contagious illness is in the classroom.

Medications

- Acetaminophen (Tylenol) or ibuprofen (Motrin) may be given for fever and pain relief with parent/caregiver permission.
- Medications may be used to control nausea and diarrhea. Consult with parent/caregiver regarding how and when to administer.

Communication

- Clarify with parent/caregiver which activities and sports are safe for child.
- Communicate with parent/caregiver whether there are contagious illnesses in the classroom given that children undergoing cancer treatment can become seriously infected quite easily.

Resource

- www.candlelighters.org

Cellulitis

Description

Cellulitis (sel u li' tis) is a serious bacterial infection of the skin that usually spreads after some type of injury to a child's skin. The initial injury typically is an open sore that gets infected; however, it can occur in areas where the skin is not broken as well. Cellulitis most commonly occurs on a child's face or lower legs. The child may complain of feeling sick and develop a fever as the infection spreads. A child who has been bitten by an animal, a saltwater fish, or a shellfish needs to be watched for signs of cellulitis. Many different types of bacteria can cause cellulitis.

Primary Group Affected

- Any child whose skin is injured from a cut, bruise, scrape, or bump
- Any children who are living with diabetes or taking medicines that affect the immune system

Signs and Symptoms

- Swelling of skin
- Tenderness
- Warm skin
- Pain
- Bruising
- Blisters
- Fever
- Headache
- Chills
- Weak feeling

- Red streaks from original site of cellulitis
- Very large area of red inflamed skin—**911**
- Numbness, tingling, or other changes in hand, arm, leg, or foot—**911**
- Skin that appears to be black—**911**
- Red and swollen area around child's eye(s) or behind child's ear(s)—**911**

Classroom Guidelines

- Have child wear protective clothing/gear during active play or sports.
- If child gets a scrape, wash site well with soap and water and then cover with a bandage.
- Notify parent/caregiver and urge to seek medical treatment if child has a large cut, deep puncture wound, or bite.
- If child has an extremity affected site, you may need to restrict activity and the child's arm or leg may need to be elevated.
- Be aware that if warm wet dressings are prescribed for infection site, they might need to be applied during school day.
- Be aware that child may be on antibiotics that adhere to a strict time schedule.

Attendance Guidelines

- Exclusion from school is not required unless prescribed by health care provider or child is hospitalized.
- Child may need rest, intravenous antibiotics, or surgery.

Medications

- Oral antibiotics (depending on antibiotic, may or may not be given with food)

Communication

- Notify parent/caregiver and urge to seek medical treatment if child has a large cut, deep puncture wound, or bite.
- Ask about activity restrictions.
- Ask about schedule of medications to be given to child.
- Ask about need for warm wet dressings during school day.

Resources

- www.kidshealth.org
- www.mayoclinic.org

Cerebral Palsy

Also known as: CP

Description

Cerebral palsy is a nonprogressive permanent neurological disorder that occurs during infancy/early childhood when the brain suffers trauma or is deprived of oxygen. The extent of this disorder varies greatly from child to child. There is no known cure for this disorder. The prognosis is dependent on the severity of the brain dysfunction. A small group of children have normal IQs with only slight evidence of motor dysfunction, while others can be profoundly cognitively disabled and incapable of any purposeful movement. Most children fall between these two extremes.

Primary Group Affected

- Affects males and females equally

Signs and Symptoms

- Motor movement having a distinctive posturing, with the majority being spastic movements
- May appear as having great difficulty in moving or unable to move at all
- May have other problems such as seizures, mental/cognitive disability (ranging from mild to profound), inability to swallow, and impairments of speech, hearing, vision, and sensory input

Classroom Guidelines

- Be aware that the needs of child will be dependent on the severity of his or her brain lesion.

- Arrange for child's safe exit from classroom in case of an unexpected event that requires students to leave classroom or school.
- Allow for child's independence as much as possible.
- Dispense medications according to schedule and school policy.
- Follow seizure precautions if child has a history of seizures (*see* Epilepsy/Seizure Disorders).
- Inquire whether child can participate in physical education/recess and, if so, to what extent.
- Ensure that child wears braces/splints as instructed.
- Provide for extra time allowance between classrooms if needed.
- Observe child's ability to maneuver the hallways/stairs, especially if using an assistance device.
- Develop a system of communication to interact with the child if he or she cannot speak.
- Be aware of the following for the child with poor motor tone/gag reflex:
  - Inability to swallow properly or to cough or bring up mucus
  - No eating/drinking via the mouth, possible use of a gastrostomy tube for feedings (*see* Procedure E)
  - Oral/nasal suctioning, possible tracheostomy (*see* Procedure D)
  - May need diapering if unable to control bowel or bladder soiling
  - May require repositioning every 2 hours
  - May require wheelchair for mobility
  - May need communication boards or a system to allow child to communicate needs

Attendance Guidelines

- Exclusion from school is not required.
- Due to the level of care required, child may have an aide assigned and may have multiple absences due to medical appointments.

Medications

- Medications vary with child's symptoms. For child unable to swallow, medications may be administered through a gastrostomy tube (*see* Procedure E).
- Child with a history of seizures may be on anti-seizure medication with a side effect of drowsiness.

Communication

- Ask parent/caregiver what activities child can do for himself or herself and those with which child requires assistance.
- Ask questions regarding child's mental/cognitive abilities.
- Ask about child's system for communication.
- Ask about child's method for mobility: independent, walker, or wheelchair.
- Ask whether child has a gastrostomy tube and, if so, whether he or she is allowed to have anything by mouth.
- Ask whether child requires medications at school and about the schedule for regular medications.
- Ask whether child has a history of seizures.
- Ask whether child has splints/braces and, if so, about the wearing schedule.

Resources

- United Cerebral Palsy Association
  1660 L Street, N.W., Suite 700
  Washington, DC 20036
  (800) 872–5827
  www.ucpa.org
- http://dir.yahoo.com/health/diseases_and_conditions/cerebral_palsy
- www.mayoclinic.org

Chicken Pox

Also known as: varicella (var i sel' ah)

Description

Chicken pox is caused by the varicella zoster virus. The disease is highly contagious but generally causes a mild illness. The disease may more seriously affect infants and persons who already have impaired immune systems. Chicken pox can also cause severe health problems in pregnant women, causing damage to their unborn infants. A child with chicken pox is contagious for 1 to 2 days before the characteristic rash begins and contagion continues until all of the lesions (pimples) have scabs. Chicken pox is spread by person-to-person contact when a susceptible person is exposed to respiratory secretions or directly to fluid from the open lesions of an infected person. The varicella virus will always remain in the body and may later take the form of shingles (herpes zoster), which is a painful skin rash. The chicken pox vaccine has been available since 1995 and is approved for healthy children over age 12 months. At least 70% of those who receive the vaccine are protected from chicken pox; the remainder will usually develop very mild symptoms with fewer lesions and lower fever and will recover more quickly. Vaccinated children who get this milder form of chicken pox can still spread the disease to others who are not protected.

Primary Group Affected

- Can occur at any age; adults more likely to have more complications
- Most common in ages 2 to 8 years
- Occurs most often in late winter and spring

Signs and Symptoms

- Itchy rash of small red lesions (pimples) that spreads to the stomach, back, and face (a few lesions to as many as 500 lesions)
- Fever
- Malaise
- Poor appetite

Classroom Guidelines

- Ensure proper hand-washing technique (*see* Procedure A).
- Ensure proper disposal of child's tissues used to wipe eyes.
- Avoid sharing of personal articles such as drinking glasses and eating utensils.
- Keep fingernails short and clean.
- Try to distract child from scratching scabs.
- Be aware that a cooler environment may lessen itching.
- Teach child to apply pressure to area that itches rather than to scratch it.
- With older children, try to help them understand that scars will form from scratching.

Attendance Guideline

- Exclusion from school is required until scabs have formed over last group of lesions (pimples).

Medication

- Topical calamine lotion to reduce itching

Communication

- Notify all staff members and parents/caregivers that a case of chicken pox has occurred.
- Contact local health department (required in some areas).

Resource

- CDC Hotline
  (800) 232–2522 (English) or (800) 232–0233 (Spanish)

Cold Sores

Also known as: herpes simplex type 1 (her' pez sim' plex), fever blisters

Description

Cold sores are a common and contagious form of the herpes simplex virus. Once a child is infected with herpes, the virus is carried for life. It can reappear on the lips as a "cold sore" or "fever blister." The virus is spread by direct contact with infected mucus or saliva, most frequently through kissing or through sharing towels or eating utensils. The herpes simplex type 1 virus can be spread even when blisters are not present. The greatest risk for contracting the virus is from the initial appearance of the blister to when it has completely crusted over. Symptoms might not be apparent for as long as 20 days after exposure. Cold sores are very different from canker sores. Canker sores are not contagious and are small sores inside the soft tissue of the mouth.

Primary Group Affected

- Children of any age who have come in contact with virus.

Signs and Symptoms

- Small, fluid-filled blisters develop on a raised red area of skin, usually the lip but sometimes the nostrils, cheeks, or fingers; blisters will break and ooze, form a yellow crust, and finally come off to uncover pinkish skin.
- If cold sores are inside of mouth, they are found on gums or roof of mouth.
- Pain or tingling often precedes blisters by 1 to 2 days.
- Small hard spot on lip is not visible.
- Fever, menses, and exposure to sun may initiate an outbreak.
- Once symptoms appear, they usually last for 7 to 10 days.

Classroom Guidelines

- Urge child not to share eating utensils or drinks.
- Urge child to wash hands frequently.
- Urge child to use sun block on lips and face before long exposure to sun if he or she is prone to cold sores.
- Be aware that a child with a cold sore should be kept away from a child with an immune system disorder or a child who has undergone an organ transplant.
- Apply ice to blister if it is painful.
- Urge child not to squeeze, pinch, or pick at blisters.
- If child complains of pain or a feeling that something is in the eye, sensitivity to light, and/or drainage from the eye, notify parent/caregiver and urge to follow up with a health care provider (eye infection with virus is a complication and can cause blindness).

Attendance Guidelines

- Each child's situation should be evaluated on an individual basis.
- Exclusion from school is required until lesions are dry.

Medications

- Antiviral medications may be ordered in some extreme circumstances.
- Over-the-counter creams may be used to provide comfort. Disposable gloves should be used in applying ointment or cream.

Communication

- Ask parent/caregiver about any medications ordered.
- Notify parent/caregiver if child complains of pain or a feeling that something is in the eye, sensitivity to light, and/or drainage from the eye.

Resources

- www.mayoclinic.org
- www.vh.org/patients/ihb/peds/infectious/oralherpes.html

Color Blindness

Also known as: color vision deficiency

Description

Color blindness is the inability to identify various colors and shades. There are several different kinds and degrees of color deficiency. It is very rare to be totally color-blind (monochromasy). Most color vision problems are present at birth due to a hereditary color vision deficiency, and there is currently no known cure or treatment. A child living with color vision deficiency may be especially challenged when confronted with color-enhanced instructional materials in the classroom (e.g., colored paper, crayons), chalk boundaries on grass (which the child does not see), or following directions of connecting lines to colored objects (which the child is unable to do). The color-blind child, when asked which color ball is the biggest ball, might not be able to respond appropriately because the names red, orange, yellow, and green are simply different names for the same color. The same may be true for violet, purple, lavender, and blue. Among the colors most often confused are pink/gray, orange/red, green/yellow, brown/maroon, and beige/green. Differentiating among pastel colors also presents a challenge for the child.

Primary Group Affected

- 5% to 8% of males and fewer than 1% of females

Signs and Symptoms

- Child may have difficulty in distinguishing among red, green, brown, and gray; red and black may look the same; pink and purple may be seen as gray or blue; dull yellow, orange, and light green may look the same; and pastels and different shades may be confusing.

- Child is not accurate in identifying colors of crayons.
- Child is challenged when it comes to drawing lines connecting certain colored objects.
- Child may have difficulty in distinguishing writing with yellow chalk on green chalkboard.
- Child may color faces, arms, legs, and the like with a crayon that does not depict normal color (e.g., may color a face green).
- Child may have difficulty in distinguishing lines on a field for a specific sports event.
- Child frequently may wear different colored socks.

Classroom Guidelines

- Label coloring utensils with names of colors.
- Use white chalk (not colored chalk) on blackboard, avoiding yellow, orange, or light tan chalk on green chalkboards.
- Photocopy textbooks or instructional materials printed with colored ink. Black print on red or green paper is not safe because it may appear as black on black to a color-blind child.
- Assign classmate to assist color-blind child with assignments that require color recognition such as different countries on a world map.
- Teach child living with color deficiency colors of common objects, such as grass, flowers, and the sky, so that he or she can use labeled coloring utensils.
- Try to teach child all of the colors. Rarely are children unable to distinguish all colors; it is usually different shades or tints that challenge them.

Attendance Guideline

- Exclusion from school is not required.

Medication

- None is required.

Communication

- If you suspect that a child has a color deficiency, request that child be tested before he or she has to learn colors or use color-enhanced instructional materials. In some school systems, the school nurse will be able to test for color blindness.

- Discuss with parent/caregiver the best approach to working with child. Attempt to be consistent in efforts and to decrease frustration for child in learning colors and performing other color-related tasks.

Resources

- www.preventblindness.org
- www.firelily.com/opinions/color.html
- www.color-vision.com
- www.dai-sho.com/colorblindness

Common Cold

Also known as: cold, stuffy nose, runny nose, upper respiratory infection, rhinovirus (ri no vi' rus), nasopharyngitis (na zo far in ji' tis)

Description

Although the common cold is usually mild, with symptoms lasting a week or less, it is the most frequent reason for children to be absent from school. On average, children have about 6 to 10 colds a year. Colds seem to be related to children's lack of resistance to infection and to contact with other children in school. There is no known cure for the common cold, especially because more than 200 viruses are known to cause cold symptoms. Most colds occur during the fall and winter. Increases in colds begin in late August or early September and the number remains high until March or April.

Primary Group Affected

- Children of any age who have come in contact with cold viruses

Signs and Symptoms

- Nasal discharge
- Difficulty in breathing through nose
- Swelling of sinus membranes (may complain of tenderness under and/or above eyes)
- Sneezing, coughing, and sore throat (and sometimes hoarseness)
- Headache
- Watery eyes
- Decreased appetite
- Fever (usually slight but reach to 102 degrees)
- Fatigue
- Symptoms that can last 2 to 14 days (symptoms that last longer may be due to an allergy)

- Infections of ear and/or sinuses (e.g., high fever, swollen glands, severe facial pain in sinuses, cough that produces mucus) that may require treatment by health care provider

Classroom Guidelines

- Urge child not to share eating utensils or drinks.
- Urge child to wash hands frequently (*see* Procedure A).
- Take child's oral temperature.
- Have child use tissue to cover nose and mouth when sneezing or coughing and then dispose of tissue in an appropriate receptacle.
- If possible, avoid prolonged contact with child who has a cold.
- Be aware that a child with a cold should be kept away from a child with an immune system disorder or a child who has undergone an organ transplant.
- If possible, clean environmental surfaces with virus-killing disinfectant; some rhinoviruses can survive up to 3 hours outside the nasal passages and on inanimate objects.
- Urge child to drink fluids if possible.

Attendance Guidelines

- Each child's situation should be evaluated on an individual basis as to whether or not child is too ill (e.g., excessive coughing, discolored or white nasal drainage) to participate in classroom activities.
- Child may return to school when there is no elevated temperature for 24 hours.

Medications

- Child may be taking over-the-counter medications, cough medicines, and/or antihistamines that may cause drowsiness.

Communication

- Notify parent/caregiver if child is too sick to participate in classroom activities.
- Ask parent/caregiver about any medications child is taking.

Resources

- www.kidsource.com/health/the.common.cold.html
- www.schoolnurse.com

Cystic Fibrosis

Description

Cystic fibrosis is a genetic disease that causes the body to produce an abnormally thick sticky mucus. This is due to the faulty transport of sodium and chloride (salt) within the cell lining. The thick mucus blocks the lungs and pancreas. Vitamin deficiencies may occur because enzymes are prevented from reaching the intestines to help break down and digest food.

Primary Group Affected

- Affects approximately 30,000 children and adults in United States
- Affects about 1 of every 2,000 white infants

Signs and Symptoms

- Salty-tasting skin
- Persistent coughing
- Wheezing or pneumonia
- Frequent respiratory infections
- Excessive appetite but poor weight gain
- Diarrhea and foul-smelling stools
- Difficulty in breathing—**911**

Classroom Guidelines

- If child is experiencing difficulty in breathing, then activate local emergency medical system if necessary.

- Consult parent/caregiver for individualized treatment routine.
- Allow child to drink fluids frequently.
- Communicate with parent/caregiver and school nurse frequently regarding child's treatments.
- Be familiar with chest physical therapy: vigorous percussion (by cupped hands) on the back and chest to dislodge the thick mucus from the child's lungs.

Attendance Guideline

- Exclusion from school is not required unless child has an elevated temperature or severe difficulty in breathing.

Medications

- Antibiotics useful for lung infections
- Enriched diets with vitamins and enzymes

Communication

- Ask parent/caregiver about the treatment plan.
- Ask about the schedule of medications.
- Ask about child's abilities and limitations.

Resources

- Cystic Fibrosis Foundation
  6931 Arlington Road
  Bethesda, MD 20814
  (800) 344–4823
  info@cff.org
- www.cff.org/living_with_cf
- www.nhlbi.nih.gov/health/public/lung/other/cf.htm

Depression

Also known as: unipolar mood disorder, clinical depression

Description

Depression is an altered mood state with a loss of interest in usually pleasurable activities and diminished interest in daily activities of living. Depression negatively influences the normal development of children who are unable to complete age-appropriate tasks. Academic progress and peer relationships are often compromised.

Primary Group Affected

- Incidence of depression in children is often underestimated. Cultural norms maintain that childhood is a carefree and happy time and that there is no reason for children to be depressed.
- In reality, at least 2.5% of children are depressed at any point in time.
- Boys and girls are at equal risk.
- Those who have family histories of depression are at higher risk.

Signs and Symptoms

Infants

- When separated from parent/caregiver, may have weepy and withdrawn behavior
- Frozen facial expression
- Weight loss and increased incidence of infections

Ages 1 to 3 Years

- Delays or regression in toileting, eating, sleeping, and intellectual growth

- Increase in nightmares
- May appear sad or expressionless
- Apathetic or more clingy

Ages 3 to 5 Years

- Loss of interest in newly acquired skills
- Nightmares with themes of annihilation
- Enuresis, encopresis, anorexia, binge eating
- May experience separation anxiety
- Frequent negative self-statements and thoughts or impulses of self-harm

Ages 6 to 12 Years

- Depressed mood, irritable, aggressive
- Academic difficulties
- Eating and sleeping disturbances
- Severe self-criticism and guilt
- Suicidal ideation and plans—**911**

Classroom Guidelines

- If child has difficulty in concentrating, present activities and lessons in short segments.
- Introduce only one topic or question at a time.
- Because thinking processes may be slowed, allow enough time for child to comprehend expectations and instructions. Clarify child's understanding through use of questions and feedback.
- Provide opportunities for success. Praise and reinforce behavior, especially positive characteristics and behavior, whenever possible.
- Ask child to compose a list of all his or her strengths (e.g., "I am honest," "I am a good friend," "I can throw a ball," "I can skip rope," "I am a good big brother").
- Because child might not have energy to interact with peers, which can result in social isolation, plan for child to interact with one other child at a time for short segments.
- Encourage child to play outside and attend gym classes because exercise is nature's way of decreasing feelings of depression. Finding a friend to exercise with child may be very helpful.

Attendance Guideline

- Exclusion from school is not required unless child is actively suicidal and in need of hospitalization.

Medications

- Antidepressant medication is given to children with severe symptoms and those with chronic or recurrent episodes.
- Medications are often given several times throughout day.

Communication

- Provide direction to parent/caregiver in supporting child in completing homework assignments using a daily planner.
- Encourage parent/caregiver to help child participate in after-school activities.

Resource

- National Foundation for Depressive Illness
  P.O. Box 2257
  New York, NY 10116
  (800) 239–1265
  www.depression.org

Diabetes

Also known as: diabetes mellitus (di ah be' tez mel'litus), sugar diabetes, type 1 diabetes (juvenile diabetes, insulin-dependent diabetes [IDDM]), type 2 diabetes (adult-onset diabetes, non-insulin-dependent diabetes [NIIDM])

Description

Diabetes mellitus is a chronic disease caused when a person either does not make enough of a hormone called insulin or the body cannot use the insulin properly. Insulin has the task of moving glucose from the blood into cells where it is converted into energy. In diabetes, because insulin is not working properly, glucose does not get moved into the cells as it should be. This results in a high blood sugar level and can lead to many other problems. The type of diabetes mellitus most commonly seen in children and teens is type 1 diabetes. In type 1 diabetes, the pancreas (pan' kre as) usually does not make any insulin. Because insulin is not made, those with type 1 diabetes will need to inject insulin and watch their diets very carefully. Type 2 diabetes occurs most commonly in adults and especially in overweight people. A person with type 2 diabetes makes some insulin and can often control his or her diabetes with just dietary changes. Oral medications that stimulate the pancreas to work better may be needed. Insulin may also be added to help control this condition. When blood sugars are not controlled well, serious complications can result, including kidney failure, heart disease, and blindness.

Primary Group Affected

- Children of any age may be affected.
- The greatest incidence for type 1 diabetes is in girls ages 10 to 12 years and in boys ages 12 to 14 years.

Signs and Symptoms

- Very thirsty
- Very hungry
- Needing to urinate often, bed-wetting
- Unexplained rapid weight loss
- Fatigue
- Sores that are slow to heal
- More infections than usual
- Tingling or numbness in hands or feet
- Sudden vision changes
- Loss of consciousness—**911**

Classroom Guidelines

- Understand signs of low blood sugar (usually from taking too much insulin or from eating too little), called hypoglycemia (hi po gli se' me ah), that include dizziness, shakiness, sweating, confusion, and the need to drink or eat sugar.
- Be aware that child may need to check blood sugar levels. This may involve puncturing skin to obtain a drop of blood.
- Recognize that many children have difficulty in accepting the diagnosis of diabetes. Be respectful of child's need for privacy with blood testing and insulin administration.
- Help child to make good food choices.
- Be aware that children with diabetes do best when they eat three meals plus two snacks per day and eat at about same time each day, avoiding or limiting foods with added sugar.

Attendance Guideline

- Exclusion from school is not required.

Medication

- Insulin given by injections or an insulin pump is used.

Communication

- Clarify with parent/caregiver the signs of hypoglycemia and what food is used to correct this (often skim milk, juice, and hard candy).
- Clarify how to assist with insulin administration if needed.

- Clarify how to assist with insulin pump use if necessary.
- Clarify acceptable and unacceptable foods to eat.

Resources

- www.childrenwithdiabetes.com
- www.idf.org

Diarrhea

Also known as: intestinal flu, stomach flu, runny bowels, loose stools, the runs

Description

Acute diarrhea (di ah re' ah), an increase in frequency and a change in consistency of bowel movements, is usually caused by bacteria, a virus, or a parasite infection. Foods, juices, laxatives, and antibiotics can also cause acute diarrhea. Most cases of acute diarrhea last 2 to 3 days and require no medical treatment other than supportive care to avoid dehydration. Chronic diarrhea lasts longer than 2 weeks and is usually caused by malabsorption syndrome, food allergies, lactose intolerance, or irritable bowel syndrome. Children with chronic diarrhea will need medical evaluations.

Primary Group Affected

- Children of any age
- More serious for infants, young children, and those with poor immune systems
- Leading cause of illness in children under age 5 years

Signs and Symptoms

- Bowel movements that are more frequent, looser, or more watery than usual
- Nausea and vomiting
- Abdominal cramps
- Headache
- Fever
- Blood in stools

- Loss of appetite
- Weight loss (chronic diarrhea)

Classroom Guidelines

- Be aware that hands should be washed after use of bathroom and before and after handling food (*see* Procedure A).
- Note that disposable paper towels should be used for hand washing.
- Clean bathroom surfaces and food preparation areas daily.
- Be aware that diapered children should be cared for by different staff in a separate room from toilet-trained children if possible.
- Use disposable table liners on changing table. Disinfect table after each diaper change.
- Because diarrhea can cause dehydration, ensure that child receives plenty of fluids.
- Because classroom pets, especially reptiles, can spread germs, wash pet cages/bowls in separate sink from where food is prepared.

Attendance Guideline

- Children who are not toilet trained and have diarrhea should be excluded from school regardless of cause.

Medications

- Anti-diarrhea medications may be used with chronic diarrhea.

Communication

- Notify parents/caregivers of children who have direct contact with child with diarrhea.
- Notify local health department if two or more children in one classroom have diarrhea within a 48-hour period.
- Notify local health department if it is learned diarrhea is due to *Shigella, Campylobacter jejuni, Salmonella, Giardia, Cryptosporidium,* or *Escherichia coli.*

Resource

- www.kidshealth.org

Down Syndrome

Also known as: trisomy 21, cognitive impairment, mental retardation

Description

Down syndrome occurs when an infant is born with three, rather than two, copies of chromosome 21. It is this extra genetic material that disrupts normal physical and cognitive development.

Primary Group Affected

- Any child may be affected. Down syndrome occurs in 1 of every 800 to 1,000 live births.
- Women over age 35 years have significantly increased risk of giving birth to children with Down syndrome.

Signs and Symptoms

- Poor muscle tone
- Facial abnormalities: flat facial profile, small nose, upward slant to eyes, abnormal shape and small size of ears, small skin folds on inner corners of eyes, enlargement of tongue in relationship to size of mouth
- Single deep crease across center of palm
- Excessive ability to extend joints
- Congenital heart defects
- Increased susceptibility to infection, respiratory problems, obstructed digestive tracts early in life, and childhood leukemia
- Chronic ear infections associated with hearing loss
- Cognitive impairment typically in mild to moderate range of disability

- Average rate of progress slower than that of nonaffected children: delayed motor development, language skills, and self-care activities

Classroom Guidelines

- Be aware that the Individuals with Disabilities Education Act (IDEA) protects rights of children in a least restrictive environment.
- Be aware that child will need an individualized education plan with inclusion in regular classroom.
- Encourage age-appropriate skills, realizing that development will be uneven in nature.
- Maintain consistency and predictability in classroom setting.
- Be aware that child may need repetitive directions and prompts about what his or her behavior should be.
- Use "time-outs" for inappropriate behavior.
- Use clear, concrete, and simple directions because child may have difficulty in understanding abstract thinking and/or non-verbal communication.
- Be geared to child's capabilities at current time.

Attendance Guideline

- Exclusion from school is not required.

Medication

- None is required.

Communication

- Understand that communication among teacher, parent/caregiver, and therapist must be clear and frequent.
- Be aware that older children should be involved in coordinated treatment plan.
- Ask parent/caregiver how to calm upset child.

Resource

- National Association for Down Syndrome
  P.O. Box 4542
  Oak Brook, IL 60522–4542
  (708) 325–9112
  www.nads.org

Dystonia

Description

Dystonia (dis to' ne ah) is a chronic neurological (brain) movement disorder that has to do with the way in which a child moves and usually develops gradually. It is rare to be born with signs of dystonia. It is characterized by involuntary skeletal muscle contractions that cause certain parts of the body to experience abnormal, sometimes painful movements or posturing that can affect any part of the body. Children living with dystonia have had their legs, arms, trunks, necks, faces, and eyelids affected. Dystonia does not affect children's intelligence, strength, vision, or hearing. Dystonia has no known cause or cure, and although it is not considered fatal, prognosis is difficult to predict.

Primary Group Affected

- Children of any race, age, or ethnicity
- Usually begins during early childhood after period of normal development; often begins in leg and foot

Signs and Symptoms

- Muscle contractions may cause twisting and repeated movements or abnormal posture.
- Child's neck may jerk in a backward position, resulting in complaints of neck stiffness or pain.
- Child might not be able to grasp pencil or write and might have poor handwriting.
- Child may frequently complain about cramps or fatigue in hands and legs.
- Child may have difficulty in sitting and walking.
- The disorder can spread to other muscles in child's body.

- Child may have "targets" (things they can do to make spasms disappear) such as sitting, walking, and touching back of head when walking.
- Child with neck dystonia may experience shortness of breath.
- Child may experience eye irritation, sensitivity to bright lights, and increased blinking.
- Child may experience face or jaw spasms, difficulty in chewing, and changes in speech.

Classroom Guidelines

- Be aware of safety concerns associated with child. Arrange for child's safe exit from classroom in case of an unexpected event that requires students to leave classroom or school.
- Plan suitable activities devised to meet needs of child.
- Treat child as normally as possible.
- Allow for handwriting difficulties.
- Be aware that dystonia that affects breathing or involvement of vocal cords may cause activity or speaking to be restricted according to medical guidelines.

Attendance Guideline

- Exclusion from school is not required unless child is recovering from surgery to lengthen tendons.

Medications

- Anticholinergics may be used.
- A combination of medications tailored to child's needs may be prescribed.

Communication

- Ask parent/caregiver about activity restrictions.
- Ask about schedule of medications to be given to child.
- Ask about known "targets" to assist in controlling spasms.
- Ask parent/caregiver/child whether child desires to inform classmates of disorder.

Resource

- www.dystonia-foundation.org

Ear Infection

Also known as: earache, otitis media (o ti' tis me' dia)

Description

Otitis media is an infection of the ear that often follows a cold, sore throat, or tonsillitis. Ear infection is the second most common childhood illness (behind only the common cold). It occurs more easily in children because of the decreased angle and length of the Eustachian (auditory) tube, which allows bacteria and viruses to be trapped inside. Otitis media can be a serious illness because lack of treatment can lead to middle ear damage and permanent hearing loss.

Primary Group Affected

- Under age 3 years, with incidence peaking between 6 months and 6 years
- Higher incidence in boys
- Incidence highest in winter and spring, incidence lowest in summer
- Often follows a cold or an upper respiratory infection
- Breathing in tobacco smoke
- Being bottle fed
- Having cleft palate
- Being Alaskan or American Indian

Signs and Symptoms

- Earache
- Ear discharge
- Fever
- Irritability

- Ringing in ears (tinnitus)
- Popping sounds
- Hearing loss
- Balance problems
- Hand held to ear, rubbing ears

Classroom Guidelines

- Dispense medications according to school regulations.
- If child is taking antihistamines that cause the body to lose water, offer opportunities to drink plenty of water.
- If child's hearing is affected, seat child to enhance hearing.
- Be aware that if tubes are in child's ears, child should wear earplugs when swimming.

Attendance Guidelines

- Exclusion from school is not required.
- Ear infections are not contagious, but exclusion from school is recommended for colds and respiratory infections that precede it.

Medications

- Decongestants, antihistamines, and/or acetaminophen (Tylenol) may be used with parent/caregiver permission.
- Aspirin should be avoided due to possible Reye's syndrome.
- Antibiotics may be used for 5 to 10 days as prescribed by health care provider.
- Tubes may be surgically inserted to drain fluid from middle ear if infections are chronic.

Communication

- Ask parent/caregiver about schedule of medications.
- Ask whether tubes have been placed in ears.
- Ask whether any hearing loss has occurred.

Resource

- www.kidshealth.org

Eating Disorder: Anorexia

Also known as: self-starvation, anorexia (an o rek' se ah) nervosa

Description

People with anorexia lose weight by dramatically decreasing their food intake and sharply increasing their amount of physical exercise.

Primary Group Affected

- Although more girls are identified as having anorexia, significant numbers of boys suffer from this disorder as well.
- Anorexia typically begins around ages 13 to 17 years, but early onset begins between ages 7 and 12 years.

Signs and Symptoms

- Nausea, abdominal pain, feeling full, unable to swallow, rapid and dramatic weight loss, irregular heartbeat, dry cracked skin
- May suffer from delayed growth and osteoporosis (thin bones)
- A desperate need to please others that results in overcompliant behavior, may overachieve in academic and extracurricular activities
- Excessive and compulsive exercise routines
- Terror of weight gain and fat
- Have no insight into disorder, believe that not eating is solution rather than problem
- Severely distorted body image, perceive self as fat even when emaciated

Classroom Guidelines

- Discourage excessive physical activity during recess and lunch break.
- Allow for snack breaks if this is part of the behavioral treatment plan.
- Avoid discussing food or physical complaints.
- Design classroom activities that will foster positive self-esteem.
- Encourage problem-solving activities and appropriate decision making.
- Avoid making statements that reinforce the culture's high value of thinness.

Attendance Guidelines

- Exclusion from school is not required.
- Be aware that if child is less than 75% of ideal body weight, he or she is likely to be placed in an inpatient eating disorder program.

Medication

- None is required.

Communication

- Ask parent/caregiver about the treatment program: specific goals and rewards and how the program should be carried out during school hours.
- Ask parent/caregiver about extracurricular activities that might be a factor in the eating disorder.

Resource

- National Association of Anorexia and Associated Disorders
  P.O. Box 7
  Highland Park, IL 60055
  Hotline: (847) 831–3438
  www.anad.org

Eczema

Also known as: atopic dermatitis (AD), chronic dermatitis, infantile eczema (ek' ze mah), contact dermatitis

Description

Eczema is a very common skin irritation, and the term actually refers to a number of different skin conditions. A red, irritated skin rash that becomes moist, oozing, and crusted characterizes this condition. The cause of eczema is unknown; however, it often appears in children who have or will later acquire allergies, hay fever, and asthma or who have family members with these conditions.

Primary Group Affected

- Most common in infants but can affect children of any age
- Affects about 10% of all infants and children
- Becomes worse during winter months

Signs and Symptoms

First Phase

- Usually ages 2 to 6 months, always by age 5 years
- Itchy, dry red bumps beginning on the face and scalp and spreading to remainder of body
- Eventually become oozy and then crusted lesions
- Symptoms that flare up and then diminish periodically

Second Phase

- Usually ages 4 to 10 years
- Round, raised, itchy scaly area on elbows and wrist as well as behind knees and ankles
- Extremely dry

Third Phase

- Usually subsides by early adulthood
- Itchy, dry scaly areas

Classroom Guidelines

- Dispense medications according to school regulations.
- Remind child not to scratch itchy areas; try distraction strategies.
- Be sensitive to emotional concerns of child.
- Urge child to avoid long hot showers/baths that dry the skin and to use warm water and mild soaps.
- Urge child to apply ointments (e.g., petroleum jelly) within a few minutes of showering.
- Urge child to try cold compresses on irritated areas.
- Avoid overheating and overstressing because both cause condition to worsen.
- Get rid of allergens that may increase flare-ups such as certain foods (eggs, milk, peanuts, soy, wheat, and seafood are common problem foods), dust, and pet dander.

Attendance Guideline

- Exclusion from school is not required.

Medications

- Topical corticosteroid creams or ointments are commonly used.
- Antihistamines may be used to help control itching.
- Oral or topical antibiotics may be used to treat secondary infections caused by itching.
- Ultraviolet light treatments may be prescribed.

Communication

- Ask parent/caregiver about schedule of medications to support/ monitor child's compliance.

Resources

- www.eczema-assn.org
- www.eczema.com

Epilepsy/
Seizure
Disorder

Description

Epilepsy (ep' i lep se) or seizure disorder is the most common serious neurological problem affecting children. Seizures occur when there are excessive electrical discharges in some nerve cells of the brain. When this happens, the brain loses control over certain muscles of the body. This loss of muscular control is temporary, and the brain functions normally between seizures. When seizures occur frequently, the disease is called epilepsy. The most familiar types of seizures are partial, complex partial, absence (petit mal), general tonic/clonic (grand mal), and febrile. There is no known cure for epilepsy, and seizures are not contagious.

Primary Group Affected

- 50% of all cases develop before age 10 years.
- 1 of every 50 children has epilepsy.
- Epilepsy can affect both females and males.

Signs and Symptoms

- Aura: a warning sign; varies from person to person; may be a change in body temperature, a feeling of tension or anxiety, a musical sound, a strange taste, a curious odor, or another individual sign

- Absence (petit mal): 5- to 15-second lapses in consciousness where child appears to be staring into space with eyes rolled upward; not preceded by an aura; activity resumed immediately afterward
- Partial seizure: strange or unusual sensations, including sudden jerky movements of one body part, distortions in hearing or seeing, stomach discomfort, and/or sudden sense of fear; consciousness not impaired
- Complex partial: appearance of being dazed and confused with purposeless behaviors such as random walking, mumbling, turning head, and pulling at clothing; possible staring and lip smacking (in children)
- General tonic/clonic: loss of consciousness, falling, and body becoming rigid at beginning of seizure; body jerking and twitching. In next phase, consciousness resuming slowly after seizure; may be preceded by an aura
- Febrile: often occurring with a fever (high temperature) at the time of an attack; generally lasting shorter than 15 minutes and not recurring within a 24-hour period; little confusion afterward

Classroom Guidelines

- Understand that safety of the child must be a key consideration. Uncontrolled seizures can present safety hazards to the unsupervised child. You need to be informed and prepared.
- Be aware that once a seizure has begun, there is nothing one can do to stop it.
- Keep calm in event of seizure. If possible, hold blanket up to screen child from other students and to give child privacy.
- Tonic/clonic seizures are most often dramatic and frightening. Other students may need to be reassured and calmed.
- Loosen child's collar and put something soft under his or her head.
- Do not try to restrain child.
- Remove hard, sharp, or hot objects from the area.
- Do not force anything between the child's teeth.
- After the seizure, turn child to one side and allow him or her to rest.
- If child has loss of bowel and/or bladder control during seizure, maintain child's privacy and allow him or her to change clothes without embarrassment.

- If seizure lasts longer than 2 to 3 minutes or if child seems to pass from one seizure to another without regaining consciousness, call **911.**
- Contact parent/caregiver.
- Reassure child and remain calm.
- Dispense medications according to school policy.

Attendance Guideline

- Exclusion from school is not required.

Medications

- Anticonvulsant therapy is preferred when possible and is effective with most children.
- Medications may include barbiturates, phenytoin, valproic acid, and Ethosuximide.
- About 50% of children who take medications will have their seizures eliminated, 30% will have their seizures reduced in intensity and frequency, and 20% will be resistant to medications or require larger doses to control their seizures.
- Side effects vary and may include drowsiness, dizziness, nausea, irritability, and hyperactivity.

Communication

- Ask parent/caregiver about child's seizures, that is, what they look like and how long they last.
- Ask parent/caregiver about treatment, medication schedule, and compliance with routine.

Resources

- Epilepsy Foundation
  4351 Garden City Drive
  Landover, MD 20785–7223
  (800) 332–1000
  www.efa.org
- National Institutes of Health
  (800) 352–9424

Eye Injury

Also known as: corneal abrasion, corneal laceration, eye scratch, eye trauma

Description

The cornea may be scratched or cut by contact with a toy, dust, dirt, sand, wood shavings, metal particles, or paper. Most often, the scratch is superficial. If the scratch becomes infected, there is a risk for developing a corneal ulcer, which is a more serious injury.

Primary Group Affected

- Children of any age, especially during outdoor activity time and in windy weather conditions
- Children engaged in doing projects such as sanding and carving wood

Signs and Symptoms

- Pain in eye (due to many sensory nerve endings in eye)
- Tears
- Blurred vision
- Sensitivity or redness around eyes
- Foreign body sticking to or embedded in eye—**911**

Classroom Guidelines

- *Do not* touch, or attempt to remove, any foreign body sticking or embedded in eye.
- If object is large and makes closing eye difficult, cover eye and object with a paper cup—**911,**
- Wash your hands (*see* Procedure A).

- Try to locate object in eye visually. Have child sit down and examine eye by gently pulling lower eyelid downward and instructing child to look at ceiling. Reverse procedure for upper eyelid; hold upper eyelid and examine eye while child looks at floor. If no penetrating object is present, tilt child's head and run lukewarm tap water over eye or splash eye with clean water, aiming for inner corner so that water washes over eye.
- If pain, vision problem, or redness persists or if flushing with water proves to be unsuccessful in removing the foreign body, apply a loose clean cloth over eye or both eyes (if child can tolerate this) and seek medical attention—**911.**
- Have child blink several times unless foreign body is penetrating, large, or obvious.
- Pull upper eyelid over lower eyelid if an object is under eyelid unless foreign body is penetrating, large, or obvious.
- Caution child *not* to rub eye because doing so can make the situation worse.
- *Do not* apply patches or ice packs to eye.
- *Do not* press on the eyeball.
- Be aware that child may experience anxiety due to vision limitations. Keep child safe and calm.
- Provide any special accommodations necessary to respond to vision limitations such as distance considerations from blackboard and visual supplements used in classroom.
- Be aware that child may have difficulty in reading and that vision may be blurred or limited during the healing process.

Attendance Guideline

- Exclusion from school is not required.

Medications

- Only as ordered by health care provider as follow-up

Communication

- Notify parent/caregiver of injury.
- Ask parent/caregiver about any restrictions or special accommodations to be implemented while eye heals.

Resource

- www.mayoclinic.org

Eye Splash

Also known as: chemical splash in eye, chemical burn

Description

Eye splash is characterized by the eye coming in contact with a chemical (alkali or acid) or radiation burns. Acid and alkali burns of the eye are often severe. Alkali burns to both eyes are more serious in the cornea (the clear transparent covering of the eye).

Primary Group Affected

- Children of any age, especially during science experiments or when using cleaning products

Signs and Symptoms

- Pain, burning in eye (due to many sensory nerve endings in eye)
- Difficulty in opening eye
- Tears
- Blurred vision, loss of vision
- Swelling or redness around eyes

Classroom Guidelines

- Immediately flush eye for at least 20 minutes (using jug if easier), tilting child's head with good eye uppermost and running cool tap water over the other eye or splashing eye with clean water. Aim for inner corner so that water will wash over eye.
- Do not let water splash in child's face. Dry child's face when finished.

- Close eyelid and apply loose, clean moist cloth over eye or both eyes and then seek emergency medical attention.
- Praise child for cooperating.
- Be aware that child may experience anxiety due to vision limitations. Keep child safe and calm.
- Provide any special accommodations necessary to respond to vision limitations such as distance considerations from blackboard and visual supplements used in classroom.
- Be aware that child may have difficulty in reading and that vision may be blurred or limited during the healing process.

Attendance Guideline

- Exclusion from school is not required.

Medications

- Only as ordered by health care provider as follow-up

Communication

- Notify parent/caregiver of eye splash.
- Request information from parent/caregiver regarding any restrictions or special accommodations to be implemented while eye heals.

Resource

- www.mayoclinic.org

Eye Stye

Description

A stye is common bacterial infection of the oil glands at the edge of the upper or lower eyelid. It can also be an infection of the hair follicle (small pit from which the eyelash grows) of an eyelash that usually goes away on its own. A stye resembles a pimple and is usually caused by bacteria that infect the gland or root of the eyelash. Contaminated mascara brushes and eye makeup have been linked with styes. A chalazion (kah la' ze on), which is a small eyelid lump resulting from a blocked mucus gland under the eyelid, is frequently mistaken for a stye. A chalazion involves painless swelling, whereas a stye is fairly painful.

Primary Group Affected

- Children of any age

Signs and Symptoms

- Small, red, pimple-like bump at base of an eyelash
- Gritty feeling as if something is in eye
- Painful

Classroom Guidelines

- Urge child to wash hands frequently because styes spread easily (*see* Procedure A).
- Urge child to use warm, moist clean compresses for 10 minutes three or four times a day.
- Remind child to not rub eye or squeeze stye because doing so can cause it to spread.

- After the stye bursts, wash it thoroughly with warm water.
- Teach children not to share washcloths or towels with a child who has a stye.
- If child has vision difficulties, the stye enlarges after 3 days and fails to drain, or there are frequent occurrences of styes, notify parent/caregiver and urge to see health care provider.

Attendance Guidelines

- Exclusion from school may be required for child depending on personal habits, pain, level of functioning, and understanding of treatment of stye.
- Return to classroom after verifying treatment.

Medications

- Antibiotic drops or ointments are usually prescribed. Do *not* let tip of bottle or tube touch eye.

Communication

- Ask parent/caregiver about any medications ordered.
- Notify parent/caregiver if child complains of vision disturbances, the stye enlarges after 3 days, the child has more than one stye, or the eye becomes red and painful and urge to seek treatment from a health care provider.

Resources

- www.aurorahealthcare.org
- www.youreyesite.com/stye.htm
- www.nlm.nih.gov/medlineplus/ency/article/001009.htm

Fetal Alcohol Syndrome

Also known as: FAS

Description

Fetal alcohol syndrome is a group of birth defects that are irreversible and can include physical, mental, and behavioral problems. Children born with fetal alcohol effects have the same symptoms, but to a lesser degree, and are less likely to have cognitive disabilities.

Primary Group Affected

- 1 of every 750 infants is born with fetal alcohol syndrome.

Signs and Symptoms

- Low birthweight
- Small head circumference and brain size
- Facial abnormalities such as small eyelid openings, flattened cheekbones, a sunken nasal bridge, an exceptionally thin upper lip, an underdeveloped groove between the nose and the upper lip, and small teeth with faulty enamel
- Heart defects
- Deformities of joints, limbs, and fingers
- Failure to thrive
- Developmental delay, poor coordination/fine motor skills
- Cognitive impairment, learning difficulties such as poor memory, inability to understand abstract concepts, poor language comprehension, and poor problem-solving skills

- Behaviors such as short attention span, hyperactivity, poor impulse control, and stubbornness
- Poor socialization skills such as difficulty in establishing friendships and in relating to groups of people

Classroom Guidelines

- Maintain consistency and predictability in classroom setting.
- Be aware that child may need repetitive directions and prompts about what his or her behavior should be.
- Use "time-outs" for inappropriate behavior.
- Use clear, concrete, and simple directions because child may have difficulty in understanding abstract thinking or nonverbal communication.
- Encourage child to make decisions within his or her capabilities.
- Because child may be socially naive, protect him or her from being taken advantage of by other children.

Attendance Guideline

- Exclusion from school is not required.

Medication

- None is required.

Communication

- Inquire about type of development and stimulation programs in which child is or has been involved.
- Ask parent/caregiver what helps child to socialize with other children.
- Discuss effectiveness of various limit-setting activities.

Resource

- National Organization for Fetal Alcohol Syndrome
  216 G Street, N.E.
  Washington, DC 20002
  (202) 785–4585
  www.nofas.org

Fever

Also known as: pyrexia (pi rek' se ah)

Description

Fever is a body temperature that is higher than normal and usually indicates that something abnormal is going on in the body. The normal oral temperature for children is 98.0 to 98.6 degrees. An increase in body temperature may also be due to exercise, hot weather, drinking hot fluids, and common childhood immunizations. Fever in itself is not an illness but rather a symptom that something is not right with the body.

Primary Group Affected

- Any children

Signs and Symptoms

- Oral temperature higher than 99.8 degrees
- Flushed face
- Hot dry skin
- Not interested in eating
- Headache
- Body ache
- Nausea and vomiting

If the following symptoms accompany a fever, call parent/caregiver and urge health care treatment immediately or activate the local emergency medical system:
- Seizures/convulsions—**911**
- Irregular breathing—**911**

- Stiff neck—**911**
- Confusion—**911**

Classroom Guidelines

- Take child's temperature if oral thermometer is available.
- Notify parent/caregiver if child has elevated temperature.
- Allow child to lie down if possible.
- Keep child from chilling.
- Have child remove coat and/or sweater if he or she is not experiencing chills.
- Reduce room temperature unless child is shivering.
- Apply cool moist compress to child's forehead.
- Give cool fluids unless child's fever is accompanied by nausea and/or vomiting.

Attendance Guideline

- Exclusion from school is required while child has elevated temperature. Child should refrain from attending school for 24 hours after a fever.

Medication

- Acetaminophen (Tylenol) may be administered according to school policy and with parent/caregiver permission.

Communication

- Notify parent/caregiver immediately and urge to see health care provider.

Resource

- www.vh.org/vch/commonproblems/commonproblems. html#fe

Fifth Disease

Also known as: human parvovirus B19, erythema (er i 'the mah) infectiosum, "slapped cheek disease"

Description

Fifth disease is an infection caused by parvovirus B19 and is spread through direct contact or through respiratory secretions. The period of infectiousness is before the onset of the characteristic face rash. Most persons who get fifth disease appear to have a cold and recover without serious consequences. However, because it can affect the red blood cells, children with sickle cell anemia, chronic anemia, or impaired immune systems may become seriously ill when infected with parvovirus B19. If a pregnant woman becomes infected, the fetus may be damaged; therefore, she should contact her health care provider for advice. The virus infects only humans and should not be confused with the parvovirus that infects cats and dogs.

Primary Group Affected

- Children of any age but most common in elementary school-age children
- Mostly in winter and spring

Signs and Symptoms

- 1 to 2 weeks after exposure, there is a low-grade fever, joint pain, and malaise.
- By 3 weeks after exposure, there is a red rash on the face, chiefly on the cheeks, giving a "slapped cheek" appearance; it lasts 1 to 4 days.
- About 1 day after the face rash appears, a pimple-like lacy rash appears on upper and lower extremities; it lasts up to 1 week

and will reappear if skin is irritated or traumatized (e.g., sun, heat, cold, friction).

- Rash may be itchy.
- Some have no symptoms at all.

Classroom Guidelines

- Ensure proper hand-washing technique (*see* Procedure A).
- Ensure proper disposal of child's tissues used to wipe eyes.
- Avoid sharing of personal articles such as drinking glasses and eating utensils.

Attendance Guideline

- Exclusion from school is not required because this condition is no longer contagious once rash appears.

Medications

- Topical calamine lotion may be used to reduce itching.
- Acetaminophen may be used for fever and joint pain.

Communication

- Notify all staff members and parent/caregiver of fifth disease outbreak.
- Be aware that pregnant women and parents/caregivers of children who have impaired immune systems, sickle cell anemia, or other blood disorders may want to consult their health care providers.
- Ask parent/caregiver about schedule for acetaminophen and how to apply calamine lotion.

Resource

- www.cdc.gov

Fractures

Also known as: broken bones

Description

A fracture is a break in the bone. A fracture happens when a bone is subjected to more stress than it can handle, possibly from a direct blow, sudden twisting motion, or crushing force. Surrounding tissues or organs may also be injured by the force that caused the break or by the force of the bone moving out of position. Fractures are described by type and extent, and they may be complete (total break through cross section of bone) or incomplete (partial break through cross section of bone). Incomplete or "greenstick" fractures are more common in children. If the bone protrudes through the skin or mucus membrane, it is an open fracture; if not, it is a closed fracture.

Primary Group Affected

- Any child is subject to a fracture in the right circumstances.
- Children participating in athletic or strenuous activities may be more at risk.
- Children not normally physically active and who are participating in strenuous activity may be at increased risk because their muscles might not be well enough developed to protect their bones.

Signs and Symptoms

- Pain is usually continuous, becoming more severe until bone is immobilized—**911.**
- A loss of use of the injured part occurs, for example, loss of ability to bear weight—**911.**

- Movement may be abnormal (e.g., too much movement, loss of or unusual mobility)—**911.**
- Deformity may be present—**911.**
- Child may feel grating sensation when he or she moves limb—**911.**
- If long bone (arm or leg) is fractured, shortening of limb may be noticed.
- Swelling or discoloration of soft tissue surrounding fracture may occur—**911.**
- Bone may protrude through the skin—**911.**

Classroom Guidelines

- *Caution:* Be aware that further damage may result from movement before immobilization.
- Be certain that child is out of further danger.
- If child must be moved for safety reasons before splint placement, firmly but gently support extremity above and below fracture, keeping the long axis of bone stable and moving slowly and cautiously.
- Immobilize joints above and below injury before moving child.
- If necessary, in the absence of an air splint or a solid splint, splint long bone with anything solid such as rolled newspaper or by securing injured part to an adjacent part.
- If bone protrudes through skin (open fracture), keep wound clean, covering with a clean (and preferably sterile), dry, lint-free cloth and call **911.**
- Inform parent/caregiver and, for obvious injury, call **911.**
- Arrange for child's safe exit from classroom in case of an unexpected event that requires students to leave classroom or school.
- Promptly report symptoms of impaired circulation if cast is present. Keep cast dry (*see* Procedure C).
- Allow for child to have extra time if going to a different classroom.
- Be aware that limb may need to be elevated to prevent swelling.

Attendance Guidelines

- Exclusion from school is not required.
- Participation in activities may be limited. Follow provider guidelines.

Medications

- Pain medications may be ordered initially.

Communication

- Ask parent/caregiver for health care provider recommendations for activity limitations and signs/symptoms to report.

Resources

- American Academy of Pediatrics
  www.aap.org/pubserv/fracture.htm
- www.mayoclinic.org

Frostbite

Description

Frostbite is an injury to body parts due to prolonged exposure of freezing temperatures. Usual sites of injury are hands, fingers, feet, toes, nose, cheeks, and ears.

Primary Group Affected

- Children who do not wear adequate protective clothing in severe cold weather

Signs and Symptoms

- Early signs are shivering, numbness, tingling, and burning in the affected area.
- Other signs include cold, white, shiny, and soft or firm skin.
- A previous history of frostbite increases the risk of frostbite in that area again.
- Child may complain of itching in the frostbite area.
- Frostbite can be mild (superficial) or deep.
- After thawing, deep or severe frostbite may be bluish in color. Blisters may develop in 1 to 7 days, and swelling may be seen.

Classroom Guidelines

- Urge child *not* to rub area.
- Remove wet clothing.
- Take temperature to check for hypothermia (low temperature is less than 95 degrees)—**911.**
- Protect area from further injury.
- Keep other areas of body warm with blankets.

- Raise affected area to decrease swelling if possible.
- Be aware that the degree of frostbite cannot be known until the affected area is rewarmed.
- Cover areas around head with warm moist soaks, keeping a constant temperature.
- Use warm immersion soaks for arms and legs until normal color returns to affected site.
- Be aware that child might not get a return to normal color for 20 to 30 minutes.
- If blisters appear, notify local emergency medical system for physician evaluation.
- Give child warm fluids.

Attendance Guideline

- Exclusion from school is not required.

Medications

- Pain medications may be used.
- Antibiotics may be ordered.

Communication

- Ask parent/caregiver about antibiotic and analgesic time schedule.
- Ask whether child has any activity restrictions.

Resource

- www.cdc.gov

Grief

Also known as: mourning, bereavement

Description

Bereavement is the feelings, thoughts, and responses that loved ones experience following the death of a person with whom they have shared a significant relationship. Bereavement also occurs in the event of any significant loss such as parental divorce, change in parent/caregiver, or death of a beloved pet. Mourning or grieving is the active process of learning to adapt to the loss. It is the progression through a series of phases that include the recognition and acceptance of the event, the experience of emotional and physical pain, and the rebuilding of a life without the loved person. Family, religious beliefs, and cultural customs influence the process of grieving.

Primary Group Affected

- Children of any age, especially with significant loss experience

Signs and Symptoms

- Death is used as a model for the process of grieving in this text.
- Children experience the same emotions of grief as do adults but are less likely to show acute grief during the initial phase and are more likely to experience the process over a much longer period of time.
- Infants may feel loss of a parent/caregiver or sibling because of the way in which they are cared for and their daily routines are disrupted. They are very sensitive to unhappy feelings of those around them and may become more anxious and needy.

- Preverbal children understand death as a separation, not as a finite end to life. They are often convinced that the deceased person could come back if he or she really wanted to do so.
- When children develop language skills at ages 2 to 3 years, they can begin the process of comprehending death and its causes, although they still believe death to be reversible. Cartoon characters who "die" and "come back to life" again may reinforce this belief.
- School-age children are able to understand basic facts about death. They tend to be more avoidant in speaking of their grief than are either preschoolers or teens, resulting in an appearance of unconcern. Because they equate death with abandonment, this age group is especially vulnerable to reacting with depression, self-blame, and low self-esteem for some months.
- At each developmental level, children rework the meaning of a family member's death from more mature cognitive and emotional functioning.
- Signs of complicated grieving include having an inability to sleep, having a prolonged fear of being alone, engaging in behavioral regression for a long time, denying that the person has died, talking repeatedly about wanting to join the dead person, withdrawing from friends, having academic difficulties, and refusing to attend school.

Classroom Guidelines

- Be aware that children benefit if usual school activities are maintained as much as possible after significant loss.
- Acknowledge death and grief. Share your feelings of sorrow with child.
- Reassure young child that dead person did not want to leave him or her and that the death was not related to anything the child did or said.
- Recognize that grieving child's attention span may be decreased and that assignments may be forgotten. Lighten homework load if necessary.
- Help other children to understand grief through stories and caring words, helping to normalize the situation for classmates and other children to become supportive toward grieving child.
- Acknowledge that the process and length of grieving is a very individual phenomenon.

- Encourage older children to write out their feelings in journals, to draw pictures showing feelings, or to scribble on pieces of paper, rip them up, and throw them away.

Attendance Guideline

- Exclusion from school is not required.

Medication

- None is required.

Communication

- Ask parent/caregiver what behaviors and feelings are being expressed at home.
- If home routine has been drastically altered due to the death of a parent/caregiver, find out who is doing the primary caregiving. Discuss your role as a supportive teacher with that person.

Resource

- www.childrensgrief.com

Headache

Also known as: head pain

Description

"My head hurts" is the most common complaint of children. Headaches are one of the most common health care problems that result in absenteeism. The majority of headaches have no underlying disease but may be related to stress, anxiety, odors, bright lights, food ingredients, and/or head injuries. Not every headache warrants going home from school. Some headaches are related to specific events such as staying up too late or being out in the sun for an extended period of time. Children whose headaches necessitate limiting their activities for a long period of time may need to be seen by their health care providers. Migraines are a type of severe and disabling headache and may be experienced by school-age children.

Primary Group Affected

- Any child may experience headaches.

Signs and Symptoms

- Complaints of "head hurting," holding head, crying
- Migraine headaches: severe and disabling pain, complaints of nausea, sensitivity to light, tingling on one side of face or body

Classroom Guidelines

- Offer to place a cold cloth to child's head.
- Allow child to lie down in a dark quiet room if possible.
- Consider referral to school counselor if, along with headaches, child appears to be withdrawn or anxious.

- If child complains of a headache and has a fever, stiff neck, rash, mental confusion, loss of balance, numbness, difficulty in speaking, and/or weakness, notify parent/caregiver immediately and urge medical treatment—**911.**
- Notify parent/caregiver and urge to seek medical treatment if child has headaches for long periods of time that restrict activity or limit participation with other students.
- Be aware that a child with diagnosed migraine-type headaches may be on medications that adhere to strict time guidelines.

Attendance Guidelines

- Exclusion from school is not required unless prescribed by health care provider.
- Child may need rest and decreased stimulus.

Medications

- Pain medications (both over-the-counter and prescription)

Communication

- Notify parent/caregiver and urge to seek medical treatment if child has frequent complaints of headaches.
- Ask about the amount of sleep the child is getting if, along with headaches, child appears to be tired.
- Ask about schedule of medications to be given to child.

Resources

- www.mayoclinic.org
- www.schoolnurse.com

Head Injury

Description

The most common sources of head injuries in younger children are falls, sporting accidents, and child abuse. Head injuries occur at the moment of impact and following the impact. Head injuries are either open or closed. An open injury involves a skull fracture in which there is a break in the barrier between the brain contents and the outside environment. A closed injury is a blunt one in which the skull and skin remain intact. Most injuries in children are mild to moderate.

Primary Group Affected

- Two to three times more common in males

Signs and Symptoms

- Depending on severity of head injury, child may experience dizziness, headache, blurred or double vision, restlessness, changes in breathing, changes in pupils of eyes, slurred speech or loss of speech, unsteady walking, uncoordination of arms or legs, decreased feeling in arms or legs, loss of consciousness, nausea, and vomiting—**911**.
- Child with skull fracture may have wound or bruise on head. In addition, a clear or pink-tinged fluid may be seen draining from the nose and/or ear—**911**.
- Blood may be showing in whites of eyes—**911**.

Classroom Guidelines

- Keep child quiet and lying down, keeping him or her immobile with slightly raised head and shoulders. If you think that the child might have a neck or spine injury, lay child flat and keep neck and spine immobile.

- Never lay child down so that head is lower than rest of body.
- Activate local emergency medical system. If child's head is bleeding, apply ice and only gentle pressure.
- Make sure that child is breathing. If breathing stops, start CPR.
- Do not give child anything to drink. If a scalp wound is present, do not clean it and do not bend neck because a fracture may be present. Place sterile dressing on wound if possible, and apply only gentle pressure on wound because bone may be broken in skull.
- Be alert for any evidence of memory impairment, unusual impulse behavior, or aggressive behavior.
- Be alert for increasing drowsiness in children with skull fractures and notify parent/caregiver and school health care provider.

Attendance Guideline

- Exclusion from school is not required once child has been seen by the health care provider.

Medication

- None is required.

Communication

- Notify parent/caregiver of any head injury because problems can occur hours later as a result of head injury.
- Report if child had seizure associated with head injury.

Resources

- www.cdc.gov
- www.biausa.org

Head Lice

Also known as: pediculosis (pe dik u lo' sis), cooties

Description

Head lice continue to be one of the most common communicable childhood infestations, and outbreaks are possible whenever there are groups of children. Head lice are small wingless insects that live on the human scalp. They are about one eighth inch in length and are dark gray in color. The lice are most frequently found on the scalp behind the ears and near the neckline at the back of the neck. Head lice can sometimes be seen crawling around in the hair or anchored to the scalp. Yellow or white nits are the eggs of lice and can usually be seen firmly attached to the hair shaft. These eggs are sometimes mistaken for dandruff or hair spray droplets. The nits take about 1 week to hatch. Head lice are rarely found on the body, eyelashes, or eyebrows.

Primary Group Affected

- Preschool and elementary school-age children, ages 3 to 10 years
- More common in girls than in boys
- Euro-American children with straight hair most apt to become infected, very rare in African American children

Signs and Symptoms

- Tickling feeling of something moving in hair
- Itching (usually an allergic reaction to insect bites), which is the most common symptom and frequently the only symptom
- Irritability
- Sores on head from scratching that may become infected
- Swollen lymph glands in back of neck (severe cases)

Classroom Guidelines

- Emphasize that anyone can get head lice and that it does not mean that child is not clean
- Isolate child from other children without embarrassing child; children with head lice are very sensitive to reactions of teacher and classmates.
- Ensure proper hand-washing technique (*see* Procedure A).
- Be aware that all children in classroom will have to be examined for head lice. Head lice will be spread so long as children play together. Contact is common during play at school, sports, sharing of lockers, and playground activities.
- Advise children not to share hats, scarves, coats, sports uniforms, or hair ornaments. Vacuum insides of sports helmets.
- Advise children not to share combs, brushes, or towels.
- If child with head lice has come into contact with objects that cannot be cleaned or heat dried, store objects in sealed plastic bag for 10 to 14 days; head lice rarely survive off of scalp for more than a week.
- Understand that lice survive only on humans and cannot infect any classroom pets.
- Be aware that head lice provide an opportunity for teachers to instruct children on responsible personal health behaviors. Children can learn communicable disease prevention concepts and be responsible for their health.

Attendance Guidelines

- Some schools have a "nit-free policy" requiring that children have all nits removed before returning to the classroom.
- Children with head lice may return to school the morning after their treatment and should be checked.
- Children with multiple infestations should be rechecked every 2 weeks until clear for two consecutive checks.

Medications

- Over-the-counter or prescription shampoos may be used at home.

Communication

- Be aware that parent/caregiver must understand "no nit" standard if mandated by school policy. Preferably, this policy should be explained prior to an outbreak and should allow for early intervention and minimize inappropriate responses.

- Encourage blame-free communication to enhance parent/caregiver involvement.
- Inform parent/caregiver or school personnel about child with head lice as soon as possible so that classmates with lice can be identified and treated.
- Instruct parent/caregiver that there are shampoos and rinses (both over-the-counter and prescription) for treatment of head lice. Stress importance of following directions. Advise parent/caregiver *not* to cut child's hair or shave child's head as a treatment.
- Suggest that parent/caregiver contact health care provider for specific instructions, especially for child with certain preexisting medical conditions and/or on certain prescribed medications. Repeated exposures to certain products for head lice infestation may put certain children, as well as families with pregnant or nursing mothers, at risk.

Resources

- www.cdc.gov
- National Pediculosis Association
  50 Kearney Road
  Needham, MA 02494
  (781) 449-NITS
  npa@headlice.org
- www.mayoclinic.org
- www.schoolnurse.com

Hearing Loss

Also known as: hard of hearing, deaf, hearing impaired

Description

Hearing loss occurs in many different degrees, ranging from slight to profound. Approximately 1 of every 1,000 children in the United States is profoundly hearing impaired (can hear almost no sound). In addition, 25 of every 1,000 children have moderate to severe hearing loss, which usually involves speech impairment, the need for speech therapy, and difficulty with normal conversation. It is estimated that 50% of hearing deficit is inherited and that exposure to rubella parentally accounts for another large percentage of hearing loss. Untreated or repeated otitis media (ear infection) can also lead to hearing impairment.

Primary Group Affected

- Children of any age; often detected during school mandatory hearing screenings

Signs and Symptoms

- Inattentiveness
- Lack of response to voice
- Confusion with instructions
- Frustration
- Need for repetition
- Speaks loudly or quietly
- Daydreaming
- Articulation errors
- Favors one ear or another

- Prefers solitary play
- Frustration

Classroom Guidelines

- Position child in classroom to promote hearing (good ear closest to you).
- Face class when speaking, move to side of room with hearing-impaired child, or stand in front of hearing-impaired child.
- Eliminate distracting noises in classroom such as machinery, fans, and music.
- Use multimodalities for presenting material (e.g., visual, auditory, interactive).
- Avoid walking while talking.
- Use round tables for group work so that child can see other speakers.
- Allow child to turn and face classmates when children behind are talking.
- Have child use "buddy system" with another classmate for note taking.

Attendance Guideline

- Exclusion from school is not required.

Medications

- Medications to reduce wax buildup or clear infection may be used.

Communication

- Ask parent/caregiver about schedule of medications.
- Determine whether tubes have been placed in ears and whether there are any restrictions.
- Determine whether any hearing loss has occurred and how to best meet child's needs.
- If hearing aids or amplifiers are used, identify any assistance child might need.

Resource

- www.kidshealth.com

Heart Disease

Also known as: cardiac disease, heart defect, congenital heart disease

Description

Most heart disorders in children occur as a result of congenital abnormalities, meaning that a problem occurred during the development of the fetus heart in pregnancy. Children can also later develop heart disorders from rheumatic fever (a disease that results following a group A beta hemolytic streptococcus infection) or Kawasaki disease (an inflammation of blood vessels that can affect many systems and lead to forming an aneurysm and heart attack). Both congenital and acquired heart disease can lead to inadequate oxygen supply to the body and can cause heart failure or infection. Children with heart disease are at risk for developing an infection called bacterial endocarditis, which affects the tissue that lines the heart and blood vessels. Most heart disorders can be helped with surgery to correct the abnormality. Sometimes, several surgeries are required during childhood.

Primary Group Affected

- Any age group

Signs and Symptoms

- Working hard to breathe—**911**
- Poor appetite
- Sweating excessively
- Pale or gray color (especially noticed on the tongue and gums)
- Sleeping excessively
- Decreased activity
- Fever
- Poor weight gain
- Frequent infections (especially respiratory infections)

- Swelling
- Choosing a squatting position for resting

Classroom Guidelines

- Ensure proper hand-washing technique to minimize the spread of infection (*see* Procedure A).
- Develop a plan to assist child in learning during time absent from school.
- Schedule frequent rest periods to accommodate child's decreased energy levels.
- Provide opportunity for frequent small snacks to aid in child's need for good nutrition.

Attendance Guideline

- Exclusion from school is not required except when contagious illness is in the classroom because child is at increased risk for infections.

Medications

- Children with heart disease are often on prophylactic antibiotics prior to surgery and dental visits.
- Children may be on medications to thin the blood (aspirin), lower blood pressure, remove excessive swelling (diuretics), or improve the strength of the heartbeat (Digoxin). Clarify administration techniques with parent/caregiver.

Communication

- Ask parent/caregiver in which activities and sports the child may participate.
- Communicate with parent/caregiver if there are contagious illnesses in the classroom because children with heart disease can become seriously infected quite easily.
- Ask whether there are food restrictions, such as high-sodium (salty) foods or high-fats foods, because of the risk of high blood pressure and high cholesterol.
- Ask about schedule of medications.

Resources

- www.kidshealth.org
- www.pediheart.org

Heat Exhaustion

Also known as: heat prostration

Description

Heat prostration occurs in young children when playing outside in hot weather for a long period of time without taking in fluids. It can also occur if children are dehydrated from diarrhea and vomiting and are outdoors.

Primary Group Affected

- Children of any age, but usually in younger school-age children

Signs and Symptoms

- Thirsty
- Lack of energy
- Complaining of muscle cramping
- Head hurting
- Nauseated and vomiting
- Normal or only slightly elevated body temperature
- Pale and damp skin
- Excessive sweating
- Light-headedness or dizziness when going from sitting to standing position and possibly fainting—**911**

Classroom Guidelines

- Activate local emergency medical system.
- Take child to a cool, shaded, and well-ventilated room and have him or her rest and remove excessive clothing.

- Have child lie down with feet elevated.
- Apply cool wet cloths to child and fan him or her.

Attendance Guideline

- Exclusion from school is not required.

Medication

- If child is not vomiting or nauseated, give sips of salt water (1 teaspoon salt per glass, one half glass every 15 minutes over a 1-hour period).

Communication

- Notify parent/caregiver if child experiences heat exhaustion.

Resource

- www.cdc.gov

Heatstroke

Description

Heatstroke is serious and may be life threatening to a child. It can cause an increased temperature of 104 degrees or higher.

Primary Group Affected

- Children playing outside in hot weather for a long period of time

Signs and Symptoms

- Temperature of 104 degrees or higher—**911**
- Dry skin
- Rapid pulse—**911**
- Increased breathing
- No sweating
- Decreased level of consciousness—**911**

Classroom Guidelines

- Activate local emergency medical system.
- Report heatstroke case to school health care provider and parent/caregiver.
- Put child in a cool, well-ventilated room if possible, and put him or her in cool water (do not add ice) and apply cool wet cloths on head and neck until temperature is decreased.
- *Do not* give stimulants such as ice tea or soft drinks with caffeine.
- *Do not* over-chill child once his or her temperature falls below 102 degrees.

- Restrict time and strenuous activities when children are outside on extremely hot days.
- Allow children to drink water more frequently on extremely hot days.
- Assess that children are dressed appropriately on extremely hot days. Make sure that they avoid sweaters, long sleeves, and the like.

Attendance Guideline

- Exclusion from school is not required.

Medication

- None is required.

Communication

- Notify parent/caregiver if child experiences heatstroke symptoms.

Resource

- www.cdc.gov

Hemophilia

Also known as: a "royal" disease because it showed up in the English, Spanish, and Russian royal families; Hemophilia A (he mo fil' e ah) (factor VIII deficiency), 80% of all cases; Hemophilia B (factor IX deficiency), also called Christmas disease, about 20% of all cases; Hemophilia C (factor XI deficiency), about 1% to 2% of all cases

Description

Hemophilia refers to a group of rare bleeding disorders that prevents the blood from clotting properly. Affected persons have problems with factor VIII, IX, or X, and their bleeding tendency varies from mild to severe. Bleeding can occur in any area of the body, including joints, bladder, bowel, and even the brain or spinal cord. Approximately 1 of every 10,000 boys are born with hemophilia in the United States. Girls are carriers of hemophilia but are rarely affected by this sex-linked genetic condition. Newborns are not usually diagnosed because it is unlikely that they would sustain injuries that would lead to bleeding; even during circumcisions, only about 30% of males with hemophilia bleed excessively. Hemophilia may be suspected once a child begins walking and a pattern of bruising and bleeding is noticed, especially if this includes bleeding in the joint. Sometimes bruises occur in unusual places, and often child abuse is suspected before the diagnosis is finally made. Hemophilia is diagnosed with several blood tests. There is no cure for hemophilia, but the condition can be managed successfully with periodic intravenous infusions of clotting factor replacement therapy.

Primary Group Affected

- Males
- Girls very rarely affected
- Jewish children: both sexes, less severe symptoms (Hemophilia C)

Signs and Symptoms

- Prolonged nosebleeds
- Excessive bleeding following apparent minor falls or accidents
- Excessive bleeding following tooth extractions
- Excessive bleeding following surgeries
- Blood in urine (hematuria)
- Pain and swelling in joints
- Heavy menstrual periods

Classroom Guidelines

- Prevent injuries in classroom.
- Alert **911** for any injury resulting in bleeding.
- While waiting for **911** response, elevate affected joint or limb, apply pressure to affected area to decrease bleeding, apply ice to affected area, and apply topical antifibrinolytic agent (if available) to nose and mouth injuries. An older child (age 8 years or over) might be able to self-administer antihemophilic factor.

Attendance Guideline

- Exclusion from school is not required.

Medications

- Clotting factor replacement therapy may be used.
- Corticosteroids may be used.
- Nonsteroidal anti-inflammatory drugs, such as ibuprofen and acetaminophen (Tylenol), may be used for pain relief.
- Persons with severe hemophilia may have permanent intravenous catheters (called portacaths) in place for rapid administration of emergency medications.

Communication

- Ask parent/caregiver which activities and sports are not safe for child (usually this includes football, boxing, and hockey).
- Ask parent/caregiver how emergency situations should be handled, including administration of medications.

Resource

- www.hemophilia.org

Hepatitis A

Also known as: infectious hepatitis (hep ah ti' tis)

Description

Hepatitis A is an acute liver disease that generally causes mild illness. It is considered to be the least harmful of the hepatitis viruses because it rarely causes permanent liver damage. The virus enters the body through the mouth, multiplies in the body, and is excreted in the feces (bowel movements). The virus is carried on the infected person's hands and is spread by touching the food or drink of another person, contaminated water, shellfish, contaminated diapers, or changing tables. The greatest period of communicability is the 2 weeks before symptoms become apparent. Many people show no symptoms at all, and most people recover in a few weeks without any complications. Once an individual recovers from the disease, he or she is immune for life and does not continue to carry the virus. Immune globulin, which protects others, can be given within 10 to 14 days of exposure for those in close contact such as household members, day care center workers for children not yet toilet trained, and institutionalized children. The hepatitis A vaccine is available and recommended for day care center workers.

Primary Group Affected

- Preschool and school-age children under age 15 years
- Common in day care settings with children in diapers

Signs and Symptoms

- Fatigue
- Poor appetite

- Fever
- Vomiting
- Dark-colored urine (tea colored)
- Jaundice (yellow) coloring of skin and whites of eyes

Classroom Guidelines

- Ensure proper hand-washing technique after using bathroom and before and after handling food (*see* Procedure A).
- Note that disposable paper towels should be used for hand washing.
- Clean bathroom surfaces and food preparation areas daily.
- Be aware that diapered children should be cared for by different staff in a separate room from toilet-trained children if possible.
- Use disposable table liners on changing tables. Disinfect table after each diaper change.
- Wash all fruits and vegetables well.
- Avoid shellfish, especially raw oysters.

Attendance Guidelines

- Exclusion from school is required until fever and jaundice have resolved and appetite has returned.
- Some health care providers may recommend 4 to 6 weeks bed rest, although this is rarely necessary.

Medication

- None is required except for symptomatic relief of fever.

Communication

- Notify parents/caregivers of children who have direct contact with a child with hepatitis A.

Resource

- www.cdc.gov

Hepatitis B

Also known as: serum hepatitis (hep ah ti' tis)

Description

Hepatitis B is a liver disease that is caused by a virus that may be found in blood, saliva, semen, and other body fluids. Hepatitis B is spread by direct contact with the body fluids of an infected person, usually by a needle stick or by sexual contact. An infected pregnant woman can pass the infection to her unborn child. Hepatitis B is diagnosed by a blood test. The usual treatment is rest; occasionally, some people need to be hospitalized if they are too ill to eat or drink. Most infected people recover completely within 6 months. However, in some instances, hepatitis B can be very harmful to a person's health, causing liver damage, cirrhosis, and an increased chance of liver cancer. Newborns are now routinely receiving the hepatitis B vaccine series. Persons in high-risk categories should be vaccinated.

Primary Group Affected

- Infants born to mothers who are hepatitis B carriers
- Drug abusers who share needles
- Health care workers who have direct contact with infected blood
- Persons who have unprotected sexual activity
- Hemodialysis patients

Signs and Symptoms

- Fatigue
- Poor appetite
- Fever

- Vomiting
- Abdominal pain
- Dark-colored urine (tea colored)
- Jaundice (yellow) skin color and whites of the eyes
- Joint pain
- Hives
- Rash

Classroom Guidelines

- Review all immunization records of children.
- Ensure proper hand-washing technique (*see* Procedure A).
- Ensure proper disposal of child's tissues used to wipe eyes.
- Avoid sharing of personal articles such as drinking glasses, toothbrushes, and eating utensils.
- Clean up blood spills immediately while wearing gloves.
- Disinfect areas of spills with freshly prepared bleach solution.
- If a child care worker has open cuts on hands, have him or her wear gloves for diaper changes.

Attendance Guideline

- Exclusion from school is required until fever and jaundice have resolved and appetite has returned.

Medication

- None is required except for symptomatic relief of fever such as acetaminophen (Tylenol).

Communication

- Notify parents/caregivers of children who have direct contact with child having hepatitis B.
- Ask parent/caregiver about schedule of medications for fever relief.

Resource

- www.hepb.org

Hepatitis C

Also known as: formerly called non A–non B hepatitis (hep ah ti' tis)

Description

Hepatitis C is a liver disease that is caused by a virus, which is usually spread by direct blood-to-blood contact between two people. The most common means of transmission is through sharing the needles or liquid drug preparation that has been exposed to hepatitis C. Another means of exposure to hepatitis C is through blood transfusion, although this risk has been greatly decreased with blood screening programs. Other methods of exposure to hepatitis C include mother passing to fetus, tattooing, body piercing, acupuncture, and sharing razors. Unlike hepatitis B, hepatitis C is not present in other body fluids such as saliva, semen, and urine. The majority of persons with hepatitis C have no symptoms for a decade or longer; some will never have symptoms, while others will have serious or even fatal liver damage.

Primary Group Affected

- Drug abusers who share needles or drug containers
- Persons who have received infected blood donations
- Infants born to mothers who are hepatitis C carriers
- Health care workers who have direct contact with infected blood
- Persons who have unprotected sexual activity if blood exchange is involved
- Hemodialysis patients

Signs and Symptoms

- Often (80% of persons) no signs or symptoms
- Fatigue
- Poor appetite

- Fever
- Vomiting
- Abdominal pain
- Dark-colored urine (tea colored)
- Jaundice (yellow) skin color and whites of the eyes

Classroom Guidelines

- Review all immunization records of children.
- Ensure proper hand-washing technique (*see* Procedure A).
- Ensure proper disposal of child's tissues used to wipe eyes.
- Avoid sharing of personal articles such as drinking glasses, toothbrushes, and eating utensils.
- Clean up blood spills immediately while wearing gloves.
- Disinfect areas of spills with freshly prepared bleach solution.

Attendance Guideline

- Exclusion from school is required until fever and jaundice have resolved and appetite has returned.

Medication

- None is required except for symptomatic relief of fever such as acetaminophen (Tylenol).

Communication

- Notify parents/caregivers of children who have direct contact with a child with hepatitis C.
- Ask parent/caregiver about schedule of medications to reduce fever.

Resources

- www.hepatitiscaware.org
- www.hepatitisinfo.com

HIV/AIDS

Also known as: human immunodeficiency virus (HIV), acquired immunodeficiency syndrome (AIDS)

Description

AIDS is a chronic, life-threatening illness caused by the human immunodeficiency virus, for which there is no cure. The virus damages the cells of the immune system (referred to as immunocompromised) and stops the body from being able to fight off infections caused by bacteria, fungi, and viruses. HIV is the virus and AIDS denotes the later stages of the HIV infection. Engaging in sexual contact, receiving blood, and/or sharing the needles or syringes of an infected person spreads the HIV virus. HIV can also be passed from an untreated mother to her infant during pregnancy, birth, or breast-feeding. Symptoms will vary depending on the phase of the disease. Some people will remain symptom free for 8 to 10 years; however, their immune systems will be slowly deteriorating. Having contact with sweat or tears, sharing food, or sharing clothing does not transmit HIV, nor does kissing someone with HIV, being bitten by a mosquito, or donating blood. Behaviors that place people at greatest risk for being infected with HIV include having sex with multiple partners and not using latex or polyurethane condoms, sharing needles with someone who is HIV positive, being a newborn of an HIV-positive mother, and having received a blood product before 1985 (when testing began).

Primary Group Affected

- Children of any age

Signs and Symptoms

HIV (early signs)

- Swollen lymph glands
- Weight loss
- Poor growth
- Diarrhea
- Fever
- Persistent cough
- Shortness of breath
- Delayed mental development
- Development of cerebral palsy

AIDS (later signs)

- Night sweats
- Fever higher than 100 degrees for several weeks, chills
- Chronic diarrhea
- Headaches
- Blurred vision
- Recurrent infections (more severe forms of otitis media, pneumonia, meningitis, and tonsillitis)
- Cancer (Kaposi's sarcoma, cervical cancer, and lymphoma)

Classroom Guidelines

- Follow guidelines to prevent blood-borne infections: wash hands (*see* Procedure A), wear gloves when changing diapers soiled with bloody stools, do not allow sharing of toothbrushes, clean up blood spills immediately using protocol set by the facility, disinfect surfaces with freshly prepared bleach solution, and cover open wounds.
- Be aware that many of child's medications are on an extremely strict schedule and that not administering on time can have grave effects for child.
- Be aware that many of child's medications must be given with food, while some are to be taken on an empty stomach.

Attendance Guideline

- Exclusion from school is required during outbreaks of infectious disease such as fifths disease (due to child's compromised immune system).

Medications

- A variety of medications are used to inhibit replication of HIV virus.

Communication

- Ask parent/caregiver about schedule of medications to support/monitor child's compliance with treatment plan.
- Ask parent/caregiver for written schedule of medications.

Resources

- STD and HIV Hotline
  (800) 342-AIDS (English) or (800) 344–7432 (Spanish)
- www.hivatis.org

Human Bites

Description

Children frequently acquire bites from other children during rough play, during arguments, or out of frustration. Because the human mouth can be a carrying place for bacteria, it is important that all bites receive attention. A child's bite can cause a wound that is deep and penetrating. It has the potential to cause an infection and is often more dangerous than an animal bite.

Primary Group Affected

- Any child may be the victim of another's child frustration or anger.

Signs and Symptoms

- Open area on the skin with surrounding teeth marks
- Possible bleeding wound

Classroom Guidelines

- Speak calmly to child to decrease anxiety.
- If wound is bleeding freely, let it do so for a few seconds before putting the bite area under running water.
- Wash wound with soap and water; use antiseptic soap if available.
- Apply sterile pressure bandage to stop bleeding.
- Be aware that ice may be applied to site to decrease swelling.
- Notify parent/caregiver and encourage to see health care provider.
- Follow school guidelines in releasing information concerning other child's health history.

Attendance Guideline

- Exclusion from school is not required.

Medications

- Antibiotics may be ordered and need to be given on schedule.
- Tetanus toxoid may be needed if child is not sufficiently immunized.
- If bite puts child at risk for hepatitis B, child might need to be immunized with hepatitis B vaccine and given immune globulin.

Communication

- Notify parent/caregiver immediately and urge to see health care provider.
- Follow school policy in documenting incident.

Resources

- www.cdc.gov
- www.nlm.nih.gov

Impetigo

Also known as: impetigo (im pe ti' go) contagiosa

Description

Impetigo is a skin infection caused by one of two bacteria: *Group A streptococcus* or *Staphylococcus aureus.* The bacteria are contagious and are likely to enter the body through broken skin and be transmitted through direct contact with the infected skin or by touching clothing or bed linens that have been in contact with infected skin. Impetigo often occurs on skin that has been previously affected by poison ivy, eczema, or allergies.

Primary Group Affected

- Most common in preschool and school-age children, with majority of children under age 2 years
- More common during summer months

Signs and Symptoms

- Most common on face around mouth and nose or at site of trauma
- *Group A streptococcus* impetigo: first tiny blisters that in time break open, then small wet patches of red skin, honey-colored crust that covers affected area, then itching
- *Staphylococcus aureus* impetigo: larger blisters containing clear and then cloudy fluid, with blisters remaining intact longer, and then itching
- Fever, diarrhea, weakness (less common symptoms)

Classroom Guidelines

- Ensure proper hand-washing technique (*see* Procedure A).
- Keep wound area as clean as possible.
- Dispense medications according to school regulations.
- Remind child not to scratch itchy areas; try distraction strategies.
- Be sensitive to emotional concerns of child.
- Eliminate any shared articles such as towels, hats, and personal articles.
- Minimize close contact with infected child until treated.

Attendance Guidelines

- Exclude from school until at least 48 hours after antibiotic treatment has started.
- Wound usually heals within 7 to 10 days with antibiotic treatment.

Medications

- Oral and topical (on the skin) antibiotics are commonly ordered.

Communication

- Ask parent/caregiver about schedule of medications to support/monitor child's compliance.

Resource

- www.emedicine.com

Inflammatory Bowel Disease

Also known as: ulcerative colitis (UC), Crohn's disease (CD), IBD

Description

Inflammatory bowel disease refers to two chronic disorders that cause inflammation in the intestines: ulcerative colitis and Crohn's disease. These two disorders have similar symptoms but two distinct differences. Both conditions can have mild to very severe symptoms with periods of flare-ups and remissions. Crohn's disease is often more disabling and has more complications. Medical and surgical treatment for Crohn's disease is often not as effective as it is with ulcerative colitis. Both diseases cause inflammation of the digestive tract. Crohn's disease can occur anywhere in the system, from the mouth to the anus (most often the small intestines), and often spreads deep into the layers of tissue. Ulcerative colitis causes inflammation and ulcerations in only the inner lining of the large intestines (colon). It is believed that environment (living in cities), diet (high in fat and refined foods), and possibly genetics play a role in both of these diseases. Smoking may also play a role in Crohn's disease. Researchers no longer believe that stress is the main causative factor, although stress can often aggravate symptoms.

Primary Group Affected

- Usually diagnosed between ages 15 and 30 years
- 30% between ages 10 and 19 years
- More common in Euro-Americans, five times more common in Jewish persons and in those of European descent
- May have parent or sibling with disease (20%)

Signs and Symptoms

- Diarrhea (sometimes bloody) (as many as 20 or more trips to the bathroom per day)
- Abdominal pain and cramping
- Fatigue
- Poor appetite
- Weight loss
- Fever
- Constipation (less common)
- Poor growth due to malnutrition
- Delay in onset of puberty

Classroom Guidelines

- Understand child's fatigue, irritability, and anxiousness.
- Provide easy access to bathroom.
- Encourage a well-balanced diet; small frequent meals throughout the day will lessen symptoms.
- Be aware that foods that tend to cause increased symptoms include seeds, popcorn, corn, foods high in fat, and sodium-laden fast-foods. Child will eventually figure out what foods trigger an attack.
- Dispense medications according to school regulations.

Attendance Guideline

- Exclusion from school is not required.

Medications

- Anti-inflammatory medications and medications to suppress the immune system may be used.
- Vitamin, iron, and folic acid supplements may be prescribed.
- Sometimes, surgery is necessary.

Communication

- Ask parent/caregiver about schedule of medications to support/monitor child's compliance with treatment plan.
- Ask parent/caregiver about foods that initiate attacks.

Resource

- www.living-better.com

Influenza

Also known as: flu, influenza A, influenza B, influenza C

Description

Influenza (in floo en' zah) is a highly contagious viral infection that can make children of any age ill. There are basically three types of influenza viruses identified as A, B, and C. Influenza A and influenza B usually cause the outbreak of respiratory illness that occurs nearly every winter. Influenza C usually causes either a very mild respiratory illness or no symptoms at all. The flu tends to pass from child to child by sneezing and coughing. The virus can also live for a short time on objects such as doorknobs, pens, pencils, telephone receivers, and eating or drinking utensils. This permits it to be spread to another child by handling an object that has been touched by an infected person. At high risk for flu are children who have asthma or other chronic lung conditions, cardiac problems, sickle cell, HIV, diabetes, or chronic kidney disease and children who are on medications to suppress their immune systems. Stomach flu is an incorrect term sometimes used to describe gastrointestinal (stomach and intestines) illnesses caused by other germs.

Primary Group Affected

- School-age children, especially those who are malnourished, are sleep deprived, and get little exercise

Signs and Symptoms

- High fever (usually 3–5 days)
- Headache
- Sneezing and coughing (may last several weeks)

- Fatigue (may last several weeks)
- Severe aches and pain
- Sore throat (in some cases)
- Nausea/vomiting (rarely seen)

Classroom Guidelines

- Notify parent/caregiver if any signs or symptoms are apparent in child.
- Urge child to wash hands to reduce (not eliminate) risk of infection (*see* Procedure A).
- Ensure that child who is coughing or sneezing covers his or her nose and mouth with a tissue to limit spread of disease.
- Provide a receptacle (bag) for used tissues.

Attendance Guideline

- Exclusion from school is required for period of time when child is showing respiratory symptoms.

Medication

- Acetaminophen may be given for fever with parent/caregiver permission.

Communication

- Notify parent/caregiver if child is exhibiting symptoms.

Resource

- http://2g.isg.syssrc.com

Inhalant Abuse

Also known as: sniffing, snorting, bagging, huffing

Description

Inhalants are used to produce a quick form of intoxication. Most commonly used are volatile solvents such as butane gas fumes, gasoline, paint thinner, spray paint, cleaning fluids, hair spray, and air fresheners. Another popular type of inhalant is nitrous oxide ("laughing gas"), which is often sold in large balloons from which the gas is released. Effects occur within minutes and last up to 45 minutes. Problems associated with inhalant abuse include cardiac arrest, depletion of oxygen in the body, and accidents while intoxicated. Inhalant abuse has reached epidemic proportions in the United States.

Primary Group Affected

- Inhalant abuse can start in grade school and continue through adolescence.

Signs and Symptoms

- Initial use: giddiness, euphoria, unsteady gait, and hallucinations followed by confusion and poor impulse control
- Continued use: anemia, hepatitis, and possible liver or kidney failure—**911**
- Toxicity: abnormal heartbeat and respiratory depression that are potentially fatal—**911**

Classroom Guidelines

- If you suspect inhalant use during school hours, confront the issue rather than ignoring the problem.

- Be aware that child should be referred for emergency medical treatment because cardiac arrest is a fatal complication.
- Look for ways in which to build child's self-esteem in classroom.
- Check with administration to provide drug information classes.

Attendance Guideline

- Exclusion from school is required when child is under the influence of inhalants.

Medication

- None is required.

Communication

- Ask parent/caregiver whether there has been a sudden change in behavior of child.
- Ask family members whether they see signs that inhalants are being used such as clothing with strong chemical odors, strong-smelling rags and empty containers hidden in closets or drawers, unusual-smelling breath, and signs of intoxication.

Resources

- www.inhalants.org
- National Clearing House for Alcohol and Drug Information (800) 729–6686
- www.health.org
- National Council on Alcoholism and Drug Dependence (800) NCA-CALL www.ncadd.org

Insect Bites
and Stings

Description

Many children suffer from insect venom allergies. There is an increased incidence related to the spread of the fire ant throughout the United States. Children stung by bees, wasps, yellow jackets, hornets, spiders, or ants can be thrust into life-and-death situations (*see* Anaphylaxis). A normal response to an insect bite is redness and swelling, but it is necessary to recognize signs of anaphylaxis. If a child has a known allergy to insect venom, an emergency kit should be available at the school and taken on all field events. Responsible persons should be trained in administering first aid for insect bites.

Primary Group Affected

- Children of any age, especially during outdoor activity time

Signs and Symptoms

- Redness
- Swelling around site of sting or bite
- Itching and hives over much of body
- Pain
- Nausea and vomiting, stomach cramps—**911**
- Confusion—**911**
- Difficulty in breathing—**911**
- Swelling in throat and tongue—**911**
- Rapid fall in blood pressure—**911**
- Shock and loss of consciousness—**911**

Classroom Guidelines

- Talk calmly to child.
- Remove stinger as soon as possible if sting is still in skin. Scrape area with swinging motion using edge of credit card or stiff cardboard. Do not use forceps or tweezers, and do not pinch or grasp stinger at top (doing so may squeeze the poison sac into the wound).
- If sting is in the mouth, then give child ice cube or Popsicle to suck, or cold water to drink, to decrease swelling.
- Wash sting site with soap and water. Then apply ice (for at least 10 minutes) and raise affected part if possible.
- For a bee sting, apply a paste of baking soda and water and leave it on for 15 to 20 minutes.
- Watch for more severe reactions. Activate the local emergency medical system and be prepared to resuscitate.
- For more severe reactions, give epinephrine (*see* Procedure I).
- Use diluted ammonia on the bite area.
- Notify parent/caregiver about the insect bite.
- Teach children methods to minimize contact with stinging insects, including refraining from wearing brightly colored clothing with flowery patterns, avoiding sweet-smelling cosmetics and hair sprays, wearing enclosed shoes to guard against stepping on insects, keeping arms and legs covered during hikes and other outings that may expose children to insects, not swatting or crushing insects, staying clear of insect nests, keeping food and garbage covered, and not drinking from open soft drink cans because insects can crawl inside and end up biting the inside of children's mouths. Instruct children that insect repellents do not work against stinging insects.

Attendance Guideline

- Exclusion from school is not required.

Medications

- Acetaminophen if parent/caregiver permission is obtained
- Antihistamines
- Corticosteroids to decrease inflammation

Communication

- Ask parent/caregiver to describe child's reaction.
- Ask parent/caregiver to provide child with severe reaction a medic alert band to wear.
- Ask whether child with severe reaction is getting venom immunotherapy.
- Ask whether child has an EpiPen or bee sting kit.

Resources

- www.allergic-reactions.com
- http://allergy.meg.edu

Juvenile Rheumatoid Arthritis

Also known as: juvenile arthritis, children's arthritis, JRA

Description

Juvenile rheumatoid arthritis (roo' mah toid ar thri' tis) is a common rheumatic inflammatory disease that results in swelling, pain, redness, and heat in the joints. It may affect only one joint or nearly all joints in the body. The majority of children with this condition have a mild disease and do quite well. In approximately 85% of these children, the disease goes into remission by adulthood. There may, however, be permanent residual joint deformities. If the mobility impairment is severe, there may be a need for total joint replacement during either childhood or adulthood.

Primary Group Affected

- Approximately 200,000 children in the United States
- Affects children under age 18 years
- Often a family history of some rheumatological condition (any variety of disorders that cause inflammation or degeneration of joints and related structures)

Signs and Symptoms

- Arthritis (e.g., pain, swelling, redness, heat) present in the joints
- Affected joints that will vary from child to child

- Stiffness, especially in the morning or after being immobile for a period of time
- Fatigue, irritability
- Anemia
- May include spiking fevers and rash
- Poor growth pattern when the disease is active

Classroom Guidelines

- If the child consistently complains of pain or exhibits difficulty in performing school activities, report these findings to parent/caregiver and school health care provider.
- Be aware that children often complain of pain for other reasons and that arthritis might not be the cause.
- Be aware that because child is very stiff in the morning, early classes may often be missed.
- Be aware that during a flare-up of the disease, child may have multiple absences due to pain.
- Allow child to get up and stretch as needed (e.g., to pass out papers, to erase the blackboard).
- Expect that child will have good and bad days and that performance will fluctuate accordingly.
- Determine whether child can tolerate a full day of classes when the disease is flaring.
- Expect that child's face and body may become more rounded due to effects of medications.

Upper Extremities

- Provide extra time for writing assignments if needed or reduce the amount of writing required.
- Be aware that penmanship may suffer.
- Ensure that child wears splints as instructed.
- Provide assistance for child with lockers, lunch tray, milk cartons, dressing, and toileting as needed.
- Determine whether child can carry books.

Back/Neck

- Investigate the need for a bookstand for desk to decrease neck strain.

Lower Extremities

- Provide indoor activities during recess when the weather is cold/damp.
- Ensure that child wears brace/splints as instructed or appropriately uses crutches/walker.
- Ensure that child has enough time to change classes.
- Arrange for child's safe exit from classroom in case of an unexpected event that requires students to leave classroom or school.

Attendance Guideline

- Exclusion from school is not required.

Medications

- Anti-inflammatory medication according to parent/caregiver instructions
- Acetaminophen (Tylenol) with parent/caregiver permission
- Possible use of low-dose chemotherapeutic (anti-cancer) drugs and/or steroids (oral or intravenous)

Communication

- Ask parent/caregiver about treatment plan, especially restriction of activities.
- Ask about schedule of medications.
- Ask what should be done when child is experiencing extremely painful episodes.
- Ask whether child has splints and, if so, what the wearing schedule is.

Resource

- American Juvenile Arthritis Organization
  1314 Spring Street, N.W.
  Atlanta, GA 30309
  (404) 872–7100
  www.arthritis.org

Lead Poisoning

Description

Lead is toxic to many tissues of the human body. It accumulates in the brain, nerve tissues, bones, and kidneys. Young children are particularly susceptible to lead poisoning because their nervous systems and brains are still developing. About two thirds of the homes built before 1940 and one half of the homes built from 1940 to 1960 contain lead-based paint. In 1978, lead paint was banned from use on the interiors and exteriors of homes. High levels of lead in the soil are attributed to leaded gasoline and paint used years ago. Children can swallow lead by playing in the dirt and then putting their fingers, clothes, or toys in their mouths. It is estimated that 9% of children in the United States under age 6 years have unsafe blood lead levels at or above 10 micrograms per deciliter.

Primary Group Affected

- Children located in older neighborhoods in nation's central cities
- Children exposed to lead through deteriorating paint or dust, air, drinking water, food, or contaminated soil

Signs and Symptoms

- Difficulty with language acquisition
- Problems with concentration, memory, and reasoning ability
- Lowered intelligence
- Hyperactivity and irritability
- Poor school performance, learning disabilities, and need for special education
- Hearing and kidney damage
- Seizures

Classroom Guidelines

- Keep play areas and school rooms as clean and dust free as possible.
- Make sure that all children wash their hands before meals and naps.
- Do not let children eat sand or dirt.

Attendance Guideline

- Exclusion from school is not required.

Medication

- A synthetic amino acid, which binds to the lead, is administered intravenously and may be given only by a licensed physician.

Communication

- Ask parent/caregiver whether home was built before 1960.
- Ask whether child has sibling or playmate who has lead poisoning.
- Be aware that if child is enrolled in Medicaid, policies require that he or she receive blood lead screening tests at ages 12 and 24 months.
- Be aware that the Centers for Disease Control and Prevention recommends universal screening of all children; however, each state determines the need for universal or targeted screening.
- Ask parent/caregiver whether screening has been done; if it has not, encourage parent/caregiver to request that blood lead levels be measured.
- Inform parent/caregiver of usual sources of lead poisoning to help inspect home environment.

Resource

- National Lead Information Center
  (800) 424-LEAD
  www.epa.gov/lead

Legg-Calvé-Perthes Disease

Also known as: LCP

Description

Legg-Calvé-Perthes (leg kal va' per' tez) disease is a serious orthopedic condition whose cause is unknown. The head of the femur (thigh bone) progressively weakens due to lack of a blood supply to the growing bone. The bone cells eventually die, and the body replaces them with new bone cells. During the time when the new cells are forming, the bone is unstable and may break and reform abnormally. The healing process may last 18 to 36 months. Both femurs are involved in approximately 10% to 15% of the cases.

Primary Group Affected

- Children from ages 3 to 12 years
- Found more frequently in boys ages 4 to 8 years

Signs and Symptoms

- Hip, thigh, or knee joint pain, ache, or stiffness (may be constant or intermittent)
- Limping on the affected side when rising and at the end of strenuous activity
- Limited movement of joint

Classroom Guidelines

- Be aware of safety concerns associated with children who are wearing special braces, casts, or leather harness slings.

- Arrange for child's safe exit from classroom in case of an unexpected event that requires students to leave classroom or school.
- Plan suitable activities devised to meet needs of child, but limit activity according to directions of health care provider.

Attendance Guideline

- Exclusion from school is required if child is placed on strict bed rest, placed in traction, or recovering from surgery.

Medications

- Anti-inflammatory medications usually must be taken on a time schedule and with food.

Communication

- Ask parent/caregiver about activity restrictions.
- Ask parent/caregiver about schedule of medications to be given to child.

Resource

- www.mayoclinic.org

Lupus

Also known as: systemic lupus (loo'pus) erythematosus (SLE)

Description

Lupus is characterized by inflammation that can affect many parts of the body (e.g., skin, joints, kidneys, blood cells, heart, lungs). It can be mild to life threatening. Flare-ups may come and go.

Primary Group Affected

- Rare in very young children
- Occurs most often ages 9 to 15 years
- Higher incidence noted in African American, Asian, and Hispanic children

Signs and Symptoms

- Complaints of weakness or feeling tired
- Rashes (butterfly-shaped rash across bridge of nose and cheeks or scaly, disk-shaped rash on face, neck, or chest that may look like severe sunburn or hives)
- Fever
- Shortness of breath
- Joints swelling and achy, pain in hip joint that may cause difficulty in walking and running
- Seizures, headaches, excitability, forgetfulness, dizziness, difficulty in concentrating, mood swings—**911**
- Nausea, vomiting, loose stools, stomach pain
- Thinning hair or loss of hair
- Sensitivity to light (photosensitivity)

Classroom Guidelines

- Take complaints of child seriously and notify parent/caregiver.
- Urge child to minimize sun exposure and to use sunscreen and wear a brimmed hat when outdoors.
- Arrange for child's desk to be away from windows with a lot of direct sunlight.
- Keep child indoors and arrange for him or her to participate in alternative activities during extremely cold weather.
- Adhere to any dietary modifications as indicated by parent/caregiver; request list of written restrictions and allowed foods.
- Provide psychological support and show patience when child has difficulty in concentrating; child may easily cry and become frustrated with himself or herself and may need to develop effective coping skills.
- Observe child for fatigue during strenuous activity and plan for involvement that decreases exertion.
- Provide for child's safety and privacy if seizures occur.
- Be aware that child should wear medic alert band regarding his or her disease and if he or she is on steroids (anti-inflammatory drugs).

Attendance Guideline

- Child may experience excessive absences depending on what symptoms are being experienced and response to medications.

Medications

- As ordered by health care provider, usually numerous medications for symptoms and pain

Communication

- Notify parent/caregiver if child complains of any symptoms during school.
- Ask for information regarding any restrictions or special accommodations to be implemented to decrease stress and fatigue.
- Ask to provide sunscreen for child when participating in outdoor activities.
- Ask whether child has experienced seizure activity associated with lupus.

- Notify parent/caregiver if child seems depressed or withdraws from other children or activities.

Resources

- Lupus Foundation of America
  1300 Piccard Drive, Suite 200
  Rockville, MD 20850–4303
  (301) 670–9292
  www.lupus.org
- www.mayoclinic.org

Lyme Disease

Also known as: Borrelia burgdorferi infection

Description

Lyme disease is an illness affecting many parts of the body. It occurs from being bitten by an infected tick commonly carried by deer, dogs, and cats. The tick must feed on the person for 36 hours or longer to transmit the disease. Development of the disease occurs in three stages. Stage 1 usually occurs 7 to 14 days after the bite and is characterized by a red rash and flu-like symptoms. Stage 2 occurs 1 to 4 months after the bite and is characterized by Lyme arthritis. Stage 3, occurring several months later, is characterized by central nervous system changes and continuing Lyme arthritis.

Primary Group Affected

- May occur in children of any age but occurs the most among children ages 5 to 10 years
- Immunity to future exposures not acquired
- Risk highest from May to July but can occur at any time
- Risk highest in areas that are heavily wooded, brushy, or grassy; higher incidence in northeastern coastal states, Wisconsin, Minnesota, and coast of Oregon and Northern California; also reported in Europe and Asia

Signs and Symptoms

- Slowly expanding red rash starts as a flat or raised red area, at site of tick bite, before spreading to form an intense red-ringed border with some clearing toward center. Blisters or scabs may develop at center, or a bluish discoloration may occur.

- Flu-like symptoms include complaints of fatigue, headache, stiff neck, mild fever, and muscle and joint aches.
- If disease is left untreated, person develops Lyme arthritis with pain and swelling of joints, most commonly in knees.
- Paralysis of facial nerves, leading to a facial palsy, is relatively common in children and occurs most often in stage 2.
- Central nervous system changes occur during stage 3 and include arm and leg weakness, Bell's palsy, encephalitis, meningitis, and sometimes depression.

Classroom Guidelines

- Be aware that when child is engaging in outdoor activities in high-risk areas, he or she should wear protective clothing to prevent exposure of skin and should tuck pant legs into socks.
- Check for ticks after outings in high-risk areas, especially ticks hidden in hair.
- Using tweezers or fingers and wearing gloves, remove a tick by gripping it gently but firmly at point where mouth parts are attached. Pull straight outward with gentle steady pressure until tick releases. Wash hands afterward.
- Do not use folklore remedies such as petroleum jelly and hot matches.
- Cleanse area with soap and water. If any tick parts are left under skin, child needs to see health care provider for removal.
- Save tick for identification in case child becomes ill.
- Be aware that child with Lyme disease might not be able to participate in vigorous activities. Allow for periods of rest.

Attendance Guideline

- Exclusion from school is not required.

Medications

- Children with early disease are usually treated with antibiotics and non-aspirin analgesics such as Tylenol for aches and mild fevers.

Communication

- Inform parent/caregiver if tick bite occurs during school hours.

- Encourage to seek medical attention promptly if parts of ticks remain after removal or if symptoms develop.
- Ask whether child is being treated with medications.

Resource

- www.cdc.gov/ncidod/diseases

Measles (German Measles)

Also known as: 3-day measles, rubella (roo bel' ah)

Description

Rubella, a virus that is spread through the air or by close contact, usually causes a mild self-limiting illness. However, this disease can also be transmitted from a mother to her fetus during early pregnancy (congenital rubella syndrome), which can lead to serious consequences (e.g., deafness, blindness, heart defects, neurological damage, miscarriage, stillbirth) for the fetus. A person can spread the virus from 1 week before the rash begins until 1 week after the onset of the rash. Immunity can be achieved by receiving the MMR (measles, mumps, rubella) vaccination. This vaccine series begins at ages 12 to 15 months and is repeated again at ages 4 to 6 years or at 11 to 12 years. The vaccine should not be given to pregnant women, and pregnancy should be avoided for 3 months after receiving the vaccine.

Primary Group Affected

- Children of any age

Signs and Symptoms

- Symptoms are often mild; 30% to 50% of cases may have no obvious symptoms.

Young Children

- Rash: usually begins on face and spreads down to feet, lasts about 3 days, sometimes itches

Older Children and Adults

- 1 to 5 days of early symptoms before rash
- Low-grade fever
- Fatigue
- Headache
- Swollen glands (neck or behind ears)
- Upper respiratory infection
- Inflammation of eyes (conjunctivitis)
- Joint pain (lasts up to 1 month)
- Rash (pink or light red spots) that occurs after 1 to 5 days of early symptoms

Classroom Guidelines

- Review all immunization records of children.
- Ensure proper hand washing with hot soapy water (*see* Procedure A).
- Ensure proper disposal of child's tissues used to wipe eyes.
- Avoid sharing of personal articles such as drinking glasses and eating utensils

Attendance Guideline

- Exclusion from school is required until 1 week after the onset of the rash.

Medication

- Acetaminophen (Tylenol) may be used to reduce fever and reduce discomfort.

Communication

- Notify staff, parent/caregiver, and school nurse.
- Notify local health department.
- Ask parent/caregiver about schedule of medications.

Resource

- www.cdc.gov

Measles (Rubeola)

Also known as: rubeola (roo bel' oah), red measles, 7-day measles, hard measles

Description

Measles is a respiratory infection caused by a virus and is known for its characteristic skin rash. Rubeola (measles) is very contagious and is spread through respiratory secretions (e.g., coughing, sneezing, kissing) to persons who are not immune. Most people with measles become very ill but usually recover with no long-lasting effects. Young infants and adults tend to become more ill and have more complications than do children and adolescents. Measles can lead to complications such as otitis media (ear infection), pneumonia, croup, and encephalitis. Measles usually last 10 to 14 days from the first symptoms until the rash disappears. People are contagious from 5 days after exposure until 5 days after the rash appears. Immunity can be achieved by receiving the MMR (measles, mumps, rubella) vaccination. This vaccine series begins at ages 12 to 15 months and is repeated at ages 4 to 6 years or at 11 to 12 years. Adults born before 1957 are considered immune because they most likely have had the disease. Adults born after 1956 should receive two doses of the MMR vaccine (one dose given after 1967 at age 12 months or over). Pregnant women should inform their health care providers of exposure because the disease can trigger miscarriage and premature delivery. This disease has been seen very infrequently since the initiation of the MMR vaccine.

Primary Group Affected

- Children of any age

Signs and Symptoms

Early Symptoms

- 1 to 8 days, usually 3 or 4 days
- Irritability
- Runny nose
- Sore throat
- Red, watery, light-sensitive eyes (photophobia)
- Hacking cough
- Fever as high as 105 degrees
- Koplik's spots: small red spots (about size of a grain of sand) with bluish white centers visible on inside of cheeks

Later Symptoms

- Continued cough
- Rash beginning on forehead and spreading down face, neck, and body
- Rash that is large and flat with red to brown blotches

Classroom Guidelines

- Review all immunization records of children.
- Ensure proper hand washing with hot soapy water (*see* Procedure A).
- Ensure proper disposal of child's tissues used to wipe eyes.
- Avoid sharing of personal articles such as drinking glasses and eating utensils.

Attendance Guideline

- Exclude from school until the fifth day after rash appeared.

Medications

- Acetaminophen (Tylenol) may be used for fever.
- Antibiotics may be prescribed to prevent secondary bacterial infections for those with poor immune systems.

Communication

- Ask parent/caregiver about schedule of medications.
- Notify staff, parent/caregiver, and school nurse.
- Notify local health department.

Resource

- www.cdc.gov

Meningitis

Also known as: viral meningitis (men in ji 'tis), bacterial meningitis, spinal meningitis

Description

Meningitis is an infection of the fluid that covers the brain and spinal cord. A virus or bacterial infection usually causes meningitis. Viral meningitis is the most common. It is a serious infection but is rarely fatal in children with normal immune systems. Less than 1 of every 1,000 persons infected with the virus actually develops meningitis. Meningococcal meningitis (bacterial) can be quite severe, occurs in epidemics, and spreads easily from child to child by droplet infection of saliva, sputum, or nasal secretions. Pneumococcal meningitis, a form of bacterial meningitis, is the most serious type and may be life threatening. Pneumococcal meningitis can be spread through contact with droplets from the nose, eyes, or mouth of an infected person. Prognosis is dependent on early diagnosis and antibiotic therapy.

Primary Group Affected

- 90% of reported cases of bacterial meningitis occur in children ages 1 month to 5 years.
- Meningococcal meningitis occurs predominately in school-age children and adolescents; there is a higher incidence in children in boarding schools and child care.
- Pneumococcal meningitis occurs frequently in very young children and in children with depressed immune systems, cancer, and AIDS.
- There is an increased incidence of bacterial meningitis in low-income children compared with other children.

- Children who have had a recent case of pneumonia or ear infection have a higher risk; however, there is a relatively low incidence.

Signs and Symptoms

- Varies from child to child; can develop over several hours or may take 1 to 3 days after contact with the infecting organism
- High fever that prevents child from eating or drinking, chills
- Severe headaches, stiff neck, drowsiness, confusion, irritability, agitation, seizures—**911**
- Skin rash (especially near armpits or on hands or feet)
- Joint pain with meningococcal infection
- Nausea and vomiting
- Ear draining fluid—**911**
- Sensitive to bright lights, noise, and other stimuli
- Confusion, decreased level of consciousness, coma—**911**

Classroom Guidelines

- Take complaints of child seriously and notify school health care provider and parent/caregiver immediately.
- Be aware that how well a child recovers may depend on how quickly he or she receives treatment.
- Isolate child from other children but keep under supervision until parent/caregiver arrives or local emergency medical system is activated.
- Teach children to wash their hands often, especially before they eat and after using the bathroom (*see* Procedure A). Ensure proper disposal of soiled tissues and diapers. Avoid sharing drinks and eating utensils to reduce chances of becoming infected.
- Wash objects and surfaces with a dilute bleach solution (made by mixing a capful of chlorine-containing household bleach with 1 gallon of water) to inactivate the virus if exposure to viral meningitis has occurred.
- Allow children to ask questions of someone knowledgeable about meningitis to decrease anxiety.
- Be aware that classmates may be placed on antibiotics or may be vaccinated if child with disease has meningococcal meningitis (*Neisseria meningitis*).

Attendance Guidelines

- Child may return to school with permission of health care provider, usually 24 hours after a fever is gone and child is on antibiotic therapy.
- Child may experience excessive absences depending on symptoms, complications from meningitis, and response to medications.

Medications

- Antibiotics as ordered by health care provider

Communication

- Notify parent/caregiver if child complains of any symptoms.
- Ask about information regarding whether meningitis is viral or bacterial in origin, and notify school nurse and administration for notification of parents/caregivers of other children in contact with infected child as per school policy.
- Ask about any restrictions of activity when child returns to school and about the administration of medications.

Resources

- www.cdc.gov
- www.choa.org/infectious/viralmenin.shtml
- Centers for Disease Control and Prevention
  1600 Clifton Road
  Atlanta, GA 30333
  (404) 639–3311

Mononucleosis

Also known as: mono, infectious mononucleosis (mon o nu kle o′ sis), kissing disease, Epstein-Barr virus (EBV)

Description

Mononucleosis is an acute, self-limiting, viral respiratory infection. The course of the disease is usually mild but can cause serious complications in rare instances. Mononucleosis is spread by person-to-person contact with infected saliva such as from sharing eating utensils, sharing drinking glasses, or intimate kissing. Children ages 4 to 15 years often have a mild form of the disease that appears to be a respiratory infection. Older persons frequently have more severe symptoms that last longer. The virus has an incubation period of 4 to 7 weeks; therefore, this amount of time will lapse from exposure before symptoms appear. There are many different symptoms, and the condition may initially be mistaken for flu or strep throat. A blood test is used to diagnose mononucleosis. However, even after diagnosis, there is no cure, only plenty of rest and symptomatic relief for aches and fever. Most symptoms will go away in about 10 days; however, it will be 2 or 3 weeks before a person can return to normal activities and often 2 to 4 months before he or she feels completely normal. If symptoms continue for longer than 6 months, it is possible that chronic fatigue syndrome may be the cause.

Primary Group Affected

- Ages 4 to 35 years; highest incidence at ages 15 to 24 years

Signs and Symptoms

- Fatigue
- Headache

- Weakness
- Sore throat
- Sore muscles
- Fever
- Swollen lymph nodes in neck and armpits
- Swollen tonsils
- Loss of appetite

Classroom Guidelines

- Avoid sharing of personal articles such as drinking glasses and eating utensils.
- Dispense medications according to school regulations.
- Reinforce the need for a well-balanced diet.
- Avoid strenuous activities and provide opportunities for rest.

Attendance Guideline

- Exclusion from school is required until fever resolves.

Medications

- Acetaminophen (Tylenol) or ibuprofen (Motrin) may be used for fever.
- Child should be encouraged to drink plenty of water.

Communication

- Inquire about schedule of medications.
- Notify staff, parent/caregiver, and school nurse.

Resource

- Chronic Fatigue Syndrome Association
  (888) 232–3228

Mumps

Also known as: infectious parotitis

Description

Mumps, caused by a virus similar to the influenza virus, is known for the parotid and salivary gland swelling noticeable in the cheeks, jaw, and neck area. One third of persons affected have minimal or no obvious symptoms. However, mumps can cause serious complications such as encephalitis (brain swelling) and hearing loss. It can also lead to spontaneous miscarriage when acquired during early pregnancy. One quarter of adolescent and adult males with the mumps will also experience swelling of one or both testicles, although this does not usually lead to sterility. Mumps is contagious and spread via direct contact with respiratory secretions. Symptoms begin to show 2 to 3 weeks after exposure; however, those affected are contagious from 12 to 24 days after the exposure. Immunity to the mumps can be achieved by receiving the MMR (measles, mumps, rubella) vaccination. This vaccine series begins at ages 12 to 15 months and is repeated again at ages 4 to 6 years or at 11 to 12 years.

Primary Group Affected

- Children of any age may be affected; mumps is uncommon under age 1 year.
- Adolescents and adults usually become more ill than do children.

Signs and Symptoms

- Swelling of the cheeks, neck, and jaw (below and in front of ear), often with one side swelling and then, as it is beginning to subside, the other side swelling

- Neck and ear pain (can be severe)
- Low-grade fever
- Headache
- Fatigue
- Loss of appetite

Classroom Guidelines

- Review all immunization records of children.
- Ensure proper hand-washing technique (*see* Procedure A).
- Ensure proper disposal of child's tissues used to wipe eyes.
- Avoid sharing of personal articles such as drinking glasses and eating utensils.

Attendance Guideline

- Exclusion from school is required until 9 days after swelling begins or until swelling subsides.

Medication

- Acetaminophen (Tylenol) may be used to reduce fever and reduce discomfort.

Communication

- Notify staff, parent/caregiver, and school nurse.
- Notify local health department.

Resource

- www.cdc.gov

Muscular Dystrophy

Also known as: MD

Description

Muscular dystrophy is a group of hereditary muscle-destroying disorders. The muscles, usually the voluntary ones, become progressively weaker. Duchenne's and Becker's muscular dystrophies are the most common form of the disease. Duchenne's is the most severe form. Becker's is a milder and slower progressing form of muscular dystrophy. Remaining physically active for as long as possible keeps the child from having to be wheelchair dependent. Sole use of the wheelchair promotes the development of contractures (abnormal shortening of muscle tissue that make the muscle resistant to stretching) and deconditioning.

Primary Group Affected

- Duchenne's: boys ages 3 to 7 years
- Becker's: older boys and young men, usually diagnosed at about age 10 years
- Children living with diabetes mellitus, Down syndrome, or Turner syndrome

Signs and Symptoms

Duchenne's

- Usually weakness in the pelvic area first and then progressing to the shoulders

- Frequent falls and having great difficulty in rising from a sitting position
- Waddling gait, with most being unable to walk by late childhood
- Enlarged calves and upper arm muscles
- Enlarged heart muscle
- Development of scoliosis (*see* Scoliosis)
- Mental deficiency common
- Often death by late teens or early 20s due to pneumonia, respiratory muscle weakness, or cardiac complications

Becker's

- Nearly identical symptoms to Duchenne's but often much less severe
- Heart problems that can be more significant
- Survival well into mid- to late adulthood

Classroom Guidelines

- Foster an atmosphere that allows child to be as independent as possible.
- Foster an atmosphere of sensitivity concerning child's knowledge of disease outcome. Because there may be other children in the extended family with this disorder, child could be aware of prognosis.
- Be aware of safety concerns associated with children who are using assistive devices such as walkers and wheelchairs.
- Arrange for child's safe exit from classroom in case of an unexpected event that requires students to leave classroom or school.
- Plan suitable activities devised to meet needs of child, but limit activity according to directions of health care provider. Plan activities in which child can be successful by using unaffected muscles.

Attendance Guideline

- Exclusion from school is not required.

Medications

- Medications to treat symptoms may be prescribed by health care provider.

Communication

- Ask parent/caregiver about child's knowledge of disease and progression.
- Ask parent/caregiver about schedule of medications to be given to child and any treatments.

Resources

- www.mayoclinic.org
- www.mdausa.org

Nosebleed

Also known as: epistaxis (ep i stak′ sis)

Description

Bleeding from the nose usually occurs as a result of increased pressure from secretions in the nose due to either respiratory tract infection, allergies, or inflammation of the sinuses. Also, bleeding can occur from nose picking and blowing, a hit to the nose, or putting something in the nose. In addition, overly dry air or a broken nose can cause bleeding.

Primary Group Affected

- Children of any age, especially during outdoor activity time and involvement in contact sports or games

Signs and Symptoms

- Bleeding from the nose (light or heavy)
- Heavy prolonged bleeding that can cause symptoms of shock

Classroom Guidelines

- Have child sit down while keeping head in an upright position, leaning slightly forward if possible.
- Using universal precautions, apply firm but not painful pressure with fingers over bleeding nostril for at least 5 minutes. Do not apply pressure to bridge of nose because this is too high up and does not stop bleeding.
- Apply ice wrapped in gauze or a cold cloth and place on bridge of nose for soothing effect.

- If bleeding does not stop in a reasonable amount of time, activate the local emergency medical system and contact parent/caregiver—**911.**
- Keep child from blowing or picking nose.
- Use proper hand-washing technique when working with the child (*see* Procedure A).
- Reassure child that bleeding is from nose and is usually not serious.
- Be calm and approach child in a positive manner.
- Discourage child from swallowing.
- Explain what you are doing to stop bleeding.

Attendance Guidelines

- Exclusion from school is not required.
- Restrict child from strenuous activities for remainder of day.

Medication

- None is required.

Communication

- Notify parent/caregiver of nosebleed episode.

Resources

- www.tipsofallsorts.com/nosebleed.html
- www.nlm.nih.gov/medlineplus/ency/article/000020.htm

Obesity

Also known as: extreme overweight

Description

Obesity is the most common nutritional disorder in the United States. Genetics appears to play a major role in obesity. Studies show that if one parent is obese, there is a 50% chance that the couple's children will be obese as well; the chance increases to 66% when both parents are obese. Other research has found that when identical twins are reared apart, they end up with similar weights regardless of the weights of their adoptive families. Prevention is more effective than treatment.

Primary Group Affected

- Children of any age may be affected.
- 22% of all children are overweight, up from 15% a decade ago.
- Minority populations, especially African American females, are disproportionately affected.

Signs and Symptoms

- Body mass index, calculated by dividing weight (in kilograms) by height (in meters) squared, of 25 to 29 (considered overweight) or of 30 or above (considered obese)
- Orthopedic abnormalities such as hip problems
- Low self-esteem
- Poor peer interactions
- Discrimination in school and from general public
- As adults, being at risk for developing a number of medical conditions: diabetes, hypertension, heart disease, gallbladder disease, arthritis, and complications of pregnancy

Classroom Guidelines

- Discuss with all children the concepts of stigma and discrimination. State clearly that those behaviors are not allowed in the school setting.
- Avoid sending negative messages about the way in which child looks.
- Limit child's access to buying junk food.
- Encourage physical activity. Model healthy lifestyle activities such as taking stairs, walking, and eating health foods.

Attendance Guideline

- Exclusion from school is not required.

Medication

- None is required.

Communication

- Because many medications for other disorders cause weight gain, ask parent/caregiver whether this is a factor for child.
- Ask parent/caregiver what strategies have been attempted and whether they have been effective.

Resources

- Weight Watchers
  (See local chapter)
  www.weightwatchers.com
- Take Off Pounds Sensibly (TOPS)
  www.tops.org

Obesity: Prader-Willi Syndrome

Description

Prader-Willi syndrome is a congenital disorder evidenced by morbid obesity by age 6 years as well as by mental and behavioral problems.

Primary Group Affected

- Estimated prevalence of 1 of every 12,000 to 15,000 children
- Both genders and all ethnic groups affected
- Congenital defect of the 15th chromosome

Signs and Symptoms

- Signs in infants that include small size, floppy muscle tone, feeding problems, poor weight gain, and delayed motor development of 1 to 2 years
- Excessive and rapid weight gain between ages 1 and 6 years
- Mild to moderate mental retardation, where those with normal IQs typically have learning disabilities
- Obsessions with food, food foraging, and excessive appetite that is physiological and overwhelming to the point where child cannot decide "not to eat"
- Behavioral problems such as temper tantrums, oppositional behavior and stubbornness, labile emotions, and compulsive behaviors such as skin picking
- Difficulties with transitions and unanticipated changes
- Sleep disturbances or sleep apnea
- Nighttime enuresis common at all ages

Classroom Guidelines

- Be aware that access to food must be rigidly enforced.
- Be aware that restricting food intake demands close supervision during lunch and snack times.
- Encourage exercise and make adaptations as needed.
- Build on areas of strength: verbal ability, visual-perceptual skills, long-term memory, reading ability, receptive language
- Understand that child may have problems with short-term auditory memory.
- Be aware that child may easily become a victim of teasing and bullying by other students. Discuss respect for all children regardless of size.

Attendance Guideline

- Exclusion from school is not required.

Medication

- None is required.

Communication

- Ask parent/caregiver what exercise activities child prefers.
- If child brings lunch to school, make provisions to prevent access to food until lunch break.

Resources

- International Prader-Willi Syndrome Organization
  Adalbert Stiffer Strasse
  8D-68259
  Mannheim, Germany
  +49 621–799–2193
  www.ipwso.org
- Prader-Willi Syndrome Association
  5700 Midnight Pass Road
  Sarasota, FL 34242
  (800) 926–4797
  www.pwsausa.org
  pwsausa@aol.com

Obsessive Compulsive Disorder

Also known as: OCD

Description

Obsessions are unwanted repetitive thoughts such as fear of dirt or germs, fear of something dreadful happening, constant doubting, or bodily concerns. Compulsions are behaviors or thoughts used to decrease the fear or guilt associated with obsessions. Examples are repetitive hand washing or bathing; repeating movements such as touching objects and getting in and out of chairs; checking doors, locks, or written work; counting silently or out loud; and needing objects to be in fixed positions. The effects of the symptoms can range from mild (less than an hour a day) to incapacitating (nearly constant).

Primary Group Affected

- There are two peak onset ages: one at around age 10 years and another during young adulthood.
- Juvenile-onset obsessive compulsive disorder has a stronger family genetic transmission, affects more boys than girls, has a higher incidence of tics and neurological symptoms, and is less responsive to treatment.

Signs and Symptoms

- Child may appear to have learning disabilities when his or her compelling need to count or recheck interferes with homework and testing.

- Child might not recognize that obsessions and/or compulsions are excessive or unreasonable.
- Child may display consuming and (sometimes) bizarre behavior.
- Child may experience "magical" thinking such as preventing an imagined future disaster by compulsive checking.
- Anxiety may range from mild to nearly constant worry.
- Constant doubts lead to difficulty with concentration and mental exhaustion; child doubts everything related to compulsion and cannot be reassured by what he or she sees, feels, smells, touches, or tastes.
- Symptoms make child very slow in solving problems but do not interfere with accuracy in problem solving.
- Affected child involves parent/caregiver and sometimes siblings in rituals, which can alter lives of all family members.

Classroom Guidelines

- Avoid forcing child to abandon compulsive behavior because this will only serve to increase his or her level of anxiety.
- Observe child for behaviors interfering with learning such as doing schoolwork repeatedly until it is perfect and taking too much time on exams seeking perfect answers.
- Recognize that until the disorder is treated effectively, child will have no control over obsessive compulsive behavior.
- Protect child from teasing or bullying in relation to bizarre behavior.

Attendance Guideline

- Exclusion from school is not required.

Medications

- May be on antidepressant medications, which often decrease the intensity of the disorder

Communication

- Describe how family has been affected by the disorder.
- Discuss accommodations needing to be made in classroom so that child can complete rituals.
- Inquire about process of behavioral therapy and what can be done to support program.

Resources

- O-C Information Center
  2711 Allen Boulevard
  Middletown, WI 53562
  (608) 827–2390
- American Academy of Child and Adolescent Psychiatry
  3615 Wisconsin Avenue, N.W.
  Washington, DC 20016–3007
  (202) 966–7300
  www.aacap.org

Organ Transplant

Description

Organ transplants are complex surgical procedures performed on persons with life-threatening conditions as a result of failure of particular body organs. The three most prevalent organ transplant procedures available for children are those for the heart, liver, and kidney.

Primary Group Affected

- Children of any age who would be considered terminal or dying without organ transplants

Signs and Symptoms

- Complaints of fatigue
- Changes in emotional responses from euphoria to depression
- Complaints of pain and discomfort
- Increased body temperature
- Nausea, vomiting
- Diarrhea
- Weight loss or gain
- Increased or decreased appetite
- Facial changes as a result of medications
- Pain over kidney, swelling of arms and legs (kidney transplant)

Classroom Guidelines

- Use proper hand-washing technique (*see* Procedure A) when working with the child.

- Avoid exposure to other children with colds, sore throats, and the like.
- Allow child to use bathroom when needed.
- Restrict physical activity if child complains of fatigue.
- Be aware that you may need to verify with veterinarian which pets would be appropriate in classroom and which pets could potentially be harmful to the child.

Attendance Guideline

- Health care provider will give permission as to when child may return to school.

Medications

- Child may be on numerous medications that follow a very strict timetable.

Communication

- Ask parent/caregiver about type of transplant.
- Ask about schedule of medications.
- Ask about any physical restrictions.
- Notify parent/caregiver immediately if an outbreak of infectious/contagious disease is prevalent in the school.

Resources

- Transplant Recipients International Organization (412) 687–2210
- www.mayoclinic.org

Panic Disorder

Also known as: panic attacks

Description

Panic disorder involves recurrent panic attacks that are usually unexpected and begin with sudden apprehension, fear, and terror.

Primary Group Affected

- May occur in children as young as age 5 years
- Often preceded by or concurrent with separation anxiety disorder
- Far more common in adolescents

Signs and Symptoms

- Four or more of following symptoms must develop abruptly and peak within 10 minutes: pounding heart; sweating, chills, or hot flashes; chest pain or discomfort; shortness of breath; nausea, stomachache, or choking feeling; dizziness or light-headedness; numbness or tingling; feelings of unreality or detachment from self; fear of losing control or going crazy; fear of dying.
- The disorder is often accompanied by a variety of specific phobias such as fear of the dark, monsters, kidnappers, bugs, small animals, heights, and open or closed-in spaces.

Classroom Guidelines

- Remain with child during times of panic. Never leave child alone during panic attack.

- Provide support and reassurance during times of panic. Speak slowly in gentle voice and use short simple sentences such as "You're OK," "I'm here with you," and "Sit next to me."
- If child has shortness of breath, ask him or her to breathe slowly, in and out, in time with your breathing. Instruct child to take deep breath through nose, hold breath for a count of three, and then exhale slowly while silently saying the word "relax."
- Reassure child that you will stay with him or her and that the attack will go away.
- During a time when child is not anxious, help to identify who in classroom helps child to feel safer.

Attendance Guideline

- Exclusion from school is not required.

Medications

- May be on antidepressant medications
- May be prescribed nonaddictive antianxiety medication (Buspar)

Communication

- Ask parent/caregiver about the usual symptoms child experiences during panic attacks and how long attacks usually last.
- Find out what measures child has developed to manage panic episodes.

Resources

- Anxiety Disorders Association of America
  11900 Parklawn Drive, Suite 100
  Rockville, MD 20852
  (301) 231–9350
  www.adaa.org
- National Mental Health Association
  1021 Prince Street
  Alexandria, VA 22314–2971
  (800) 969-NMHA
  www.nmha.org

Pediatric Autoimmune Neuropsychiatric Disorder

Also known as: PANDAS

Description

Pediatric autoimmune neuropsychiatric disorder is a neurological complication of streptococcal infections in some children. The antibodies produced to fight the streptococci bacteria can trigger an autoimmune reaction. This reaction is most frequently directed against cells in the heart and joints and is referred to as rheumatic fever. In 20% to 30% of the complicated cases, the central nervous system becomes inflamed, causing brain dysfunction. In some children, the disorder resolves completely; in others, symptoms continue with less severity; and a few children will have periods of acute symptom relapse.

Primary Group Affected

- Children with streptococcal infections
- Children with obsessive compulsive disorder, Tourette's syndrome, or attention deficit/hyperactivity disorder at higher risk

Signs and Symptoms

- Sudden and dramatic onset of obsessive compulsive disorder, attention deficit/hyperactivity disorder, or Tourette's syndrome, where child is described as having changed overnight

- Classic obsessive compulsive disorder: excessive hand washing, rigid nighttime rituals, checking behavior, obsessions about death
- Classic attention deficit/hyperactivity disorder: peculiar "squirminess" where child tries very hard to sit still but constantly wiggles and fidgets
- Classic Tourette's syndrome: sudden uncontrollable movements, grunts, and/or facial grimaces
- Emotional swings with unprecipitated bouts of crying or hysterical laughter and increased irritability
- Separation anxiety
- Nighttime difficulties such as severe nightmares and new bedtime fears or rituals

Classroom Guidelines

- Avoid forcing child to abandon compulsive behavior because this will only serve to increase the level of his or her anxiety.
- Observe child for behaviors that will interfere with learning such as doing schoolwork repeatedly until it is perfect.
- Ask child to repeat what he or she heard of instructions before beginning a task.
- Allow child to carry out one instruction before being given another and provide positive feedback for completion of each step.
- Create a classroom climate of acceptance, belonging, and security. Do not allow teasing or bullying of these children in the face of their seemingly "strange" behavior.

Attendance Guideline

- May need to be on bed rest until signs of active infection have disappeared

Medication

- May be on antibiotics

Communication

- Because the symptoms have a sudden onset, call parent/caregiver immediately and urge them to make an appointment with family health care provider.

- Ask about accommodations that need to be made in classroom so that child can complete rituals.
- Discuss any significant social problems with child's peers.

Resource

- American Academy of Child and Adolescent Psychiatry
  3615 Wisconsin Avenue, N.W.
  Washington, DC 20016–3007
  (202) 966–7300
  www.aacap.org

Phobia: Social

Also known as: extreme shyness, selective mutism

Description

Fearfulness is experienced with both other children and adults. Children fear that they will act in a way that will be humiliating or embarrassing. Avoidance of others may become so extreme that it interferes with the development of normal social relations, which can lead to a sense of isolation and/or depression. Selective mutism, a form of social phobia, is the steady failure to speak in specific social situations where speaking is expected. Obviously, this disability interferes with education and social relationships.

Primary Group Affected

- Social phobias can occur as early as the preschool years.
- Selective mutism usually begins between ages 3 and 6 years and occurs more frequently among girls.

Signs and Symptoms

- Distressing events occurring mostly (60%) at school
- Reluctant to speak in class, unable to write on blackboard
- Stands at perimeter during recess
- Refuses to attend pleasant events such as parties
- Refuses to use public bathrooms
- Test anxiety
- Refuses to eat in front of others
- Physical symptoms such as choking, flushes, palpitations, and headaches

Classroom Guidelines

- Do not force child to behave in a way that will intensify fears. Protect child from escalating anxiety.
- Have class discussions on how children establish and maintain friendships.
- Discuss assertive skills and encourage child to practice these skills in classroom.
- Discuss conflict resolution skills and help child to practice negotiating with peers.

Attendance Guideline

- Exclusion from school is not required.

Medication

- None is required.

Communication

- Ask parent/caregiver whether there is more than one fear situation.
- Ask how family has tried to resolve the problem and discuss what has worked and what has not worked.
- If child is in treatment, ask how you can support skills on which child is working.

Resources

- Anxiety Disorders Association of America
  11900 Parklawn Drive, Suite 100
  Rockville, MD 20852
  (301) 231–9350
  www.adaa.org
- National Mental Health Association
  1021 Prince Street
  Alexandria, VA 22314–2971
  (800) 969-NMHA
  www.nmha.org
- Social Phobia/Social Anxiety Association
  www.socialphobia.org

Phobia: Specific

Also known as: fear of [situation or object]

Description

A specific phobia is an intense persistent fear of a specific situation or object that poses no real danger. Fears may involve animals or insects, storms, heights, water, closed places, blood, and injuries as well as injections or other invasive medical procedures. These phobias are usually not disabling in children, and they tend to disappear with age.

Primary Group Affected

- Common among young children

Signs and Symptoms

- Exposure to the feared situation or object results in an immediate anxiety response such as restlessness, muscle tension, stomach complaints, shortness of breath, headaches, and/or dizziness.
- If phobia is of some object in classroom or of closed places, child may have difficulty in concentrating at school.
- If phobia is of dogs, child may have difficulty in walking to school.

Classroom Guidelines

- Avoid reinforcing child's fear by agreeing with perceived danger.
- Do not minimize or discount child's fear. Speak slowly and calmly.

- Prepare child in advance for any stressors related to phobia.
- Model appropriate responses to phobic situation or object.

Attendance Guideline

- Exclusion from school is not required.

Medication

- None is required.

Communication

- Ask parent/caregiver what measures child has developed to manage associated anxiety.
- If child is in behavioral treatment program, ask what must be done in classroom to support intervention.

Resources

- Anxiety Disorders Association of America
  11900 Parklawn Drive, Suite 100
  Rockville, MD 20852
  (301) 231–9350
  www.adaa.org
- National Mental Health Association
  1021 Prince Street
  Alexandria, VA 22314–2971
  (800) 969-NMHA
  www.nmha.org

Pica

Also known as: dirt eating, geophagia

Description

People with pica (pi' kah) most often crave and eat nonfood items. Although eating some of these items may be harmless, pica is considered to be a serious eating disorder, sometimes leading to serious health problems such as lead poisoning and iron deficiency anemia. Children with pica do more than taste a variety of substances in their environment. Some children may imitate a pet dog or cat. They repeatedly eat the items despite efforts to stop them. Some cases of pica are in response to dietary deficiencies. Iron deficiency anemia is a common underlying condition in pregnant women with pica. In other cases, pica may be a behavioral response to stress or a habit disorder.

Primary Group Affected

- As many as 10% to 20% of children experience pica at some time before adulthood.
- Children under age 18 months put everything in their mouths, which is considered normal behavior.
- Pica may occur in people who have epilepsy, cognitive impairment, mental disorders, or brain injuries.
- Pica most frequently occurs in women before or during pregnancy and breast-feeding; those in lower socioeconomic groups seem to be at higher risk.
- People who diet and try to ease hunger with low-calorie, nonfood substances may be affected.
- For some individuals, family, ethnic, or religious customs include eating particular nonfood substances.

Signs and Symptoms

- The most frequent items ingested are dirt, clay, paint chips, plaster, chalk, corn starch, baking soda, coffee grounds, cigarette ashes, and insects.
- Complications include bowel problems, parasites from the soil, and lead poisoning.

Classroom Guidelines

- Understand that if a nonfood substance is readily available in classroom, removal of the item or close supervision of child may be necessary.
- Discuss with all children ways in which to eat appropriately.
- Provide healthy alternative snacks.
- If child has developmental disability, tailor interventions to his or her developmental level.
- Be aware that if child develops abdominal pain or problems with his or her bowels, immediate medical attention should be sought.

Attendance Guideline

- Exclusion from school is not required.

Medication

- None is required.

Communication

- Ask parent/caregiver what nonfood items child eats at home.
- Discuss strategies that seem to work in decreasing the eating of these substances.
- Ask whether the disorder seems to increase under stressful conditions.

Resource

- www.eating-disorder.org/pica

Pink Eye

Also known as: conjunctivitis (kon junk ti vi' tis)

Description

Pink eye, an inflammation (redness) of the conjunctiva (white part of the eye), can be caused by bacterial or viral infections, allergic reactions, or a foreign object or chemical in the eye. Most cases do not cause any serious damage, but in rare situations infectious conjunctivitis can cause permanent damage or even blindness. Pink eye that is caused by a virus or bacteria is easily spread from one person to another.

Primary Group Affected

- Children of any age

Signs and Symptoms

- Pus-like drainage
- Crusting on eyelids
- Reddened conjunctiva
- Swollen eyelids
- Both eyes usually affected
- *Bacterial:* white drainage from eyes, crusting of eyelids (especially on awakening), swollen eyelids, reddened lining of eye, sensitivity to light, moderate tearing, blurred vision that clears with blinking, minimal itching, usually both eyes affected
- *Viral:* usually occurs with a cold, watery drainage from eyes, reddened lining of eye, swollen eyelids, minimal itching, constant tearing, usually one eye affected and then both eyes, sensitivity to light

- *Allergic:* itching and burning of eyes, watery to thick drainage, reddened lining of eye, swollen eyelids, constant tearing, lining of nose swollen and pale in color
- *Foreign body:* tearing, pain, reddened lining of eye, usually only one eye affected

Classroom Guidelines

- Ensure proper hand-washing technique (*see* Procedure A).
- Ensure proper disposal of child's tissues used to wipe eyes.
- Urge child to avoid touching or rubbing eyes.
- Monitor other children for signs of pink eye.
- Disinfect any articles that have been contaminated.
- Eliminate any shared articles such as towels.
- Isolate child from others, especially if child has an immune system disorder or has undergone an organ transplant.
- Keep eye clean. Be aware that warm moist compresses are helpful for removing crusts but should not be kept on eye due to the chance of promoting bacterial growth. Wipe drainage from inner part of eye and outward, away from opposite eye.
- If child complains of sensitivity to light and there is drainage from the eye or redness, notify parent/caregiver and urge follow-up with health care provider.

Attendance Guidelines

- If child has white or yellow discharge, exclusion from school is required until child has been treated with an antibiotic for at least 24 hours.
- Exclusion from school is not necessary when child has watery eye discharge.
- Exclusion from school is not required when child has allergic conjunctivitis caused by a foreign body.

Medications

- Eye drops are used about four times a day for 1 week.
- Eye ointments may be used but can cause blurring of vision and therefore are usually reserved for nighttime.
- Clean eyes of crust/discharge by using a clean cotton ball or washcloth and warm water. Wipe from inner portion of eye to outer eye. Use a separate cotton ball or corner of washcloth

each time you wipe, and for each eye, to prevent further spread of infection.

Communication

- Advise parent/caregiver and school nurse.
- Ask parent/caregiver about schedule and procedure for instilling eye drops or ointment.

Resource

- www.cdc.gov

Pneumonia

Description

Pneumonia (nu mo' ne ah) is a general term that refers to an infection of the lungs that can be caused by bacteria, a virus, chemical irritants, dusts, and allergies. A cold, sore throat, or influenza may often precede pneumonia. The term "double pneumonia" means that both lungs are affected. The term "walking pneumonia" means that the symptoms are mild enough that the infected person might not even know that he or she has it and can continue to "walk" around. Most cases of pneumonia are cured in 2 weeks if treated properly; however, some children will need to be hospitalized to receive intravenous medications and breathing treatments. There are vaccines to prevent various viral or bacterial types of pneumonia. Vaccines are especially recommended for children with chronic illness or with compromised immune systems such as those with cancer or HIV.

Primary Group Affected

- Children of any age, but most common during infancy and early childhood
- Most common in late winter and early spring
- Children with weakened immune systems (e.g., due to cancer or HIV)

Signs and Symptoms

- Cough
- Difficulty in breathing—**911**
- Fever
- Wheezing—**911**

- Breathing faster than usual
- Chest pain—**911**
- Poor appetite
- Very fatigued
- Vomiting
- Irritable
- Restless
- Bluish or gray lips in very ill children—**911**

Classroom Guidelines

- Ensure proper hand-washing technique (*see* Procedure A).
- Dispense medications according to school regulations.
- Encourage child to drink plenty of water.
- Encourage child to spit up mucus (phlegm).
- Avoid sharing of personal articles such as drinking glasses, toothbrushes, and eating utensils.

Attendance Guideline

- Exclusion from school is required until fever is resolved and energy level returns.

Medications

- Usually an antibiotic is prescribed by health care provider for bacterial pneumonia.
- The antibiotic should be given until it is all gone.
- Acetaminophen (Tylenol) or ibuprofen (Motrin) may be given for fever and pain relief with parent/caregiver permission.
- Cough medicine may be prescribed.

Communication

- Ask parent/caregiver about schedule of antibiotics to support/ monitor child's compliance with treatment plan.

Resource

- www.allkids.org

Poisoning

Description

Children can be exposed to a variety of poisoning agents. It is imperative that you find out what a child may have ingested, inhaled, or touched so as to take appropriate steps in responding to this emergency situation. The local poison control center number should be readily available. The poison control center is the best resource for information.

Primary Group Affected

- Children, especially younger school-age children

Signs and Symptoms

- Pain in the stomach
- Nausea, vomiting
- Loss of consciousness—**911**

Classroom Guidelines

- Remain calm and immediately contact local poison control center. (Insert local poison control center telephone number here: _____.)
- Remove poison from contact with child.
- Be prepared to initiate CPR if child loses consciousness and stops breathing.
  Eye
  - Turn child's head to the side and gently wash with lukewarm water for at least 15 minutes from inner to outer part of eye.
  - Have child blink as much as possible while running water over eye.

- *Do not* allow child to rub eye.

Skin

- Remove contaminated clothing from child.
- Wash poison from skin with large amounts of water for 15 minutes or longer.

Mouth

- Remove poisoning agent from mouth by hooking out with finger anything you can see.
- Examine mouth for any burns, cuts, irritations, or unusual coloring.

Inhaled

- Immediately get child to fresh air.
- If child is not breathing, begin CPR.
- Avoid breathing the fumes.
- Open all doors and windows.

Swallowed

- *Do not* give anything by mouth until calling for advice from local poison control center. Ask whether you should make child vomit.
- See whether school has poison control kit.
- For chemical or household products, give water or milk as directed by local poison control center.
- Provide poison control center with the following information: your name and the name of child who came in contact with poison, your telephone number (in case you are accidentally disconnected), age and approximate weight of child, signs of ingestion (e.g., pills found in mouth), and any unusual behavior on part of child. If possible, read the label of the poison container and estimate how much poison was taken.
- *Instructions to induce vomiting:* Use syrup of ipecac–(usually 1 tablespoon for children age 1 year or over) given with glass of water. If child does not vomit within 15 minutes, you may need to give another dose with water. *Do not* use salt water to induce vomiting because this may be potentially dangerous. Never induce vomiting if child is unconscious or having convulsions, if a caustic substance was swallowed, or if a petroleum-based product was swallowed.
- If you are instructed to take child to hospital, take plant, drug container, and/or poison and its container with you.
- Avoid potential poisonings in classroom by keeping all dangerous supplies locked up with "Mr. Yuk" stickers on

containers, never putting dangerous chemicals in beverage containers or recycled food containers, knowing names of plants in your classroom, and verifying with poison control center whether plants are dangerous. Do not rely on child-proof caps; do not store drugs/vitamins in purses, drawers, or cabinets; and never refer to medicine as "candy."

- Know availability of poison control kit in your school and telephone number of local poison control center.

Attendance Guideline

- Exclusion from school is not required.

Medications

- Medications only as directed by local poison control center or health care provider

Communication

- Notify parent/caregiver of incident.

Resources

- www.mayoclinic.org
- www.cdc.gov/ncipc/factsheets/poisoning.htm
- Poison Control Center
  (See local center)

Poison: Oak, Ivy, and Sumac

Also known as: poison oak dermatitis

Description

Children who come in contact with any of three poisonous plants (ivy, oak, and sumac) may experience localized, streaked or spotty, oozing, and painful sores. Poison oak grows as a shrub or vine, especially near lakes, rivers, and streams. All parts of the plant have an oil that contains the irritant. The fur or saliva of an animal that is contaminated with the oil may transfer the poison to a child. Shoes, tools, and toys can be a source of contamination to a child. As soon as the child touches the oil, it penetrates the skin and initiates a reaction. Even the smoke from a burning shrub or vine can cause a skin reaction and may be dangerous to the lungs if inhaled. It is important, however, to remember that poison ivy sores are not contagious and that children who are exposed to the oil do not need to be isolated from other children.

Primary Group Affected

- Children of any age in contact with offending shrub or plant

Signs and Symptoms

- Rash (not contagious—only contact with sap may cause rash)
- Itching or burning sensation (itching stops in 10 to 14 days)
- Multiple blister-like sores oozing fluids
- Sores that last 2 to 4 weeks (usually the full-blown reaction is seen after about 2 days)
- Swelling

Classroom Guidelines

- Remain calm and immediately flush irritant site with *cold* running water (cold water neutralizes oil not yet attached to the skin), preferably within 15 minutes. Do not use harsh soaps or scrub skin. Wear gloves when washing or bathing skin.
- If there is a stream, allow child to enter water (clothes and all) and let water rinse oil from both skin and clothes.
- Have child completely change clothes if possible. Clothing should be laundered in hot water and detergent. Sap can be present on unwashed clothes for 12 to 24 hours after contact with leaves.
- Try to prevent child from scratching contact site. Calamine lotions or vinegar compresses may serve to decrease itching.
- Avoid warm or heated compresses because they serve to increase itching.
- Prior to outdoor field events that may make children vulnerable to contact with poison ivy, oak, and sumac, teach students how to recognize shrub or vine.

Attendance Guideline

- Exclusion from school is not required unless itching interferes with classroom activities.

Medications

- Apply calamine-drying lotion, washing off old lotion prior to new application. Do *not* use products containing the "caine" anesthetic or lotions.
- Child may be taking prescribed oral corticosteroids for severe reactions for prevention or relief of inflammation.
- Child may be applying prescribed topical corticosteroid gel for prevention or relief of inflammation.

Communication

- Notify parent/caregiver of child's contact with poison ivy, oak, or sumac.

Resources

- www.cdc.gov
- www.knoledge.org/oak

Posttraumatic Stress Disorder

Also known as: PTSD

Description

Posttraumatic stress disorder may occur after a traumatic event usually involving a serious threat to a child or a family member's life. The types of disasters that may lead to this disorder are natural disasters (e.g., earthquakes, tornadoes, floods), accidental disasters (e.g., car or airplane crashes, large fires, collapsed structures), and human-made disasters (e.g., acts of terrorism, shootings, assaults, kidnappings, torture, war, bombings). Human-made disasters result in a more severe and longer lasting posttraumatic stress disorder.

Primary Group Affected

- Children of any age

Signs and Symptoms

- Symptoms usually appear within first 3 months after trauma but, in some instances, do not surface until months or years after stressful event
- Reexperience trauma through repetitive play containing themes similar to initial trauma
- Lose newly acquired developmental skills and regress to an earlier level of development
- Somatic complaints such as headaches and stomachaches
- May withdraw from play groups and friends, compete more for attention from adults, fear going to school, lose concentration, show drop in school performance, or become aggressive
- May develop fear of strangers, dark, or being alone

Classroom Guidelines

- Be aware that very young children need a lot of cuddling as well as verbal support.
- Reassure child of safety and your presence.
- Be aware that the goal of interactions with traumatized child is to regain some degree of control over his or her life.
- Answer questions about disaster honestly, but do not dwell on frightening details or allow subject to dominate classroom time indefinitely.
- Encourage child to express feelings through talking, drawing, or painting.
- If child becomes preoccupied with death, has unusual accident proneness, or makes suicidal threats, inform school administration and refer to primary health care provider—**911.**

Attendance Guideline

- Exclusion from school is not required.

Medication

- None is required.

Communication

- Ask parent/caregiver whether child has had more than one major stress incident within year before this disaster.
- Ask whether child has had to move out of home because of disaster.
- Discuss coping measures that child has developed to manage anxiety.

Resources

- American Academy of Child and Adolescent Psychiatry
  3615 Wisconsin Avenue, N.W.
  Washington, DC 20016–3007
  (202) 966–7300
  www.aacap.org
- National Youth Crisis Line
  (800) 999–9999

Psoriasis

Description

Psoriasis (so ri' ah sis) is a skin disease that is the result of a faster than normal life cycle of the skin. Normal skin takes about a month for new cells to move from the lowest layer to the outer layer. In psoriasis, this process speeds up to a cycle of 3 or 4 days, leaving a buildup of dead cells on the outer layer. The buildup of dead skin cells causes a scaly appearance to patches of skin over the scalp, elbows, knees, and lower back. Annually, 20,000 children under age 10 years are diagnosed with psoriasis. Some cases of psoriasis are hardly noticeable, while others cover large patches on the individual's body. Psoriasis affects people both physically and emotionally. The condition will have cycles of exacerbation and then go into remission for weeks or months. Factors that cause exacerbations are systemic infections, injury to skin, stress, alcohol, exposure to some chemicals, and reaction to medications and vaccines. Self-help methods that improve psoriasis include balanced diet, adequate rest, avoidance of scratching/ itching, daily bath (avoid hot water), specially formulated soaps and shampoos, and exposure to moderate sunlight (avoid sunburn).

Primary Group Affected

- 10% to 15% under age 10 years
- Slightly more prevalent in females than in males
- Average age of onset 28 years, although sometimes seen in newborns and in individuals as old as age 90 years

Signs and Symptoms

- Pink or red raised patches of skin covered with flaky white or silver scales

- Small scaling dots (most common in children)
- Most commonly occurs on scalp, elbows, and knees
- Pitted fingernails
- Stiff swollen finger and toe joints (arthritis psoriasis seen in 10% of cases)

Classroom Guidelines

- Dispense medications according to school regulations.
- Remind child not to scratch psoriasis areas; try distraction strategies.
- Be sensitive to the emotional concerns of child.

Attendance Guideline

- Exclusion from school is not required.

Medications

- Creams and ointments may be applied.
- Some oral medications that help to block skin growth may be used.
- Ultraviolet light treatments may be used.

Communication

- Ask parent/caregiver about schedule of medications to support/monitor child's compliance.

Resources

- National Psoriasis Foundation
  (800) 723–9166
  www.psoriasis.org
- www.aad.org

Reye's Syndrome

Description

Reye's (rāz) syndrome is a rare but serious disorder that can affect the brain, blood, and liver. Children who have viral infections may develop Reye's syndrome if they are specifically given aspirin or aspirin-containing medications during the infection. Because it can develop rapidly, it is important to notify a health care provider if a child is showing symptoms of the syndrome. It is also important that children do not receive aspirin or cold remedies containing aspirin (Alka-Seltzer, Anacin, Bufferin, some Excedrin products, and Pepto-Bismol) in treating chicken pox or flu-like illnesses.

Primary Group Affected

- Children between ages 2 and 16 years who have been given salicylates for viral infection

Signs and Symptoms

- Usually occurs within 1 week after viral infection
- Persistent nausea and vomiting
- Decreased level of consciousness; can lead to disorientation or combativeness—**911**
- Unusually sleepy—**911**
- Seizures or convulsions—**911**

Classroom Guidelines

- Notify parent/caregiver if any signs or symptoms are apparent in child.

- Activate local emergency medical system for transport to an emergency facility.

Attendance Guideline

- Exclusion from school is not required once child has recovered.

Medications

- Do not administer aspirin to children unless ordered by the health care provider.
- Child may be prescribed a variety of medications during recovery period.

Communication

- Ask parent/caregiver to provide information regarding child's prognosis and any side effects associated with disorder.

Resource

- www.mayoclinic.org

Rheumatic Fever

Description

Rheumatic fever (roo mat' ik fe' ver) is an inflammatory disease that occurs approximately 2 to 3 weeks following a group A beta-hemolytic streptococcal infection, more commonly known as strep throat. Not all children who suffer from this infectious organism will acquire rheumatic fever. About 1% to 5% of known strep infections will result in rheumatic fever. The most common sites affected by the disease are the joints and the heart. A child's prognosis is dependent on the severity of the heart involvement. There is an excellent prognosis if the child does not develop heart involvement during the initial attack. Future strep infections that may occur can increase the child's chance of developing heart disease.

Primary Group Affected

- Affects fewer than 2 of every 100,000 children
- Boys and girls equally affected
- Most common between ages 5 and 15 years
- Greater genetic susceptibility for ethnic minorities

Signs and Symptoms

- Past history of a streptococcal infection (e.g., sore throat, fever, upper respiratory infection)
- Possible sudden onset of symptoms
- Joint pain, usually in the larger joints such as the knee
- Inflammation of the heart, which can cause murmurs and chest pain with an increased heart rate—**911**
- Fever

Classroom Guidelines

- Report fever, joint pain, and/or chest discomfort to parent/caregiver and school health care provider—**911.**
- Notify parents/caregivers of other students that a classmate was diagnosed with a streptococcal infection.
- Dispense medications according to school regulations.
- Ensure that child follows activity restrictions.
- Allow child to work at his or her own pace if joint pain develops.
- Be aware that child may initially have difficulty in tolerating a full day of school activities.

Attendance Guidelines

- Child with strep infection may return to school after completing the first 24 hours of antibiotic therapy.
- Child may be restricted from attending school by the physician if the heart is involved. Child with severe heart inflammation may require bed rest or a reduced activity level.

Medications

- Antibiotic therapy for 10 days to eradicate the infection if still present
- Aspirin or anti-inflammatory drugs to reduce inflammation in the joints/heart
- Steroids to control inflammation in the heart
- Prophylactic antibiotic to prevent future group A beta-hemolytic streptococcal infections

Communication

- Ask parent/caregiver whether child has a diagnosed streptococcal infection.
- Ask whether child requires medications to be given during school hours.
- Ask whether there are any activity restrictions for child.
- Ask whether child is allowed to attend school or will require home tutoring.

Resources

- Arthritis Foundation
  www.arthritis.org

- American Heart Association National Center
  7272 Greenville Avenue
  Dallas, TX 75231
  www.americanheart.org
  You, Your Child, and Rheumatic Fever (brochure available at above address)

Rocky Mountain Spotted Fever

Also known as: RMSV, Rickettsia rickettsii

Description

Rocky Mountain spotted fever is the most severe and most frequently reported tick-spread illness in the United States. Bacteria that are carried by the American dog tick and the Rocky Mountain wood tick cause the disease. In general, about 1% to 5% of the tick population is infected. If not treated, the bacteria infect the cells lining blood vessels throughout the body. The bacteria may also damage the respiratory system, central nervous system, gastrointestinal system, and/or renal system. Without prompt treatment, the infection can be fatal. As many as 3% to 5% of affected individuals still die from the infection.

Primary Group Affected

- Any children bitten by infected ticks may develop this illness.
- Two thirds of cases occur in children under age 15 years.
- The peak age for these cases is 5 to 9 years.
- More than 90% of affected individuals are infected from April through September.
- More than half of these infections are reported in the South Atlantic region of the United States.
- Those states with the highest incidences are North Carolina and Oklahoma.

Signs and Symptoms

- Symptoms usually develop 5 to 10 days after being bitten by an infected tick.

Early Symptoms

- Nonspecific and may resemble variety of other illnesses
- Fever
- Nausea and vomiting
- Severe headache
- Muscle pain
- Lack of appetite

Later Symptoms

- Joint pain
- Abdominal pain
- Diarrhea
- Characteristic red spotted rash (younger victims usually develop rash earlier than do older persons)—**911**

Classroom Guidelines

- Be aware that when children are engaging in outdoor activities in high-risk areas, they should wear protective clothing to prevent exposure of skin and tuck their pant legs into their socks.
- Check for ticks after outings in high-risk areas, especially for ticks hidden in hair.
- Using tweezers or fingers and wearing gloves, remove a tick by gripping it gently but firmly at the point where its mouth parts are attached. Pull straight outward with gentle steady pressure until tick releases. Wash hands afterward.
- Do not use folklore remedies such as petroleum jelly and hot matches.
- Save tick for identification in case child becomes ill.
- Cleanse area with soap and water. If any tick parts are left under the skin, child needs to see a health care provider for removal.

Attendance Guidelines

- Infected person is usually hospitalized until condition is stabilized.
- Exclusion from school is not required following acute illness.

Medication

- Tetracycline (an antibiotic) is usually administered in two doses a day.

Communication

- Inform parent/caregiver if tick bite occurs during school hours.
- Encourage to seek medical attention promptly if parts of tick remain after removal or if symptoms develop.
- Ask whether child is being treated with medications.

Resource

- www.cdc.gov/ncidod/dvrd/rmsf/prevention

Scabies

Also known as: mites, 7-year itch, itch mites

Description

Scabies (ska' bez) is a skin infestation caused by a tiny mite called *Saroptes scabiei*. The pregnant female mite burrows under the skin and deposits eggs and fecal material that causes minute, linear, thread-like lesions. The reaction causes very severe itching. The rash and itching occur after the individual becomes sensitized to the mite, usually 30 to 60 days after the initial contact. If an individual has been previously sensitized to mites, the itching will begin much sooner (48 hours after exposure). The rash is most commonly found on the wrists, on the elbows, under the arms, and between the fingers. In infants, the rash may appear anywhere but most commonly appears on the feet and ankles. Scabies is spread by extended skin-to-skin contact or by sharing an infected person's clothes. It takes about 45 minutes for a mite to burrow under the skin; therefore, brief contact is not likely to cause transfer of the mite.

Primary Group Affected

- Children of any age

Signs and Symptoms

- Intense itching
- Rash, especially common over wrists, over elbows, and between fingers

Classroom Guidelines

- Ensure proper hand-washing technique (*see* Procedure A).
- Discourage children from sharing personal articles and clothing.

Attendance Guideline

- Exclusion from school is required until 24 hours after treatment is completed.

Medications

- Usually a one-time application of an over-the-counter scabicide lotion (e.g., Elimite) is used as follows. Bathe thoroughly, apply scabicide lotion liberally from head to soles of feet (not just on rash sites), using toothpick to apply lotion under fingernails and toenails. The lotion should remain on the skin for 8 to 14 hours and then be removed by bathing. Launder bed linens, towels, and clothing in very hot water and dry at the high setting in the dryer.
- A second treatment 10 days later may be necessary.
- It will take 2 to 3 weeks after treatment for itching and rash to subside.

Communication

- Notify staff, parent/caregiver, and school nurse, especially those with extended contact with infested child.

Resource

- www.headlice.org

Scarlet Fever

Description

Scarlet fever is caused by an infection with the group A streptococci bacteria (*see* Strep Throat). Some children experience a rash with this illness. Scarlet fever is usually associated with a strep throat infection but sometimes can be due to a skin infection such as impetigo (*see* Impetigo). The symptoms begin suddenly, and the child should be seen by a health care provider. Incidence is highest in temperate climates and usually occurs in late winter or early spring.

Primary Group Affected

- Most common in children ages 6 to 12 years

Signs and Symptoms

- High fever (103–104 degrees)
- Headache
- Chills or body aches
- Loss of appetite
- Nausea and vomiting
- Fatigue
- Swollen glands in the neck
- Usually a sore throat (throat and tonsils may have a white covering or appear very red)
- Skin rash (12–48 hours after fever and/or sore throat): initially resembles a bad sunburn with tiny bumps and may itch; will turn white when child presses on the bumps; usually appears first on the neck and face but not around the mouth; appears mainly on the body trunk and skin folds and spreads to rest of the body; usually lasts for 1 week

- Whitish or yellowish coating on the tongue initially, then turning a strawberry color
- Increased pulse

Classroom Guidelines

- Notify parent/caregiver/school health provider if any of these symptoms appear.
- Isolate child from other children. Scarlet fever is contagious and can be passed through contact with nasal or throat fluids of someone with a strep throat infection; by touching the infected skin of someone who has strep impetigo; or by sharing towels, clothing, or bed linen.
- Encourage children not to drink from other children's glasses or to eat with other children's eating utensils.
- Ensure proper hand-washing technique with antibacterial soap if possible (*see* Procedure A).

Attendance Guideline

- Exclusion from school is required. Usually health care provider will indicate when child may return.

Medications

- Antibiotic treatment (usually penicillin) will reduce symptoms, minimize transmission, and reduce the likelihood of complications. Acetaminophen (Tylenol) may be used for pain and fever every 4 hours.
- Lozenges, hard candy, and warm saline gargles may soothe sore throat.

Communication

- Ask parent/caregiver the schedule for medications.

Resource

- www.kidshealth.org

Schizophrenia

Also known as: acute psychosis

Description

Schizophrenia (skit so fre' ne ah) is a devastating disorder of the brain that affects not only the individual but family and friends as well. The person with schizophrenia has difficulty in thinking clearly, knowing what is real, managing feelings, making decisions, and relating to others.

Primary Group Affected

- The vast majority develop this disorder during adolescence or young adulthood.
- Childhood schizophrenia (diagnosis before age 12 years) is a very severe form of the disorder and may have a stronger genetic predisposition.

Signs and Symptoms

- Most children who develop schizophrenia appear normal at birth and during first years of life.
- Subtle behavioral and cognitive characteristics often precede the first acute episode; these include higher than expected rates of abnormal speech and motor abnormalities such as clumsiness and abnormal movements.
- Other preceding characteristics include social withdrawal and isolation, a decline in IQ over several years, and diminishing school performance.
- Prior to full-blown symptoms, there is a high rate of special education placement and failed grades.

- Delusions (fixed false beliefs) are a common symptom; the content of children's delusions comes from their experiences (e.g., children may believe that cartoon villains are out to get them).
- Hallucinations (occurrences of sounds, sights, touches, smells, or tastes without external stimuli to sensory organs) may be triggered by anxiety and changes in the brain.
- Children with schizophrenia may exhibit bizarre behavior, hyperactivity, decreased self-care, inappropriate affect, an inability to experience pleasure, and disorganized thinking.
- Attention impairment and memory deficits cause severe day-to-day difficulties for many of these children; lack of motivation often gets them into academic difficulties.

Classroom Guidelines

- Accept child for who he or she is and try to understand child's perspective. This will help to empower child and assist in achieving his or her highest levels of functioning.
- If child is having trouble in communicating, interrupt politely but firmly and ask questions that will help him or her to communicate in a more direct manner; for example, say "I'm not understanding what you are saying. Could we try that again?"
- Put child in quietest part of classroom to enhance his or her ability to listen and concentrate.
- Be aware that special education classes should include social skills training to improve these children's level of social functioning with peers and adults.
- Look for opportunities to give positive reinforcement.
- Note that art class could include having all students make collages that tell something about themselves and their interests. In this way, you can emphasize the positive qualities that each collage reveals.
- Set limits on hyperactivity by providing firm direction.
- Strive toward a balance between being protective and encouraging independence.

Attendance Guideline

- Exclusion from school is not required unless child is acutely ill.

Medications

- Antipsychotic medications

Communication

- Because so many people are afraid of and uninformed about schizophrenia, many families try to hide it from others. Reach out to these families and offer them support and a listening ear.
- Ask for particulars on practical solutions on how to manage on a day-to-day basis.

Resources

- American Schizophrenic Association Hotline (800) 847–3802
- www.schizophrenia.org

Scoliosis

Also known as: curvature of the spine

Description

Scoliosis (sko le o' sis) is a sideways curving of more than 10 degrees of the spine. Scoliosis can occur in either the upper back or the lower back. It very rarely is seen in the neck region. The cause for most curvatures of the spine is unknown (idiopathic scoliosis). Scoliosis is usually noticed at the onset of puberty and is most frequently identified during school screenings. About 1 of every 10 persons has some curving of the spine.

Primary Group Affected

- Girls, usually noticed at onset of puberty (ages 10–14 years)

Signs and Symptoms

- Uneven shoulders or hips (girls frequently complain that the bottoms of their skirts or slacks do not hang evenly)
- Shoulder blade ribs stick out
- Rise of one side of shoulder area when bending and curve noted in spinal column

Classroom Guidelines

- Be aware of safety concerns such as falls, stairs, and loss of balance associated with children who are wearing special braces or who have had surgery for spine realignment.
- Arrange for child's safe exist from classroom in case of an unexpected event that requires students to leave classroom or school.

- Plan suitable activities devised to meet the needs of child, but limit activity according to directions of health care provider.
- Be aware that school-age children being treated for scoliosis may need continual positive reinforcement, encouragement, and as much independence as can safely be assumed. Socialization with peers should be encouraged through group activities.

Attendance Guideline

- Exclusion from school is not required.

Medications

- Pain medications may be prescribed.

Communication

- Ask parent/caregiver about activity restrictions associated with treatment plan.

Resources

- www.wh.org/patients/ihb/ortho/peds/scoliosis/questions/scoliosis.html
- www.mayoclinic.org

Sensory Integration Dysfunction

Also known as: sensory integration disorder, sensory integrative dysfunction, SI dysfunction

Description

Sensory integration dysfunction is the inability to process information received through the senses. In this disorder, the brain has difficulty in analyzing, organizing, and connecting (integrating) sensory messages. Because of this dysfunction, the child cannot respond to sensory information and behave as expected. The child is frequently described as being oversensitive or undersensitive to his or her surroundings and people. Interacting and relating with others and functioning in daily life may be affected. The child may also have difficulty in using sensory information to plan and organize what needs to be done and may experience learning difficulties. The child in the classroom may find performing ordinary tasks and responding to everyday activities to be enormously challenging. Because of the uniqueness of every child's brain, symptoms of sensory integration disorder vary from child to child. Some children may have mild dysfunction, while others may live with moderate to severe impairment. In addition, sometimes children will exhibit signs of the disorder one day and not the next.

Primary Group Affected

- Any child

Signs and Symptoms

- Unusually high or low activity level, from always being "on the go" and easily excited to moving slowly and showing little interest in the world
- Impulsivity: lack of self-control, unable to stop after starting an activity
- Easily distractible: short attention span, disorganized, forgetful
- Problems with muscle tone and motor coordination: awkwardness, clumsiness, accident prone
- Lack of definite hand preference by age 4 or 5 years
- Poor eye-hand coordination: trouble with crayons, art project, puzzles, tying shoes, and handwriting (may be sloppy or uneven)
- May want to wear the same clothes over and over again or wear clothes with a specific logo or picture
- Resists new situations or experiences
- Difficulty in moving from one situation to another: may seem stubborn and uncooperative
- High level of frustration: gives up on projects easily, poor game player
- Self-regulation problems: may be unable to show emotion easily or calm down once aroused
- Academic problems: difficulty in learning new skills and concepts
- Social problems: difficulty in making friends, playing in group activities, and sharing toys
- Emotional problems: overly sensitive to change, stress, and hurt feelings; disorganized, inflexible, and irrational (low self-esteem is one of the most telling symptoms of poor sensory integration)

Classroom Guidelines

- Be aware that sensory integration dysfunction is often confused with attention deficit/hyperactivity disorder. The major symptoms of sensory integration dysfunction are a child's unusual responses to touching and being touched and/or to moving and being moved.
- Reduce sensory overload in the classroom. You may need to seat the child in a spot where he or she feels safe, surrounded by children who sit quietly and pay attention; avoid sitting child by doors, windows, or fluorescent lights. Prepare worksheets with

a minimum of instructions to read and problems to solve. White space around each written problem helps the child to focus on one at a time.

- Provide comfortable furniture if possible. Find chair that has cushion and does not tip; child's feet should be flat on the floor.
- Keep chalkboards and worksheets clean with a minimum of instructions.
- Attempt to develop a consistent routine. Give child some time to adjust to changes.
- Encourage child to be an active learner rather than a passive one, and give him or her time to learn.
- Provide a choice of writing instruments.
- Emphasize the positive, keep voice low, and keep expectations realistic.
- Anticipate problems and provide alternatives, but not too many. Assist child in making choices.
- When you want to be certain that the child is paying attention, get up close and look the child in the eyes.

Attendance Guideline

- Exclusion from school is not required.

Medication

- No medications required.

Communication

- Discuss with parent/caregiver the child's behavior and strategies that work best.

Resource

- http://home.earthlink.net./~sensoryint/faq.html

Sexual Acting Out

Description

Sexual acting out must be distinguished from normal childhood sex play, which involves children of similar ages, sizes, and abilities engaging in activity that is consensual. Young children normally hug, kiss, roll on top of one another, and explore each other's genitals. When such activity is actively discouraged, children either stop the behavior or continue it secretly. Children who engage in inappropriate sexual behavior may be said to be acting out sexually. Some children have been abused, some feel a sense of control, some are curious about sexual behaviors they have heard about or seen, and some do not know it is wrong to make others engage in sexual behaviors. In general, the behavior is problematic when there is a 3-year age difference or a power difference such as size or cognitive abilities.

Primary Group Affected

- Children who act out sexually at an early age are more likely to have been sexually abused themselves.
- Of children who start molesting at age 6 years or under, 72% report being sexually abused.
- Of children who start molesting at ages 7 to 11 years, 42% report being sexually abused.
- Of children who start molesting at ages 11 to 12 years, 35% report being sexually abused.
- The median age of victims is 7 years.

Signs and Symptoms

- Nonconsensual touching and genital fondling
- Sexual gestures

- Sexual talk
- Exposing of genitals
- Public masturbation
- Peeping
- Oral sex
- Sexual intercourse

Classroom Guidelines

- Be aware that the curriculum should include age-appropriate facts about human reproduction, contraception, and sexually transmitted infections.
- Do not leave acting-out child alone with younger children.
- Supervise any situations where children may be changing clothes together.
- Teach bathroom privacy expectations.
- Interrupt sexual language or jokes and discuss how such language or jokes can harm others.
- Give clear and consistent messages about what behavior is and is not appropriate. If child starts to act out, calmly interrupt the behavior, state why it is not acceptable, and help child to figure out how to control it.

Attendance Guideline

- Children who act out sexually need to receive specialized treatment so that the problem will not worsen over time.

Medication

- None is required.

Communication

- Discuss with parent/caregiver whether the sexually acting-out behavior is limited to school setting or whether it occurs in other situations as well.
- Refer to school social worker or psychologist for further assessment.
- Inform family that all suspected cases of child sexual abuse are mandated to be reported to legal authorities.

Resources

- www.sexualdeviancy.com
- Safer Society Foundation
  (802) 247–5141

Sickle Cell Anemia

Description

Sickle cell anemia (sik' l sell ah ne' me ah) is a genetic disorder in which normal hemoglobin is replaced by sickle hemoglobin. If the child carries only one of these recessive genes, he or she is identified as having sickle cell trait and shows no symptoms. The sickle hemoglobin causes the red blood cells to become elongated in shape, and this impairs their ability to flow freely through blood vessels and causes small obstructions known as a vaso-occlusive crisis. When this occurs, pain results due to the lack of circulation. Conditions that can cause such a crisis include low oxygen supply (e.g., high altitude), lack of fluids, infection, and exposure to cold temperatures, which causes the small blood vessels to vaso-constrict. Over time, children may experience damage to many body systems. Common areas affected are the eyes, stomach, intestines, and kidneys. In addition, there are two more serious types of crises. Sequestration crisis occurs when there is an excessive pooling of blood in the liver and spleen. This significantly reduces the total blood volume; the child appears to be in shock, and it can be fatal if not treated promptly. Aplastic crisis occurs when the production of red blood cells is markedly reduced and the child suffers from severe anemia.

Primary Group Affected

- Most common among those with ancestors from Sub-Sahara Africa, South America, Cuba, Central America, Saudi Arabia, India, and the Mediterranean countries
- In the United States, occurs in 1 of every 1,000 to 1,400 Hispanic American births and in 1 of every 500 African American births

Signs and Symptoms

- Pain during an acute crisis
- Pale color, fatigue, and shortness of breath with activities—**911**
- Decreased vision, abdominal pain, and urinary incontinence in long-standing disease

Classroom Guidelines

- Dispense medications according to school regulations.
- Ensure that child follows his or her activity restrictions.
- Refer child to school health professional if pain or fever develops.
- Allow child to drink fluids and use the washroom facilities as needed.
- Be sure that child dresses warmly on cold days, especially with gloves and boots.
- Assist child if pain interferes with his or her ability to walk.
- Arrange for child's safe exit from classroom in case of an unexpected event that requires students to leave classroom or school.
- Notify parent/caregiver if infectious/contagious illness is present in classroom.

Attendance Guidelines

- Exclusion from school is not required.
- Child may have multiple absences if frequent pain crises occur.

Medications

- Pain medications
- Prophylactic antibiotic use sometimes employed in the younger population to prevent infections that might cause a crisis

Communication

- Ask parent/caregiver how often child experiences pain crises.
- Ask how much fluid child should drink per day and whether child follows this plan independently.
- Ask whether child requires medications to be given during school hours.
- Ask whether child's pain medications will interfere with the ability to function in school.

- Ask whether there are any activity restrictions for child, especially regarding contact sports.
- Ask whether child is to participate in outdoor activities on cold days.

Resources

- www.sicklecell.org
- Midwest Association for Sickle Cell Anemia
  65 E. Wacker Place
  Chicago, IL 60601–7203
  (312) 663–5700
- Sickle Cell Disease Association of Illinois
  200 N. Michigan Avenue, Suite 605
  Chicago, IL 60601–5980
  (312) 345–1100
  Sickle Cell Trait (brochure available at above address)

Skin Infections: Fungal

Also known as: tinea (tin' e ah) pedis (athlete's foot), tinea cruris (jock itch), tinea capitis (ringworm of the scalp)

Description

Tinea is the medical word for a group of related fungal infections. Fungal infections, caused by several types of mold-like organisms called dermatophytes (der mah' to fits), live on the dead tissue of skin, hair, and nails. The infection can be passed from shared clothing, combs, and pets. All fungi grow best in a warm moist environment. Athlete's foot (tinea pedis), the most commonly occurring fungal infection, affects the soles of the feet and between the toes. Jock itch (tinea cruris) causes itching and burning in the groin area, including the inner thighs, buttocks, and anal area. Ringworm often occurs over the scalp and neck area (tinea capitis). As the name implies, there is a ring appearance; however, it is not caused by a worm. The Latin names refer to the locations of the fungal infections, not the actual fungal types.

Primary Group Affected

- Children of any age

Signs and Symptoms

- Ringworm of scalp: patchy areas with dandruff-like scaling, hair loss, and broken stubbles of hair
- Jock itch: itching or redness on inner thighs, buttocks, and anal area

- Athlete's foot: itching, burning, and redness on soles of feet; stinging on soles of feet; possible peeling, flaking, and cracking of skin; possible discolored and thick nails

Classroom Guidelines

- Ensure proper hand-washing technique (*see* Procedure A).
- Encourage good hygiene.
- Eliminate sharing of towels, hats, and personal articles.
- Minimize close contact with infected child until treated.
- Urge children to dry well after showering or swimming.
- Urge children to wear waterproof shoes to protect feet in shower and gym areas.
- Urge children to avoid wearing same shoes all of the time and to avoid synthetic material shoes.
- Urge children to wear cotton socks.

Attendance Guideline

- Exclusion from school is not required once treatment has begun; however, child should avoid touching affected area.

Medications

- A fungicidal medication (lotion, shampoo, cream, spray, or powder) may be applied to affected area.
- Oral medications may also be prescribed.
- Treatment may be prolonged (weeks or months).

Communication

- Advise parent/caregiver and school nurse.
- Inquire about schedule of medications.

Resource

- www.mayoclinic.org

Sleep Disorders

Also known as: night terrors, sleepwalking, sleep apnea

Description

Sleep disorders include problems such as insomnia, night terrors, sleep-walking, and sleep apnea. Insomnia includes problems in falling asleep, staying asleep, or waking earlier than desired. Although night terrors do not actually waken children, they are very frightening episodes for the parents/caregivers to witness. Sleepwalking is characterized by complex motor activities that usually last from several minutes to half an hour or longer. Sleep apnea is obstruction of the airway during sleep. Getting enough sleep gives children energy and motivation for the day. Children ages 2 to 5 years need about 11 hours of sleep at night along with a nap during the day. Children generally stop napping around age 5 years. For most children, 8 hours of sleep is adequate. Excessive day-time sleepiness may cause attention problems throughout the day, and these can affect school performance. Sleep-deprived children may be moody, irritable, and/or hyperactive during the day.

Primary Group Affected

- Night terrors are most common between ages 2 and 6 years and are more common in boys than in girls.
- Sleepwalking is most common between ages 5 and 12 years and is more common in boys than in girls.
- Sleep apnea is more likely to occur in children with enlarged tonsils or adenoids.

Signs and Symptoms

- Night terrors: sits up in bed, screams, seems very frightened and confused, returns to peaceful sleep after several minutes, has no memory of episode

- Sleepwalking: partial waking, eyes open, dazed expression, walking or other activities, confusion or disorientation if awakened
- Sleep apnea: snoring, labored breathing, or gasping for air when sleeping

Classroom Guidelines

- Keep consistent nap times for younger children.
- With older children, discuss aids to sleep such as quiet activities for hour before bedtime, being read to, or learning simple meditations to slow their bodies down in preparation for sleep.

Attendance Guideline

- Exclusion from school is not required.

Medication

- None is required.

Communication

- Suggest that parent/caregiver set fixed bedtimes and wake-up times.
- Suggest that bed be used only for sleeping, not for homework, playing, or watching television.
- Suggest that child consume only decaffeinated drinks and food during the evening.

Resource

- National Sleep Foundation
  1522 K Street, N.W.
  Suite 500
  Washington, DC 20005
  (202) 347–3471
  www.sleepfoundation.org

Snakebites

Description

Children need to be taught that even though most snakes are not poisonous, they should not pick up or play with snakes. Infections or allergic reactions from the bites of "harmless" snakes can occur in children. However, there are snakes whose venoms are poisonous and require activation of the local emergency medical system or immediate treatment by a health care provider. The appropriate antivenin given within a specific time may save a child's life. Children who frequent wilderness areas or who camp, hike, picnic, or reside in snake-inhabited areas should be observant of the dangers posed by some snakes. Rattlesnakes, coral snakes, copperheads, and cottonmouth water moccasins all are snakes considered to cause poisonous bites.

Primary Group Affected

- Any child in contact with snakes

Signs and Symptoms

- Open bloody wound on skin with surrounding fang marks—**911**
- Swelling at site of bite
- Severe localized pain
- Burning at site of bite
- Blurred vision—**911**
- Excessive sweating
- Convulsions—**911**
- Diarrhea
- Dizziness—**911**
- Weakness—**911**

- Fainting—**911**
- Fever—**911**
- Increased thirst
- Loss of muscle coordination, inability to walk—**911**
- Nausea and vomiting
- Numbness and tingling—**911**
- Difficulty in breathing—**911**
- Increased salivation—**911**
- Rapid pulse—**911**
- Skin discoloration—**911**

Classroom Guidelines

- Carry child to safety. Do not allow child to walk or perform any type of exercise.
- Activate local emergency medical system immediately. Either you or the emergency medical technicians should call ahead to emergency room so that antivenin will be ready when child arrives. Inform emergency medical system responders and/or emergency room if child is allergic to horse products. (Because antivenin is obtained from horses, snakebite victims sensitive to horse products must be carefully managed.)
- Speak calmly to child to decrease anxiety.
- Wash bite site gently with soap and water.
- Remove any rings or constricting items on affected extremity.
- Help child to sit or lie down, immobilize bitten area, and keep it *lower* than heart.
- Apply clean moist bandage.
- Immobilize area using padding and binder.
- Monitor breathing and pulse.
- Notify parent/caregiver.
- Be aware that American Red Cross guidelines recommend that if child cannot receive medical care within 30 minutes, a bandage should be applied and wrapped 2 to 4 inches above the bite site to help slow the venom. The bandage should not be constricting and should be loose enough to slip a finger under it. If a suction device is available, apply it over the bite to help draw venom out of the wound without making a cut (a suction device is often included in commercial snakebite kits).
- Follow school guidelines reporting the snakebite.
- *Do not* apply a tourniquet, *do not* cut into the snakebite, *do not* give child anything by mouth, *do not* raise the site of the bite

above the level of child's heart, *do not* try to suction venom with your mouth.

- Discuss with children how to protect themselves from snakebites. Urge them to avoid picking up or playing with any snake, to not put their hands or feet into any area if they cannot see the area, to tap ahead of themselves with a walking stick before entering an area they cannot see (most snakes will attempt to avoid people if the snakes are given a warning), to wear thick boots and remain on hiking paths as much as possible, to stay out of tall grass areas, to not pick up rocks or firewood unless they are out of a snake's striking distance, to be cautious and alert when climbing rocks (and to leave snakes alone), and to not get too close to a snake.

Attendance Guideline

- Exclusion from school is not required, but observe child for signs/symptoms of infection and notify parent/caregiver if there are any.

Medications

- Antivenin

Communication

- Notify parent/caregiver immediately and urge to see health care provider.
- Follow school policy in documenting incident.
- If child is receiving series of rabies vaccine and antiserum injections, ask parent/caregiver for information concerning reactions.

Resource

- www.healthcentral.com

Spider Bites

Description

Most spiders that children encounter are harmless with the exception of the black widow and the brown recluse (violin spider). These spiders are usually found in warm climates. A bite from either of these spiders necessitates prompt medical attention and activation of the local emergency medical system.

Primary Group Affected

- Children of any age, especially children playing in or around basements, closets, or attics

Signs and Symptoms

- Bite marks (black widow spider's double fang marks)—**911**
- Pain and swelling
- Nausea and vomiting—**911**
- Difficulty in breathing and swallowing—**911**
- Redness at site—**911**
- Brown recluse spider symptoms: deep blue or purple area around the bite, surrounded by white-colored ring and large red outer ring; sometimes described as a bull's eye; blister that turns black, headache, body aches, rash, fever, nausea, vomiting—**911**
- Black widow spider symptoms: immediate pain, burning, swelling, and redness at site; cramping pain and muscle rigidity in stomach, chest, shoulder, and back; headache, dizziness, rash, itching, restlessness, anxiety, sweating, nausea/vomiting, tearing of eyes, eyelid swelling, increased saliva, weakness, tremors, inability to move (especially legs)—**911**

Classroom Guidelines

- For all spider bites, wash the area well with soap and water, apply a cold pack or ice pack to the site, and elevate the site of the bite if possible. Notify parent/caregiver and urge visit to health care provider.
- For black widow spider bites, do all of the above *plus* apply an antibiotic cream (if available) to protect against infection *plus* activate local emergency medical system.

Attendance Guideline

- Exclusion from school is not required.

Medications

- Give acetaminophen (Tylenol) for pain with parent/caregiver permission.
- Depending on severity of the spider bite, health care provider may prescribe a variety of medications.

Communication

- Notify parent/caregiver of spider bite.
- Ask parent/caregiver for information regarding prescribed medications.

Resource

- http://2g.isg.syssrc.com/non_trauma/spider.htm

Spina Bifida

Also known as: neural tube defect, meningocele, myelomeningocele

Description

Spina bifida is one of the more serious (and most common) types of birth defects. Spina bifida occurs when the spinal cord fails to close properly before birth. Children with spina bifida will have varying degrees of disability. The extent of a child's problems is directly related to the level of the spinal cord defect. The higher the level of the defect, the more problems the child will experience. Spina bifida occurs in three forms: spina bifida occulta (mildest and usually without symptoms), meningocele (rarest and can be repaired with very little damage to nearby nerves), and myelomeningocele (severest and often with some degree of inability to walk, loss of control of bowel and bladder, and fluid on the brain, a condition known as hydrocephalus).

Primary Group Affected

- Begins at birth and affects 1,500 to 2,000 babies in the United States each year
- More frequently seen in Hispanics and whites of European ancestry; less commonly seen among Ashkenazi Jews, most Asian groups, and blacks

Signs and Symptoms

- Inability to move (paralysis) or weakness in the legs requiring braces, crutches, or wheelchair
- Club feet
- Spine problems

- Loss of control of bowel and bladder
- Normal intelligence, although many may experience learning disabilities
- Accumulation of fluid on the brain that may be decreased by surgically inserting a device ("shunt") in the brain of some children

Classroom Guidelines

- Be aware of safety concerns associated with child. Arrange for child's safe exit from classroom in case of an unexpected event that requires students to leave the classroom or school.
- Plan classroom schedule to allow child to participate in a successful bladder management program (many children learn to catheterize themselves at a very early age).
- Be aware that children with histories of hydrocephalus may experience learning problems. They may have difficulty in paying attention, expressing or understanding language, and grasping reading and math. Reduce the amount of information presented at one time and allow for extra time for learning. Emphasize key points in a logical sequence. Reinforce conceptual learning through practical activities related to child's life or interests. Provide alternatives, perhaps using a tape recorder for creating writing activities. Encourage organized study habits at both home and school.
- Encourage child, within the limits of safety and health, to be independent and to participate in activities with nondisabled classmates.
- Avoid the use of latex in the classroom. Many children with spina bifida have a greater risk of this allergy (*see* Allergy: Latex).
- Promote positive self-esteem in child. Depression is seen in many of these children (*see* Depression).
- Consider the use of a wheelchair for long-distance activities.
- If a child with a shunt suddenly experiences a severe headache, vomiting, fever, or abdominal pain, notify parent/caregiver and school health provider—**911.**

Attendance Guideline

- Exemption from school is not required unless child is recovering from surgery related to disability.

Medication

- Not applicable unless related to specific symptoms or complications

Communication

- Notify parent/caregiver immediately if child experiences sudden headache, vomiting, fever, or abdominal pain.
- Inquire about any medications and schedules.
- Inquire about child's schedule for bladder control.
- Inquire about activity restrictions for child.
- Inquire about child's acceptance of condition.
- Inquire about any known latex allergy of child.
- Inquire about any known learning disabilities or psychological testing reports of child.
- Inquire whether child desires to inform classmates of the disorder.

Resource

- Spina Bifida Association of America
  4590 MacArthur Boulevard, N.W., Suite 250
  Washington, DC 20007–4226
  (800) 621–3141
  www.sbaa.org

Spinal Cord Injury: Acute Care

Also known as: paraplegia (par ah ple' je ah), quadriplegia (kwod ri ple' je ah)

Description

Most traumas to the spinal cord in children are the result of motor vehicle accidents, blows to the head, back falls, or other athletic activities. The injury may affect any of the spinal nerves; the higher the injury in the spinal column, the more severe the damage. Children who live with complete or partial loss of movement of the lower extremities are said to have paraplegia, while those who cannot function or have limited functional abilities of the four extremities live with quadriplegia. A high cervical cord injury can result in a child being ventilator dependent to breathe. The care of a child living with spinal cord injury is complex and challenging. In the classroom, the child may experience many physical and psychological barriers.

Primary Group Affected

- Boys more often than girls

Signs and Symptoms

- Blunt force or indirect trauma to head or spinal cord
- Inability to move one or more extremities
- Loss of consciousness

Classroom Guidelines

- In any event where spinal cord injury is suspected or is a possibility and where child is conscious, speak calmly to child and tell him or her *not* to move. Child should be moved only by trained personnel who have the ability to immobilize child's head and trunk and move child on a backboard.
- Assess child's breathing and be prepared to administer CPR.
- Activate the local emergency medical system and notify parent/caregiver.

Attendance Guideline

- Child should be transported to the nearest hospital emergency center.

Medication

- Not applicable

Communication

- Parent/caregiver should be notified as soon as possible regarding the injury and where child is being taken so that parent/caregiver can go directly to the emergency center.

Resources

- www.spinalcord.org
- www.spinalinjury.net

Spinal Cord Injury: Long-Term Care

Description

Recent advances in emergency care and rehabilitation now permit many children with spinal cord injury to survive and be present in the classroom. The types of disability associated with a spinal cord injury vary depending on the severity, nerve fiber damage, and level of the injury. Children with higher level spinal cord injury will be more challenged in participating in classroom activities. In addition, children with long-term spinal cord injury are prone to develop bladder infections, lung infections, and bed sores (e.g., pressure ulcers, decubitus ulcers). Other symptoms, such as pain or sensitivity to stimuli and muscle spasms, may develop over time.

Primary Group Affected

- Boys more often than girls

Classroom Guidelines

- Arrange for child's safe exit from classroom in case of an unexpected event that requires students to leave the classroom or school.
- Be familiar with school policy regarding any ventilator or oxygen equipment safety concerns and procedures.
- Allow child to maintain adequate fluid intake to prevent dehydration.

- Plan classroom schedule to allow child to participate in a successful bladder/bowel management program (many children, depending on the level of injury, learn to catheterize themselves at a very early age).
- Be aware that children with injuries at the Thoracic 6 or above are at risk for the medical emergency of autonomic dysreflexia. Signs of autonomic dysreflexia may include the following:
  - Sudden headache
  - Sweating
  - Increased blood pressure
  - Flushed or reddened skin
  - Goosebumps
  - Blurry vision or seeing spots
  - Anxiety
  - Difficulty in breathing
  - Tightness in chest
- Be aware that any child having any of these signs or symptoms should be placed immediately in a sitting position or with the head raised 90 degrees. Loosen anything tight (e.g., belt, pants/slacks, underwear) on child, check blood pressure if possible, check to make sure that any catheter tube is not kinked (most common cause seems to be overfilling of the bladder), and call **911.**
- Be aware that environmental temperature controls such as air-conditioning can affect child's body temperature, especially with injuries high on the spinal cord. Urge child to avoid getting sunburns and to use sunscreens when outside.
- Assist or permit child to change positions frequently (every 2 hours) to avoid pressure ulcers. Make sure that child is positioned in wheelchair correctly. If assisting child with positioning, be sure to lift and not pull child to decrease pressure ulcer injury. Pressure relief may be obtained by leaning child forward, with chest toward the thighs, and carefully tipping the wheelchair back 65 degrees.
- Be aware that child may need to be in a lying down position for part of the school day to decrease risk for pressure ulcers.
- Encourage child, within the limits of safety and health, to be independent and to participate in activities with nondisabled classmates.
- Observe child for signs of depression (*see* Depression).

Attendance Guideline

- Exclusion from school is not required unless child is recovering from complications related to spinal cord injury.

Medications

- A combination of medications tailored to child's needs may be prescribed.

Communication

- Ask parent/caregiver about child's activity abilities and restrictions.
- Ask about special procedures, extra equipment, and specific instructions regarding equipment.
- Ask about schedule of any medications to be given to child.
- Ask whether child desires to inform classmates of what it is like to live with a spinal cord injury.
- Notify parent/caregiver of any health problems noted in the classroom.

Resources

- www.sci-info-ages.com/faq.httm
- www.spinalcord.org
- www.spinalinjury.net

Splinters

Description

Small wooden splinters can usually be successfully removed without much difficulty. However, large items such as fishhooks, pieces of glass, deeply embedded objects, and objects that are difficult to see may need the attention of a health care provider.

Primary Group Affected

- Any children

Signs and Symptoms

- Small object protruding near surface of skin

Classroom Guidelines

- Wash hands (*see* Procedure A) and apply disposable gloves if available.
- Clean area around splinter with soap and water, being careful not to break splinter.
- Gently remove splinter with tweezers that have been cleaned with alcohol or with a flame if available. If a flame is used, allow tweezers to cool before using.
- Squeeze wound to encourage bleeding that will flush out dirt.
- Wash area again, pat dry, and apply sterile bandage over site.
- Be aware that cactus spines may be removed by placing piece of cellophane tape, sticky side down, over spine and lifting off.
- Understand that if the splinter breaks or will not come out, child should be seen by his or her health care provider for removal.

Attendance Guideline

- Exclusion from school is not required.

Medication

- None is required.

Communication

- Notify parent/caregiver if splinter breaks.

Resources

- www.med.jhu.edu/peds
- www.choa.org/first_aid/splinter.shtml

Staph Infection

Also known as: staphylococcus aureus (staff low kuh' kus are' ee us) infection, impetigo (im pe ti' go), pyoderma (pi o der' ma), folliculitis (fol ik u li' tis), cellulitis (sel u li' tis), scalded skin syndrome

Description

Staphylococcus aureus is a bacterial organism that is normally found on the skin; therefore, it is the organism most commonly involved in skin infections. Many different kinds of infections, such as impetigo, pyoderma, boils, cellulitis, and scalded skin disease, are caused by staphylococcus aureus. Impetigo frequently is found around the noses and mouths of toddlers and preschoolers and is more commonly seen during the summer months. It begins with a reddened area that becomes full of fluid (vesicle) and eventually opens and oozes and leaves a heavy, honey-colored crust that causes itching. Pyoderma involves a deeper infection from staphylococcus aureus into the skin, leading to fever and inflammation and pus at the affected area. Folliculitis is where a hair follicle becomes infected and can cause a pimple, a boil (furuncle), or multiple boils (carbuncle). It can be caused when hair is pulled back tightly with barrettes and rubber bands. Folliculitis can range from a mild inflammation at one hair follicle site to multiple sites that can be very inflamed and can cause fever and extreme tiredness. More severe folliculitis may need to be opened, drained, and treated with antibiotics. Cellulitis involves tissue beneath the skin leading to inflammation of tissue and local lymph nodes. With cellulitis, an abscess, fever, and extreme tiredness are common and often require hospitalization and antibiotics. Scalded skin syndrome has a "sandpaper" reddened appearance, with areas of fluid-filled pockets that may also require hospitalization and antibiotic treatment.

Primary Group Affected

- Any age group

Signs and Symptoms

- Fluid-filled areas of skin called vesicles
- Reddened inflamed skin
- Honey-colored crusted areas
- Itching
- Pus-filled lesions/hair follicles
- Fever
- Extreme tiredness
- Swollen lymph nodes (glands)
- "Sandpaper" reddened skin

Classroom Guidelines

- Ensure proper hand-washing technique (*see* Procedure A).
- Remind child not to scratch or rub affected area; infection is found under the fingernails.

Attendance Guideline

- Exclusion from school is required until areas are crusted over.

Medications

- Antibiotic medications or ointments may be prescribed.

Communication

- Ask parent/caregiver how medication should be given.

Resource

- www.kidshealth.org

Stomachache

Description

Stomachaches are a common complaint of children. Some children experience lactose intolerance and complain of a "hurting" stomach 30 minutes to 1 hour after eating a lunch that includes milk or other dairy products. In addition, some children complain of a stomachache as a response to stress. It is important that stomachaches be taken seriously because they may be a symptom of a more serious health problem.

Primary Group Affected

- Children of school age

Signs and Symptoms

- Pain in stomach
- Nausea/vomiting

Classroom Guidelines

- Notify parent/caregiver and urge to see health care provider if child complains of severe stomach pain, if pain does not go away after 30 minutes, or if child is having difficulty in breathing.
- Allow child to lie down. Provide a receptacle in case of vomiting.
- Do not give child anything to eat.
- If child has acute pain in middle of abdomen that settles in lower right abdomen, increased temperature, nausea, vomiting, and diarrhea, notify parent/caregiver and urge to seek emergency care (*see* Appendicitis)—**911.**
- If child is diagnosed as lactose intolerant, adhere to restrictions and inform cafeteria personnel so that they do not encourage

child to drink milk or consume other dairy products with lactose.

Attendance Guideline

- Exclusion from school is not required unless complaints of pain are for an extended period of time.

Medications

- Over-the-counter stomach relief medications may be suggested by health care provider.

Communication

- Notify parent/caregiver if child is exhibiting symptoms.
- Ask parent/caregiver about possibility of child being lactose intolerant (higher incidence found in children of Asian, Southern European, Arab, Israeli, and African American ethnicity/race).

Resource

- www.cdc.gov

Strep Throat

Also known as: tonsillitis, pharyngitis

Description

Strep throat is one of the most common bacterial infections of the throat during childhood. The infection is caused by group A streptococcus bacteria. This infection can be confirmed only by a throat culture. This illness is spread by direct close contact with other people via respiratory droplets (coughing or sneezing). Untreated people are most infectious for 2 to 3 weeks after the onset of the infection. Symptoms appear 1 to 5 days after exposure to the infection. People are no longer infectious within 24 hours after treatment begins. Without treatment, serious complications can occur such as scarlet fever, rheumatic fever, abscesses, and kidney problems.

Primary Group Affected

- Most common in children ages 2 to 14 years

Signs and Symptoms

- Sore, scratchy throat
- Difficulty swallowing
- Throat reddened with white patches
- Tender, swollen glands (lymph nodes)
- Enlarged, red tonsils (may have gray or white coating)
- Headache
- Fever
- Poor appetite
- Muscle pain
- Abdominal pain

- Stiffness of joints
- Rash

Classroom Guidelines

- Dispense medications according to school regulations.
- Allow child to drink fluids.
- Teach children not to drink from the same glass or straw or to eat with another child's eating utensils.
- Encourage proper hand-washing technique (*see* Procedure A).
- Remind children to cover their noses and mouths whenever they sneeze or cough.
- Notify parent/caregiver of any child in classroom with a history of congenital heart defects, organ transplantation, chemotherapy treatment, or immune deficiency disorders.

Attendance Guideline

- Child may return to school after he or she has been on antibiotics for a full 24 hours and no longer has a fever.

Medications

- A combination of antibiotics may be prescribed by health care provider.

Communication

- Ask parent/caregiver for the schedule of medications.

Resources

- www.kidshealth.org
- www.naid.nih.gov/factsheets

Suicide

Also known as: taking one's life

Description

Suicidal behavior is defined as either the behavior and thoughts leading up to the act of suicide or the act of taking one's own life. The end result—survival or death—is described as either attempted suicide or completed suicide. Suicide is not a random act. It is a way out of a problem, a dilemma, or an unbearable situation.

Primary Group Affected

- Children as young as ages 3 to 5 years have been known to commit suicide.
- Suicide is the fourth leading cause of death among children ages 10 to 14 years, for whom the suicide rate has increased 100% since 1950.

Signs and Symptoms

- A pervading sense of hopelessness has a very high association with suicide—**911.**
- Verbal cues include statements such as "It won't matter much longer," "I won't be here when you come back on Monday," and "Will you miss me when I'm gone?"—**911.**
- Behavioral cues may include a change in school performance, an increased tendency toward accidents, and giving away personal belongings—**911.**
- Suicidal intentions may show up in writing, drawing, or doodling—**911.**
- Children may have fantasies about continuing on after their own deaths; there may be talk about being able to see how their parents or friends will react to their deaths—**911.**

Classroom Guidelines

- Remember that children who are suicidal are afraid and believe that no one cares.
- Understand that children who are suicidal might not introduce the topic because they fear being punished or being considered "crazy."
- Introduce the topic by asking, "Often, when children are feeling very upset or sad, they have thoughts of hurting or killing themselves. Have you had any of these thoughts?"
- Take all suicidal thoughts very seriously.

Attendance Guideline

- Exclusion from school is not required unless child needs to be hospitalized to remain safe.

Medications

- None is required.

Communication

- Inform parent/caregiver immediately when there are any signs of suicidal thoughts or behaviors.

Resources

- Crisis Line
  (800) 521–4000
- Suicide Hotline
  (888) SUICIDE
- Light for Life Foundation for the Prevention of Youth Suicide
  P.O. Box 644
  Westminster, CO 80030–0644
  (303) 429–3530
- www.yellowribbon.org

Swimmer's Ear/Foreign Object in Ear

Also known as: external otitis (o ti' tis), otitis externa

Description

Swimmer's ear is an inflammation or infection in the ear canal. The inflammation occurs because the environment in the ear canal has been changed by swimming or bathing, increased humidity, decreased earwax, trauma, or even a foreign body (e.g., eraser, peanut, bean). In rare situations, the infection may lead to hearing loss.

Primary Group Affected

- Any children spending long periods of time in water
- Preschool and school-age children who might place foreign bodies in ears

Signs and Symptoms

- Severe ear pain that increases when outer ear is touched or moved
- Itching in ear canal
- Greenish-yellowish discharge or pus from ear
- Hearing loss
- Fever
- Swollen ear canal

Classroom Guidelines

Swimmer's Ear

- Be aware that prevention includes being in water for less than 1 hour, making sure that ears are completely dry (1–2 hours) before returning to water, shaking head and using corner of towel to dry ears; placing a 50/50 combination of alcohol and white vinegar (SwimEar) in both ears in morning, at bedtime, and after each swimming session, leaving in ears for 5 minutes (avoid cotton-tipped applicators or bobby pins).

Foreign Body

- Be aware that soft objects such as paper and insects can be removed with forceps/tweezers.
- Be aware that small hard objects such as pebbles can be removed with water irrigation.
- Be aware that vegetative matter such as beans and pasta should not be removed with irrigation because this will cause the object to swell and become more difficult to remove.

Attendance Guideline

- Exclusion from school is not required.

Medications

- Analgesics such as acetaminophen (Tylenol) or ibuprofen (Motrin) may be used for pain.
- Antibacterial and corticosteroid preparations may be instilled into ear canal for 7 to 10 days.

Communication

- Ask parent/caregiver about schedule of medications.
- Ask parent/caregiver how long child is to be kept out of water (usually 10–14 days).

Resource

- www.kidshealth.org

Tattooing Infection/ Reaction

Description

Tatooing infection/reaction is a response of the body to any indelible design, letter, scroll, figure, symbol, or other mark placed with the aid of needles or other instruments and done with scarring on or under the skin.

Primary Group Affected

- Teenagers

Signs and Symptoms

- Infection reactions to a tattoo may include pain, redness, swelling, increased body temperature (higher than 99 degrees), drainage that has a foul smell, fatigue, nausea, and vomiting.
- Allergic reactions can occur due to dyes and pigments; nodules may form around tattoo.
- Extensive scarring may occur.
- Skin reactions are increased with red and yellow dyes; in rare cases, hepatitis B and hepatitis C can be contracted from the tattooing process.

Classroom Guidelines

- Notify parent/caregiver and school health provider if child complains of any signs and symptoms after getting tattoo.

- Instruct child to wash tattoo using warm soapy water, rinse with cold water, and pat dry (do not rub with towel).
- Be aware that tattoo should not be directly exposed to sunlight for 4 weeks.
- Urge child to avoid school or other public pools until tattoo has healed.

Attendance Guideline

- Exclusion from school is required when child has increased temperature.

Medications

- Antibiotics and analgesics may be ordered for child, and schedule needs to be followed.

Communication

- Ask parent/caregiver whether there are any special restrictions due to the tattoo.

Resource

- www.mayoclinic.com

Thyroid Disorder

Also known as: thyroiditis, Hashimoto's (hash i mo' toz) thyroiditis

Description

Hashimoto's disease is the most frequent cause of thyroid enlargement in children. This disorder accounts for the largest percentage of juvenile hypothyroidism (low levels of thyroid hormone). Hashimoto's disease affects body growth and results in childhood obesity.

Primary Group Affected

- Found more frequently in girls after age 6 years, peaking during adolescence
- Occurs more frequently in Euro-American children than in African American children
- Children living with diabetes mellitus, Down syndrome, or Turner syndrome

Signs and Symptoms

- Short stature
- Weight gain
- Enlarged thyroid gland that may be noticeable when swallowing
- Fatigue
- Falls asleep easily
- Puffy face
- Cold extremities, discolored patchy skin
- Change in activity level

Classroom Guidelines

- Be aware that a child with long-standing hypothyroidism may experience marked changes in classroom behavior; child may have difficulty in concentrating, complain of feeling cold and of having a lack of energy, and appear tired even when awake.
- Child living with thyroid disorder may wear a sweater even in warm weather and complain of being cold.

Attendance Guideline

- Exclusion from school is not required.

Medications

- Thyroid medications usually must be taken on a time schedule.

Communication

- Ask parent/caregiver about schedule of medications to be given to child.
- Discuss with parent/caregiver any ongoing medical recommendations.

Resources

- www.mayoclinic.org
- www.thyroid.org/resources/patients/brochures/hypothyroidism.html

Tooth Abscess

Also known as: oral abscess

Description

Tooth abscess is an accumulation of pus near the tooth root that causes the gum to be swollen and reddened, and that causes moderate to severe pain. One side of face may appear to be swollen. Tooth abscess occurs more frequently in primary teeth and sometimes follows a filling fracture or tooth fracture.

Primary Group Affected

- Children of any age

Signs and Symptoms

- Pain with pressure
- Pain with extremely hot or cold fluids
- Swollen gum
- Swollen jaw
- Irritability
- Holding hand to area

Classroom Guideline

- Place a cold compress on affected side of child's face to decrease pain.

Attendance Guideline

- Exclusion from school is not required.

Medications

- Pain, anti-inflammatory, and antibiotic medications may be prescribed and administered as directed by health care provider. Antibiotic therapy is usually for 7 to 14 days as ordered by health care provider.

Communication

- Notify parent/caregiver and urge immediate follow-up with a dentist.
- Ask about treatment given.
- Request information about medication schedule.

Resource

- www.nlm.nih.gov

Toothache

Also known as: dental caries, cavities

Description

Toothache usually refers to pain around the teeth or jaw. Toothaches are one of the most common problems that affect children at all ages. They are the leading mouth problem in children. Toothaches due to cavities must be taken seriously because if they are left untreated, they can cause the loss of the involved teeth. However, a cracked tooth (fractured tooth), an exposed tooth root, gum disease, or a disease of the jaw can also cause a toothache. Sometimes, a toothache in a child has nothing to do with the teeth but rather is a symptom of an earache or a sinus infection or, in more serious cases, a symptom of a heart problem.

Primary Group Affected

- Children of any age

Signs and Symptoms

- Throbbing sensation in mouth that can be either continuous or intermittent
- Swollen jaw
- Pain when eating sweets and extremes of hot and cold liquids
- With toothache due to cracked tooth, pain after child chews or bites hard objects such as hard candies, pencils, and nuts

Classroom Guidelines

- Place a warm cloth over side of face affected by pain.
- Urge children not to bite or chew on pencils, pens, and the like.

Attendance Guideline

- Exclusion from school is not required.

Medications

- Pain medications may be prescribed and administered as directed by health care provider.

Communication

- Notify parent/caregiver and urge follow-up with dentist.
- Ask parent/caregiver for information about medication schedule.

Resources

- www.floss.com
- www.mayoclinic.org
- www.nlm.nih.gov

Tooth Injuries

Also known as: knocked out tooth, fractured tooth, broken tooth, dental emergency

Description

Any injury to the head and neck region in children can cause a fracture or even knocking out of a tooth. A child's front upper teeth are most at risk for being injured. A dentist may restore baby teeth that are broken. However, baby teeth that are knocked out completely are not usually reimplanted. If a school-age child has a permanent tooth knocked out, you must respond *quickly* for the best chance of saving the child's tooth.

Primary Group Affected

- Children of any age who are active

Signs and Symptoms

- Missing tooth or teeth
- Bleeding gums

Classroom Guidelines

- Be aware that a knocked out tooth may cause a large amount of bleeding and may frighten child.
- Use a calm approach and provide gentle reassurance to reduce anxiety.
- Wash hands and put on disposable gloves.
- Locate tooth after instructing children who are assisting in this process not to touch tooth but rather to notify you if they find it.
- Pick up tooth by the crown (white part) rather than the root and rinse gently with milk, contact lens solution, child's saliva, or

saline. Use water to clean the tooth only if no other means are available. Do not scrub or scrape tooth clean, even if the tooth has been found outdoors. Be sure to insert plug in sink or basin to avoid dropping tooth down drain.

- Insert tooth into socket and have child maintain tooth in place. If child is reluctant to have tooth put into socket or if you fear that he or she may swallow tooth, place tooth in a commercially available Tooth Saver or Save-A-Tooth jar; these jars contain an ideal medium for transport of the tooth. If these products are not available, use milk. If milk is not available, place tooth in water. (A tooth that is left to dry must be replanted within 30 minutes. A tooth that is kept in milk must be reimplanted within 30 minutes to 1 hour. After 90 minutes, there is little chance for successful replanting of tooth.) If broken tooth fragment is found, it should be taken to the dentist for bonding. Tooth fragments should also be kept moist.
- Place clean gauze over tooth socket, making sure that the dressing allows the child to bite on the gauze and not the other teeth.
- Remove gloves and wash hands (*see* Procedure A).
- Encourage children to use mouth guards when playing sports (both organized and on playground).

Attendance Guideline

- Exclusion from school is not required.

Medications

- Pain and antibiotic medications may be prescribed and administered as directed by health care provider.

Communication

- Notify parent/caregiver of injury as soon as possible and urge immediate follow-up with dentist.
- Ask about any activity restrictions.
- Ask for information about medication schedule.

Resource

- www.schoolnurse.com

Tourette's Syndrome

Also known as: tic disorder

Description

Tourette's syndrome is a disorder of the brain characterized by sudden, rapid, recurrent motor and vocal tics.

Primary Group Affected

- Usually starts between ages 5 and 9 years
- Can begin as early as age 1 year and as late as the teen years
- More frequent among males

Signs and Symptoms

- Motor tics include eye blinking, facial grimacing, head jerking, neck movements, shoulder shrugging, hand movements, hopping, touching people, and pulling on clothing.
- Common vocal tics include throat clearing, grunting, coughing, sniffing, stuttering, yelling or screaming, and making animal sounds.
- A small minority exhibit coprolalia (involuntary use of obscene words)
- 80% also have attention deficit/hyperactivity disorder (*see* Attention Deficit/Hyperactivity Disorder).
- 50% to 70% exhibit obsessive and compulsive symptoms (*see* Obsessive Compulsive Disorder).

Classroom Guidelines

- Understand that children with Tourette's syndrome need assistance to maintain healthy self-esteem in the face of their seemingly "strange" behavior.
- Create a classroom climate of acceptance, belonging, and security. Do not allow teasing or bullying of these children.
- Explain to all students basic concepts of this disorder and the involuntary nature of various tics.
- Celebrate child's achievements, no matter how small.
- Encourage positive self-talk such as "I can do this" and "I am a worthwhile person."
- At end of day, have child review the following questions. What have I tried that was new today? What have I done today better than before? Who are the people I have helped today? Who has helped me today? What has given me the most pleasure today?

Attendance Guideline

- Exclusion from school is not required.

Medications

- Catapres (clonidine), an antihypertensive medication, reduces motor tics in many individuals with Tourette's syndrome.
- A nicotine patch may have a beneficial effect in relieving some symptoms.

Communication

- Ask parent/caregiver what coping mechanisms child has developed to cope with or disguise motor and vocal tics.
- Communicate significant social problems with peers.

Resource

- Tourette Syndrome Association
  42–40 Bell Boulevard
  Bayside, NY 11361–2820
  (800) 237–0717
  www.tsa.mgh.harvard.edu

Tuberculosis

Also known as: TB

Description

Tuberculosis (tu ber ku lo' sis) is a highly contagious chronic bacterial infection that affects the lungs, although in some cases other organs of the body are involved. The tubercle bacillus (responsible germ) is found in air droplets from someone infected with the tubercle bacillus when that person coughs or sneezes. All children should be screened yearly for tuberculosis if they live in high-risk areas such as those with overcrowded living conditions or homelessness. Children who have emigrated from other countries with many cases of tuberculosis are also at risk. It is important for teachers to be aware that there is a difference between being infected with the tubercle bacillus and having "active" tuberculosis disease. Tuberculosis infection occurs when a person has the tuberculosis bacteria in his or her body, has no symptoms, and is not contagious. The risk of developing the disease for these persons is highest during the first 1 to 2 years after infection. Having "active" tuberculosis means that the person has symptoms and is contagious.

Primary Group Affected

- Minority children seemingly more susceptible than Euro-American children
- Children who are malnourished
- Children living with HIV/AIDS
- Children who have lived in or are coming from other countries where tuberculosis is prevalent (e.g., Latin America and the Caribbean, Africa, Asia, Eastern Europe, Russia)
- Children living in poverty, migrant camps, or homeless shelters

- Children living in medically underserved communities
- Children living with family members diagnosed with tuberculosis
- Children who have traveled to high-risk countries

Signs and Symptoms

- Fatigue
- Fever
- Loss of weight
- Night sweats
- Coughing
- Chills
- Enlarged lymph nodes (rarely)
- Positive tuberculin test
- Positive chest X ray

Classroom Guidelines

- Explain to other children in classroom the need to be tested for tuberculosis.
- Be sensitive to the emotional needs of child living with tuberculosis.
- Explain that children may be tested again in 10 to 12 weeks.
- Explain to children that tuberculosis can almost always be cured with medicine.
- Plan suitable activities devised to meet the needs of child living with tuberculosis, but limit activity according to directions of health care provider.
- Open windows or place a fan in windows to pull in fresh air if possible.

Attendance Guidelines

- Exclusion from school is required for children with active tuberculosis of the lungs or throat; however, once treatment begins, child is not usually considered contagious provided that he or she follows the treatment regimen prescribed by health care provider.
- Exclusion from school is not required for children who test positive but do not have symptoms.
- Health care provider or health department will determine when child can safely return to school.

Medications

- Several different drugs are prescribed for children with active tuberculosis to kill all bacteria.

Communication

- Ask parent/caregiver about activity restrictions.
- Ask about schedule of medications to be given to child and side effects. It takes about 6 to 12 months of medications to kill all the tuberculosis bacteria.
- Ask parent/caregiver for suggestions as to how child may devise drug reminder schedule for medications needing to be taken during school hours.

Resources

- www.mayoclinic.org
- www.cdc.gov
- www.kidshealth.org

Urinary Tract Infection

Also known as: UTI, bladder infection (cystitis) (sis ti' tis), urethra infection (urethritis) (u re thri' tis), kidney infection (pyelonephritis) (pi e lo ne fri' tis)

Description

A urinary tract infection may involve the bladder, urethra, or kidneys and is caused by bacteria (germs) that get into the urinary tract. Causes include taking bubble baths, wearing tight-fitting clothing, wearing nylon underwear, holding urine for too long, and wiping from back to front (girls), which brings bacteria from the bowel toward the urethra/bladder.

Primary Group Affected

- More likely in girls than in boys
- Most common between ages 4 and 8 years

Signs and Symptoms

- Pain or burning when urinating
- Stomach or lower back pain
- Urine that smells bad and/or looks cloudy or reddish from blood
- Needs to go to bathroom more often than usual
- Fever
- Vomiting
- Wetting clothes even if potty trained

Classroom Guidelines

- Dispense medications according to school regulations.
- Reinforce instructions for girls to wipe from front to back after they urinate.
- Reinforce instructions to urinate regularly and not to hold in urine for a long time.
- Be aware that if child has repeated urinary tract infections, then you may need to encourage urination every 30 minutes to 2 hours.
- Provide opportunities for drinking plenty of water (8–10 glasses per day).

Attendance Guideline

- Exclusion from school is not required.

Medications

- Usually an antibiotic is prescribed by health care provider.
- Antibiotic should be given until it is all gone.
- Acetaminophen (Tylenol) may be given for fever and pain relief with parent/caregiver permission.

Communication

- Ask parent/caregiver about schedule of antibiotics to support/ monitor child's compliance with treatment plan.

Resource

- www.familydoctor.org

Vision Problems

Also known as: nearsightedness (myopia) (mi o′ pe ah), farsightedness (hyperopia) (hi per o′ pe ah), astigmatism (ah stig′ mah tizm), nystagmus (nis tag′ mus)

Description

Vision problems include the inability to see clearly, focus, or process visual material. These problems can be caused by heredity, eye injury, disease, or neurological injury. Degrees of vision impairment may vary from minimal to legally blind. Mandatory vision screening in grades 1, 3, 8, and 10 allows for many vision problems to be identified and corrected. Such problems include tunnel vision (has less than 20 degrees in peripheral vision), nearsightedness (myopia) (sees things near but has difficulty with distance and will need glasses, contacts, or refractive surgery for distance vision), farsightedness (hyperopia) (sees things far or distant but has difficulty with close vision and will need glasses, contacts, or surgery for reading and close work), astigmatism (has irregular shape of cornea causing blurred vision and will need glasses, contacts, or refractive surgery), and nystagmus (has rapid involuntary movements of eyeballs that may impair vision).

Primary Group Affected

- Children of any age, often detected in school mandatory vision screening

Signs and Symptoms

- Squinting
- Blinking
- Red eye

- Eye pain
- Headaches
- Unnecessary eye movements (twitching)
- Photophobia (sensitivity to light)
- Difficulty in identifying letters, shapes, and/or colors
- Assumes an unnatural position to focus on chalkboard or text
- Holds things close to face when reading or moves to front of class during work on chalkboard

Classroom Guidelines

- Encourage child to wear glasses when needed for schoolwork.
- Modify classroom seating to accommodate child's vision needs.
- Observe for signs and symptoms of persistent vision problems.
- Preserve child's self-esteem.
- Do not allow other children to tease child about glasses.

Attendance Guideline

- Exclusion from school is not required.

Medications

- Correction to best visual acuity through wearing of glasses or contact lenses
- Surgical correction

Communication

- Report symptoms observed to parent/caregiver.

Resources

- www.allabouteyes.com
- Lions Club
  (See local chapter)

Whooping Cough

Also known as: pertussis (per tus' is)

Description

Pertussis, a highly contagious, acute respiratory infection, can lead to lung damage and recurrent bronchial infections if left untreated. In infants, it can even lead to brain damage and death. This disease can be prevented with the combination vaccine DPT (diphtheria, pertussis, tetanus) given at ages 15 months, 2, 4, and 6 and a booster between ages 4 and 6 years.

Primary Group Affected

- Children of any age
- 75% under age 5 years

Signs and Symptoms

- Initial symptoms resemble those of a common cold (e.g., sneezing, runny nose, low-grade fever, mild cough).
- Within 2 weeks, characteristic cough begins with episodes of numerous rapid coughs followed by crowing or high-pitched whoop.
- Thick clear mucus is common.
- Vomiting with coughing is common.
- Coughing phase lasts up to 6 weeks.

Classroom Guidelines

- Ensure proper hand-washing technique (*see* Procedure A).
- Ensure proper disposal of child's tissues used to wipe eyes.

- Avoid sharing of personal articles such as drinking glasses and eating utensils.
- Be aware that child can become easily dehydrated. Provide opportunities to drink water.
- Advise any child or staff member with persistent cough to seek care from a health care provider.

Attendance Guidelines

- A child who does not receive antibiotics can transmit pertussis from 7 days following exposure to 4 weeks after onset of coughing episodes.
- Exclusion from school is required for child who receives antibiotics until 5 days after starting antibiotics; antibiotics will not reduce severity of illness but will reduce infectiousness of pertussis.

Medications

- Often an antibiotic is prescribed (antibiotics are of no use once the whooping cough stage begins).
- Codeine may be prescribed to help relieve cough.
- Some children are hospitalized (especially under age 1 year).

Communication

- Ask parent/caregiver about schedule of medications.

Resource

- www.cdc.gov

Worms

Also known as: pinworms, roundworms, hookworms, whipworms

Description

Pinworms are a common occurrence in children. It is believed that as many as 15% of children in the United States have a yearly infection. Humans are the only hosts for pinworms. Dogs and cats do not carry or transmit pinworms. The adult female worm lives in the intestines and at night migrates to the rectum, laying a large number of eggs on the surrounding skin. The eggs are capable of living for 2 to 3 weeks and are unknowingly transferred to the mouth. After the eggs are swallowed, they hatch in the small intestine and migrate down to the large intestine. Humans are not part of the normal life cycles of the worms that affect dogs and cats (roundworms and hookworms). The eggs, however, can enter the body through the mouth (roundworm) or directly through the skin (hookworm).

Primary Group Affected

- Pinworms are spread person-to-person by clothing, bedding, food, dust, and air; schoolchildren are at highest risk for pinworm infection.
- Roundworms and hookworms are most likely to affect young children between ages 1 and 4 years and are picked up from direct skin contact with contaminated soil or grass.
- Whipworms are most common in warm moist climates and occur most often in undernourished children living in unsanitary conditions.

Signs and Symptoms

Pinworms

- Severe itching of anal area at night
- Insomnia, irritability, and restlessness
- Occasional abdominal pain
- Can spread to vagina and cause a vaginal discharge (girls)

Roundworms and Hookworms

- Mild infections: may have mild anemia and malnutrition
- Moderate infections: loss of appetite, weight loss, fever, intestinal colic, irritability, and nervousness
- Severe infections: intestinal obstruction, appendicitis, liver damage, and lung damage

Whipworms

- Mild infections: no symptoms
- More severe infections: abdominal pain and bloating and diarrhea

Classroom Guidelines

- Be aware that proper hand washing (*see* Procedure A) may prevent pinworms from passing from one child to another.
- Encourage children to wash around their nails very carefully.
- Be aware that outside sandboxes should be covered when not being used to prevent cats from using them as litter boxes.
- Do not let children play outside in bare feet.

Attendance Guideline

- Exclusion from school is not required.

Medication

- Pinworms are easily treated with Vermox.

Communication

- If there is an outbreak of pinworms in the classroom, notify all parents/caregivers to make appointments with their primary health care providers.

- Report any signs of severe anal itching to parent/caregiver.
- If child's family has a new kitten or puppy, parent/caregiver should talk with veterinarian about deworming pet.

Resource

- www.mayoclinic.org

PART III

Health Policies
and Procedures

Procedure A

Hand Washing

Hand washing is the single most effective practice that prevents the spread of germs that can cause colds, flu, pneumonia, diarrhea, and somtimes even more serious diseases. You can stop the spread of germs by washing your hands and teaching your students good hand-washing practices.

Steps to Good Hand Washing

Step 1: Wet both hands with warm running water.

Step 2: Apply a liquid or bar soap (antibacterial soaps may be used but are not required) to hands, and rub hands together for 15 to 20 seconds. Wash all surfaces thoroughly, including wrists, palms, backs of hands, fingers, and under fingernails. (Note that it takes approximately 20 seconds to say the Pledge of Allegiance, sing the *Happy Birthday* song, or recite the poem "Twinkle, Twinkle, Little Star.") Rub longer if hands are visibly soiled. This is the most important step of washing away germs.

Step 3: Rinse hands thoroughly under running water. Leave the water running until after drying hands.

Step 4: Dry hands with a disposable paper towel. Pat your skin to avoid cracking or chapping. Activate hand dryer with your elbow.

Step 5: Turn off water with a different dry paper towel to prevent the germs from the faucet from getting back onto your hands.

Step 6: Consider applying a hand lotion after washing to prevent and soothe dry skin.

When You Should Wash Your Hands

- *Before you* eat food, treat a cut or sore, tend to a sick child, or insert or remove contact lenses
- *After you* go to the bathroom, help a child with toileting, help a child who is vomiting or has diarrhea, touch an animal or pet cage, take off plastic or vinyl gloves, handle garbage, blow your nose, cough, sneeze, handle money, when your hands are visibly dirty, or you handle uncooked foods

When to Wear Gloves

Disposable gloves should be worn to provide a protective barrier and to prevent contamination of hands when touching blood, body fluids, mucus membranes (inside mouth), and nonintact skin (e.g., cut, sore).

Remember: The wearing of disposable gloves does *not* replace the need to wash your hands. Gloves may have very small defects or may be torn during use, both of which can lead to hands becoming contaminated when taking off the gloves. Wash hands immediately after disposing of gloves. Hands are to be washed even if they are not visibly contaminated.

When Water Is Not Available

When running water is not available, towelettes may be used as a temporary measure until hands can be cleaned under running water. Water basins should not be used as an alternative to running water. If there are no alternatives to a water basin as a temporary measure, clean and disinfect the basin between each use. The Centers for Disease Control and Prevention has stated that disease outbreaks have been linked with sharing wash water and wash basins.

Spills Cleanup

The Occupational Safety and Health Administration has addressed concerns about transmission of certain diseases through contact with blood or body fluids. Each school system should have policies and procedures related to these concerns accessible to staff. The appropriate recent: made solutions of a mixture of chlorine bleach and water and specific procedures related to cleanup should be readily available.

Resources

- www.gphealthsmart.com/teaching/index.asp
- www.asmusa.org
  (Can download a free poster about the importance of hand washing)
- www.cdc.gov
- www.mayoclinic.org

Procedure B

Care of Minor Cuts/Abrasions and Lacerations

Bleeding From Minor Cuts or Abrasions

Small wounds and abrasions (scrapes) do not pose any serious threat to children. In the event of a minor injury that results in a small amount of bleeding, do the following:

- Rinse the area with warm water to clean away dirt.
- Wash with a mild soap and water.
- Cover the area with a sterile bandage/gauze.
- If the dressing becomes wet or soiled, remove and replace with a new sterile dressing.
- Be aware that once a scab has formed, the wound no longer needs a dressing.
- Note that signs of improper healing include increasing redness, swelling, heat, and drainage (pus).

Bleeding From Larger Cuts or Lacerations

Large wounds require more immediate attention. Do the following:

- Rinse the area with warm water to clean away dirt.
- Wash with a mild soap and water.
- Cover the area with a sterile bandage/gauze.
- Protect yourself by wearing latex gloves.
- If the wound is bleeding, raise the bleeding area above the level of child's heart.
- Apply pressure over the wound with the palm of your hand for 5 minutes.
- Do not apply a tourniquet or lift pressure to check the wound.

- If the dressing becomes soaked with blood, leave it in place and put another dressing over the first one. Continue to apply pressure.
- Call **911** in the following instances:
  - Child does not seem alert or responsive.
  - Bleeding does not stop after 5 minutes of pressure.
  - Wound is on the face, neck, or head.
  - Something is stuck in the wound (do not remove protruding objects).
  - Cut seems to be deep.

Resources

- www.kidshealth.org
- www.mayoclinic.org

Procedure C

Care of Casts

There are basically two types of casts that are used for children in immobilizing specific body parts. Instructions regarding cast care are based on the type of cast that is applied, either synthetic (fiberglass) or plaster. Synthetic casting material is lighter, dries in 30 minutes, has a rough exterior, and is water resistant. Plaster casts take 10 to 72 hours to dry and have a smooth exterior.

Guidelines for Synthetic Casts

- Be aware that weight may be placed on a newly casted leg or arm 30 minutes after it is applied unless you are otherwise informed by parent/caregiver or health care provider.
- Be aware that the rough surface makes the cast harder to autograph.
- If cast becomes damp, dry thoroughly with a blow dryer on a cool setting. Failure to dry the cast may cause sores under the cast.
- Follow guidelines for plaster casts.

Guidelines for Plaster Casts

- Check with parent/caregiver regarding any restriction of activity. Child may need to avoid strenuous activities for the first few days.
- Be aware that weight may be placed on the newly casted leg after 48 hours unless you are otherwise informed by parent/ caregiver or health care provider.
- Be aware that child should use crutches with a leg cast.

- Elevate the child's casted extremity if possible. Avoid allowing the casted extremity to hang down for any length of time. Restrict standing for too long even with the use of crutches.
- Place a wet cast on a pillow or soft pad. (Avoid using fingers to move a wet cast; use the palm of the hand to avoid indentations. Avoid placing a wet cast on a hard surface because this may dent wet plaster.)
- Do not allow child to scratch under the cast or put any objects inside the cast because this may irritate the skin and cause sores.
- If child has a boot for the cast, make sure that child wears it whenever he or she is walking. Not doing so, even for short periods of time, can cause the cast to crack and soften.
- Keep the cast dry. If child needs to walk in the rain or snow, make sure that the cast is protected with a plastic or waterproof covering or a cast shoe.
- Immediately notify school health care personnel and parent/caregiver if child complains of the cast feeling too tight or too loose; if the cast becomes broken or cracked; if child feels painful pressure areas or increased swelling; if child complains of tingling, pain, or numbness that is not relieved by elevating the casted extremity; if you notice an excessive odor (although some perspiration odor from the cast is normal); if the skin becomes darker or lighter than the comparable extremity; if you notice reddened skin or bleeding around the edges or on the cast itself; or if child has a temperature higher than 101.3 degrees.
- Arrange for child's safe exit from classroom in case of an unexpected event that requires students to leave the classroom or school.

Resource

- www.vh.org/patients/ihb/ortho/castwear.html

Procedure D

Care of Tracheostomy

Tracheotomy or tracheostomy is a procedure in which a cut (incision) is made into the windpipe (trachea) that forms either a temporary or permanent opening (ostomy). The opening or hole (stoma) allows for the insertion of a short tube that permits the child to get air and remove mucus. Instead of the child breathing through the nose and mouth, the child now breathes through the tracheostomy opening. In the school setting, the child may need to be suctioned (remove secretions) to keep the tube clear of mucus that can block the tracheostomy and hinder breathing. Some children require suctioning prior to eating. In some cases, older school-age children may be able to perform this procedure without assistance. Be aware that some modification may be needed for this procedure depending on the child's specific tracheostomy tube and/or equipment.

Guidelines for Tracheostomy Suctioning

- Ask parent/caregiver the reason for child having a tracheostomy. Request any specific instructions from health care provider regarding the procedure such as when suctioning should be performed, whether sterile saline drops should be instilled in the tracheostomy opening prior to suctioning, length of catheter insertion, disposal of used equipment, and care of suction machine and connecting tube. Ask whether suctioning technique should be following clean or sterile procedure. Ask parent/caregiver for any activity restrictions due to the tube (e.g., swimming, showers). Request that parent/caregiver initially demonstrate the tracheostomy suctioning.
- Wash hands prior to suctioning (*see* Procedure A). Put on protective eyewear.

- Remove the suction catheter (tube) from the package. Do not touch the part of the catheter that goes directly into child's tracheostomy. Put a sterile glove on the hand that will be touching the catheter.
- Attach the suction catheter to the suction machine tubing.
- Turn on the suction machine with the nongloved hand.
- *If* saline drops are to be instilled, put in the drops at this time.
- With your thumb *off* the opening, insert the catheter without touching the part of the tube that goes into the opening. Never apply suction when inserting the catheter. Insert the catheter just beyond the length of the tracheostomy tube. Ask parent/ caregiver the specific length of catheter insertion.
- Stand to the side of child when suctioning. This procedure may produce a cough reflex, and the mucus may propel out of the stoma on you if you are standing directly in front of child.
- With your thumb *on* the opening *intermittently*, withdraw the catheter with a rotating or twisting motion. When first inserting the catheter, it is helpful to count "1-one thousand, 2-one thousand, 3-one thousand, 4-one thousand." Or, you may choose to take a breath and hold it when you start inserting the tube and remove it when you are no longer able to hold your breath. Remember that suctioning can cause children to be anxious as they cannot breathe during suctioning and that they may need time to rest afterward. If you need to suction again, wait at least 30 to 60 seconds before suctioning and rinse the catheter by putting the tip in the water and applying suction until the catheter is free of any mucus.
- Note any changes in color, thickness, or smell of the mucus, and report such changes to parent/caregiver.
- Turn off the suction machine. Dispose of equipment per procedure without letting the tip touch anything else.
- Offer comfort to child as needed.
- Remove gloves and wash hands.

Communication

- Share with parent/caregiver how suctioning is progressing.
- Notify parent/caregiver of any changes in color, thickness, or smell of the mucus.
- Ask parent/caregiver to list specific activity restrictions and how stoma is to be protected on the playground. Ask to list specific

safety concerns associated with child having a tracheostomy such as avoiding swimming pools and streams. Parent/caregiver may request that child remains indoors on very windy days to prevent small items from entering stoma.

Resources

- http://tracheostomy.com
- www.cafamily.org.uk
- http://wellness.ucdavis.edu/child_health/special_needs/pediatric_tracheostomy

Procedure E

Tube Feedings

This procedure is also referred to as gastric gavage, nasogastric gavage, or gastrostomy. A child who is unable to take nourishment or medications by mouth for a variety of health problems may have a tube inserted through the nose (NG-tube), mouth (OG-tube), or stomach (G-tube) or into the intestines (J-tube). Most school-age children will have a gastrostomy (stomach) tube or a gastrostomy button. Usually, children receive commercially prepared feedings continuously (bag and pump) or intermittently (bolus or bag) designated at certain times of the day. The health care provider and/or dietitian determine the type and amount of nourishment. Depending on the health care provider's instructions, children with tube feedings may also be taking some nourishment by mouth. Initially, the thought of tube feeding a child in your classroom may seem frightening, but with instructions it can be done.

Guidelines for Intermittent G-Tube Feedings

- Ask parent/caregiver the reason for child having a tube feeding and for any specific instructions from health care provider such as feeding schedule, amount of feeding and any special preparations, rate of flow of the feeding, and about how long feeding child should take. Ask whether child is to also eat solid food or drink fluids by mouth. Ask for any activity restrictions due to the tube (e.g., swimming, showers). Request that parent/caregiver initially demonstrate the tube feeding.
- Wash hands prior to tube feeding (*see* Procedure A) and put on disposable gloves.
- Gather equipment: large syringe (30–50 ml) without plunger or needle or funnel, tap water (unless otherwise indicated), and formula or medications usually given at room temperature.

- Be aware that most children are fed in a semi-reclining or sitting position. Position child with his or her head higher than the stomach. It is important to have contact with child during the feeding time; interact with and talk to child.
- *Bolus Feeding:* Attach funnel or syringe without plunger to feeding tube. Pour tap water (usually 1–2 ounces unless otherwise instructed) and then feeding into a syringe, not allowing air into the tubing or syringe. Raising or lowering the funnel/syringe controls the rate of feeding. When nourishment is completed, add tap water to clear tube and clamp or kink tubing. Disconnect syringe/funnel from the tube. Clamp/cap and secure tubing unless otherwise instructed. Be aware that, depending on child and tube/button, some children will need a decompression tube to vent air after the feeding.
- *Feeding Bag:* Clamp tubing. Fill bag and tubing with feeding. Hang bag from a pole or hook about 12 inches above child's stomach. Open the clamp and regulate the drip according to instructions. You may initially need to squeeze the bag to start the feeding. Control rate of flow with the clamp. The feeding should take 15 to 30 minutes. If feeding is given too fast, child may complain of sweating, nausea, vomiting, or diarrhea.
- Keep child in sitting position 30 to 60 minutes after feeding to prevent reflux (backward or return flow).
- Remove gloves and wash hands (*see* Procedure A).
- Wash feeding equipment with hot soapy water, rinse well, and air dry. Feeding supplies may be reused.

Communication

- Share with parent/caregiver how feedings are going, including any problems or changes. Ask for a written feeding plan to keep track of the schedule, amount, and type of feeding. Revise and update plan as necessary.
- Notify parent/caregiver if skin around the G-tube is warm, tender, bright red, swollen, or bleeding. Notify parent/caregiver immediately if site is red and sore or has green or white liquid where the tube enters the skin and the child has a fever or is vomiting.
- Notify parent/caregiver that the child may experience sweating, nausea, vomiting, or diarrhea.

- Notify parent/caregiver if the tube is blocked and you cannot remove blockage or if the tube is pulled out. With a blocked tube, try to *slowly* push water into the tube with a syringe. Use very slow and easy pushing. Never try to push any object into the tube to unclog it.
- Notify parent/caregiver if child has a temperature higher than 101 degrees.

Resources

- www.cincinnatichildrens.org
- www.pedslink.com
- www.oralcancerfoundation.org/dental/tube_feeding.htm

Procedure F

Medical Emergencies

The following are examples of child medical emergencies that may warrant immediate medical attention:

- Experiencing chest or abdominal pain or pressure
- Difficulty with breathing or shortness of breath
- Large puncture wounds (including human bites)
- Bite from an unknown animal, snake, or insect
- Fall that results in a loss of consciousness
- Fall where child ends up on his or her back
- Hitting the head or suffering a head injury
- Burns
- Suspected of inhaling, swallowing, or touching poisonous substances
- Suspected of taking an overdose of drugs
- Bleeding that does not stop after applying pressure
- Unable to move or has difficulty in moving; feels strange sensations or acts peculiar (or different in some way) after a fall or an injury
- Sudden slurred speech
- Hitting the head, followed by bleeding or drainage from the ears, nose, and/or eyes
- Injection with the EpiPen (*see* Procedure I)
- Broken bones
- Severe asthmatic episode
- Severe allergic reaction
- Severe pain in any part of the body
- Cannot stop vomiting, bleeding from the face, or having diarrhea episodes
- Complaints of sudden dizziness, weakness, or change in vision
- Expression of suicidal or homicidal feelings

- Victim of abuse
- Experiencing hallucinations and being incoherent in thoughts
- Complaining of a stiff neck along with a fever or headache
- Having pupils that are unequal or experiencing sudden blindness
- Inability to walk without staggering
- Experiencing persistent seizure activity
- Stopped breathing

Any time you are not comfortable with a medical situation, call for assistance by activating the local emergency medical system. You may save a child's life!

Be ready to give the following:

- Your location, including cross streets and landmarks
- The telephone number you are calling from in case you become disconnected
- Your name
- What happened
- Who is injured and how many are injured
- Condition of child needing assistance (e.g., conscious or unconscious, location of bleeding if any, whether breathing on own, whether complaining of pain)
- What is being done to help child

Do not hang up first. Let the dispatcher hang up first.

Procedure G

Pets in the Classroom

Guidelines for Keeping Pets in the Classroom

- Be aware that pets/reptiles kept in the classroom should not be handled unless appropriate hand-washing and cleanup facilities are available and made accessible.
- Be aware that after any handling of pets/reptiles, hands should be washed with soap (antibacterial preferred) and water (*see* Procedure A).
- Keep pets/reptiles away from areas where food is stored, prepared, or eaten.
- Do not use the same sink to clean pet/reptile accessories or caging material where food is prepared.
- Do not allow children to touch food or eating utensils after touching pets/reptiles.
- Keep pet/reptile cages as clean as possible.
- Do not permit unsupervised handling of pets/reptiles by children.
- Clean caging material with rubber gloves.
- When washing pet/reptile cages/accessories, avoid splashes to the face or wear goggles.
- Do not use bathroom facilities for pet-/reptile-related activities unless they are thoroughly disinfected.
- Consult veterinarian or pet care professional for recommendations on soaps and other products useful for disinfecting hands and surfaces.
- Avoid keeping reptiles in places with very young children.
- Be aware that disinfectant lotions, sprays, or similar products should be carried whenever reptiles are going to be handled and hand-washing facilities may be absent such as on field trip events.

Selected Infectious Diseases Related to Pets

Infectious Disease	Pets	Susceptibility
Cryptococcus (krip toe kok' us)	Birds (especially pigeons)	Children with immune disorders
Psittacosis (sit uh ko' sis)	Birds (especially parrots and parakeets)	Bird owners
Cat scratch disease	Cats	Cat owners and children with immune disorders
Cryptosporidium (krip toe spor id' ee um)	Cats	Children with immune disorders
Dipylidium	Dog and cat fleas and tapeworms	Children of women who were infected during pregnancy and children with immune system disorders
Hookworms	Puppies and kittens	Owners of puppies and kittens, children, pregnant women, and persons who are malnourished
Rabies	Unvaccinated dogs, cats, skunks, foxes, raccoons, coyotes, and bats	Children who have been bitten by animals with rabies
Hantavirus	Rodent droppings, urine, and saliva (virus can spread through the air and on dust particles)	Children who are camping, hiking, or engaging in outdoor hobbies
Ringworms	Cats and dogs	Children and owners of cats and dogs
Toxocariasis (tox o cari' a sis) (roundworms)	Dogs (especially puppies) and cats	Children
Salmonellosis	Small animals/reptiles such as hamsters, gerbils, pet mice, pet rats, guinea pigs, rabbits, lizards, snakes, turtles, and iguanas	Children, owners of these pets/reptiles, children with immune disorders, children with organ transplants, and children undergoing radiation therapy
Lymphocytic choriomeningitis (lim fo sit' ik kor ee o men in ji' tis)	Pet mice or hamsters	Owners of pet mice or hamsters and children whose mothers became infected during pregnancy

Procedure H

Immunizations

The Advisory Committee on Immunization Practices (ACIP) is a national advisory group made up of experts from the Centers for Disease Control and Prevention (www.cdc.gov), the American Academy of Pediatrics (www.aap.org), and the American Academy of Family Physicians. Each year, the ACIP issues an updated Recommended Childhood Immunization Schedule (www.cdc.gov/nip/acip). Its Web site also features fact sheets, statistics, a glossary, and links to organizations offering additional information.

State-by-state school entry vaccination requirements may be found at the National Network for Immunization Information (NNii) Web site (www.immunizationinfo.org). The NNii is a partnership of the American Academy of Pediatrics, the American Academy of Family Physicians, the American Nurses Association, and several other medical societies concerned with school health.

Recommended Childhood and Adolescent Immunization Schedule -- United States, 2003

Vaccine ▼ / Age ▶	Birth	1 mo	2 mos	4 mos	6 mos	12 mos	15 mos	18 mos	24 mos	4-6 yrs	11-12 yrs	13-18 yrs
Hepatitis B[1]	HepB #1	only if mother HBsAg (-)									HepB series	
		HepB #2			HepB #3							
Diphtheria, Tetanus, Pertussis[2]			DTaP	DTaP	DTaP		DTaP	DTaP		DTaP	Td	Td
Haemophilus influenzae Type b[3]			Hib	Hib	Hib	Hib	Hib					
Inactivated Polio			IPV	IPV		IPV		IPV		IPV		
Measles, Mumps, Rubella[4]						MMR #1				MMR #2	MMR #2	MMR #2
Varicella[5]						Varicella	Varicella			Varicella	Varicella	
Pneumococcal[6]			PCV	PCV	PCV	PCV	PCV		PCV	PCV / PPV	PPV	
Hepatitis A[7]										Hepatitis A series	Hepatitis A series	
Influenza[8]						Influenza (yearly)						

Vaccines below this line are for selected populations

This schedule indicates the recommended ages for routine administration of currently licensed childhood vaccines, as of December 1, 2002, for children through age 18 years. Any dose not given at the recommended age should be given at any subsequent visit when indicated and feasible. ▨ Indicates age groups that warrant special effort to administer those vaccines not previously given. Additional vaccines may be licensed and recommended during the year. Licensed combination vaccines may be used whenever any components of the combination are indicated and the vaccine's other components are not contraindicated. Providers should consult the manufacturers' package inserts for detailed recommendations.

Approved by the Advisory Committee on Immunization Practices (www.cdc.gov/nip/acip), the American Academy of Pediatrics (www.aap.org), and the American Academy of Family Physicians (www.aafp.org).

**Footnotes: Recommended Childhood Immunization Schedule
United States, 2002**

1. Hepatitis B vaccine (Hep B). All infants should receive the first dose of hepatitis B vaccine soon after birth and before hospital discharge; the first dose may also be given by age 2 months if the infant's mother is HBsAg-negative. Only monovalent hepatitis B vaccine can be used for the birth dose. Monovalent or combination vaccine containing Hep B may be used to complete the series; four doses of vaccine may be administered if combination vaccine is used. The second dose should be given at least 4 weeks after the first dose, except for Hib-containing vaccine which cannot be administered before age 6 weeks. The third dose should be given at least 16 weeks after the first dose and at least 8 weeks after the second dose. The last dose in the vaccination series (third or fourth dose) should not be administered before age 6 months.

Infants born to HBsAg-positive mothers should receive hepatitis B vaccine and 0.5 mL hepatitis B immune globulin (HBIG) within 12 hours of birth at separate sites. The second dose is recommended at age 1-2 months and the vaccination series should be completed (third or fourth dose) at age 6 months.

Infants born to mothers whose HBsAg status is unknown should receive the first dose of the hepatitis B vaccine series within 12 hours of birth. Maternal blood should be drawn at the time of delivery to determine the mother's HBsAg status; if the HBsAg test is positive, the infant should receive HBIG as soon as possible (no later than age 1 week).

2. Diphtheria and tetanus toxoids and acellular pertussis vaccine (DTaP). The fourth dose of DTaP may be administered as early as age 12 months, provided 6 months have elapsed since the third dose and the child is unlikely to return at age 15-18 months. **Tetanus and diphtheria toxoids (Td)** is recommended at age 11-12 years if at least 5 years have elapsed since the last dose of tetanus and diphtheria toxoid-containing vaccine. Subsequent routine Td boosters are recommended every 10 years.

3. *Haemophilus influenzae* type b (Hib) conjugate vaccine. Three Hib conjugate vaccines are licensed for infant use. If PRP-OMP (PedvaxHIB® or ComVax® [Merck]) is administered at ages 2 and 4 months, a dose at age 6 months is not required. DTaP/Hib combination products should not be used for primary immunization in infants at age 2, 4 or 6 months, but can be used as boosters following any Hib vaccine.

4. Inactivated poliovirus vaccine (IPV). An all-IPV schedule is recommended for routine childhood poliovirus vaccination in the United States. All children should receive four doses of IPV at age 2 months, 4 months, 6-18 months, and 4-6 years.

5. Measles, mumps, and rubella vaccine (MMR). The second dose of MMR is recommended routinely at age 4-6 years but may be administered during any visit, provided at least 4 weeks have elapsed since the first dose and that both doses are administered beginning at or after age 12 months. Those who have not previously received the second dose should complete the schedule by the visit at age 11-12 years.

6. Varicella vaccine. Varicella vaccine is recommended at any visit at or after age 12 months for susceptible children (i.e. those who lack a reliable history of chickenpox). Susceptible persons aged ! 13 years should receive two doses, given at least 4 weeks apart.

7. Pneumococcal vaccine. The heptavalent **pneumococcal conjugate vaccine (PCV)** is recommended for all children aged 2-23 months and for certain children aged 24-59 months. **Pneumococcal polysaccharide vaccine (PPV)** is recommended in addition to PCV for certain high-risk groups. See *MMWR* 2000;49(RR-9);1-37.

8. Hepatitis A vaccine. Hepatitis A vaccine is recommended for use in selected states and regions, and for certain high-risk groups; consult your local public health authority. See *MMWR* 1999;48(RR-12);1-37.

9. Influenza vaccine. Influenza vaccine is recommended annually for children age ! 6 months with certain risk factors (including but not limited to asthma, cardiac disease, sickle cell disease, HIV and diabetes; see *MMWR* 2001;50(RR-4);1-44), and can be administered to all others wishing to obtain immunity. Children aged ∀12 years should receive vaccine in a dosage appropriate for their age (0.25 mL if age 6-35 months or 0.5 mL if aged # 3 years). Children aged ∀ 8 years who are receiving influenza vaccine for the first time should receive two doses separated by at least 4 weeks.

Additional information about vaccines, vaccine supply, and contraindications for immunization, is available at www.cdc.gov/nip or at the National Immunization Hotline, 800-232-2522 (English) or 800-232-0233 (Spanish).

Procedure I

EpiPen

EpiPen is a portable auto-injecting device available from Dey, L. P. (Napa, CA). EpiPen can be used in an emergency to administer epinephrine in response to a severe allergic reaction (anaphylaxis). A complete guide to using EpiPen can be found at Dey's Allergic Reaction Central Web site (www.allergic-reactions.com).

NDC 49502-500-01 (EPIPEN)
NDC 49502-500-02 (EPIPEN 2-PAK)
NDC 49502-501-01 (EPIPEN JR)
NDC 49502-501-02 (EPIPEN JR 2-PAK)

> **EPIPEN® & EPIPEN® JR**
> (epinephrine) Auto-Injectors
> *For allergic emergencies (anaphylaxis)*

IMPORTANT INFORMATION
Both EPIPEN® & EPIPEN® JR
-- are disposable, prefilled automatic injection devices
-- are for allergic emergencies
-- contain a single dose of epinephrine (intramuscular)
-- are available by prescription only (Rx)
-- contain **no latex**

Amount of epinephrine delivered
EPIPEN®   = one dose of **0.30mg** epinephrine *(USP, 1:1000, 0.3mL)*
EPIPEN® JR = one dose of **0.15 mg** epinephrine *(USP, 1:2000, 0.3mL)*
-- *Note:* most of the liquid (about 90%)
        stays in the auto-injector after use and cannot be reused

When to Use

Use the **EPIPEN®/EPIPEN® JR** auto-injector *only* if you are a hypersensitive (allergic) person and your doctor has prescribed it for allergic emergencies. Such emergencies may occur from insect stings or bites, foods, drugs, latex, other allergens, exercise-induced anaphylaxis, or unknown causes (idiopathic).

Emergency Treatment of Allergic Reaction (Anaphylaxis)

-- If you experience the signs and symptoms described by your physician:
  -- Use the **EPIPEN®/EPIPEN® JR** auto-injector immediately, **through clothing if necessary.**
  -- Repeat injection with an additional **EPIPEN®** or **EPIPEN® JR** may be necessary- consult your physician.
  -- Follow "Directions for Use" section carefully.
  -- Then follow steps in "Immediately After Use" section.
  -- Avoid exertion.
-- If you have been stung by an insect:
  -- Remove insect stinger with your fingernails if possible.
  -- Do <u>not</u> squeeze, pinch, or push it deeper into the skin.
  -- If available, apply ice packs or sodium bicarbonate soaks to the stung area.

Care & Storage

-- Keep the **EPIPEN®/EPIPEN® JR** auto-injector ready for use at all times.
-- Store:
  -- in a dark place at room temperature (59-86°F)
  -- plastic carrying tube provides added UV light protection
  -- do NOT refrigerate
  -- do NOT expose to extreme cold or heat
-- Note expiration date on the unit (month & year)
  -- example: "Aug. 02" = Aug. 31, 2002
  -- replace it before the expiration date
  -- see below to enroll in the Expiration Reminder Program
  -- always have at least one unexpired unit on hand
-- Examine contents in clear window of auto-injector periodically
  -- replace the unit if the solution is discolored or contains solid particles (precipitate)
  -- the physician may recommend emergency use of an auto-injector with discolored contents rather than to postpone treatment

WARNING

-- **Never put thumb, fingers, or hand over black tip.** Needle comes out of black tip. Accidental injection into hands or feet may result in loss of blood flow to these areas. If this happens, go immediately to the nearest emergency room.
-- **EPIPEN®/EPIPEN® JR** should be injected *only* into the outer thigh (see "Directions for Use").
-- **Do <u>NOT</u> remove gray activation cap until ready to use.**

DIRECTIONS FOR USE

--Follow these directions *only* when ready to use.
--**Never put thumb, fingers, or hand over black tip.**
--**Do <u>NOT</u> remove gray activation cap until ready to use.**

1) Familiarize yourself with the unit.

Black Tip (needle comes out during use)   Clear Window   Gray Activation Cap (do **NOT** remove until ready to use)

<--- - - Auto-Injector - - - ->

2) Grasp unit, with the black tip pointing downward.
3) Form a fist around the auto-injector (black tip down).
4) With your other hand, pull off the gray activation cap.

5) Hold black tip near outer thigh.

6) Swing and **jab firmly** into outer thigh so that auto-injector is perpendicular (at a 90° angle) to the thigh.

7) Hold **firmly in thigh** for several seconds.

8) Remove unit, massage injection area for several seconds.

9) Check black tip:
   -- if needle is exposed, you received the dose
   -- if not, repeat steps #5-8

10) *Note:* most of the liquid (about 90%) stays in the auto-injector and cannot be reused.

11) Bend the needle back against a hard surface.

12) Carefully put the unit (needle first) back into the carrying tube (*without* the gray activation cap)

13) Recap the carrying tube.

14) See "Immediately After Use" box on right side.

IMMEDIATELY AFTER USE

-- **Go immediately to the nearest hospital emergency room.**
You may need further medical attention.

-- Tell the physician that you have received an injection of epinephrine (show your thigh).

-- Give your used EPIPEN®/EPIPEN® JR to the physician for inspection and proper disposal.

MANUFACTURED FOR DEY,
NAPA, CALIFORNIA 94558, U.S.A.
by Meridian Medical Technologies, Inc.
Columbia, MD 21046, U.S.A.
U.S. Patent No. 4,031,893
03 535 00A 12/00

Bibliography

American Dental Association, Council on Scientific Affairs. (1999). The dental team and latex hypersensitivity. *Journal of the American Dental Association, 130*, 257–264.

Anderson, J. A. (1997). Milk, eggs, and peanuts: Food allergies in children. *American Family Physician, 56*, 1365–1374.

Ball, J., & Bindler, R. (1999). *Pediatric nursing: Caring for children.* Upper Saddle River, NJ: Appleton & Lange.

Behrman, R., & Kleigman, R. (1998). *Nelson's essentials of pediatrics.* Philadelphia: W. B. Saunders.

Bernardo, L. M., & Bove, M. (1993). *Pediatric emergency nursing procedures.* Boston: Jones & Bartlett.

Boynton, R. W., Dunn, E. S., & Stephens, C. R. (1998). *Manual of ambulatory pediatrics* (4th ed.). Philadelphia: J. B. Lippincott.

Bradley, B. J. (1996, October). Tinea capitis today: What nurses need to know about identifying and managing fungal infections of the scalp in the school setting. *Journal of School Nurses* (Special supplement).

Bragdon, A. D., & Gamon, D. (2000). *Brains that work a little bit differently.* Cape Cod, MA: Brainwaves Center.

Brewer, E., & Angel, K. (1992). *Parenting a child with arthritis.* Los Angeles: RGA Publishing Group.

Burns, C., Barber, N., Brady, M., & Dunn, A. (1996). *Pediatric primary care: A handbook for nurse practitioners.* Philadelphia: W. B. Saunders.

Casella, J. F., Bowers, D. C., & Pelidis, M. A. (1997). Disorders of coagulation. In K. B. Johnson & F. A. Oski (Eds.), *Oski's essential pediatrics* (pp. 1472–1491). Philadelphia: J. B. Lippincott.

Cassidy, J., & Petty, R. (1990). *Textbook of pediatric rheumatology* (2nd ed.). New York: Churchill Livingstone.

Chandra, R. K. (1997). Food hypersensitivity and allergic disease: A selective review. *American Journal of Clinical Nutrition, 66*, S526-S529.

Cherry, J. D. (1999). Parvovirus infections in children and adults. *Advances in Pediatrics, 46*, 245–269.

Coakley-Maller, C., & Shea, M. (1997). Respiratory infections in children: Preparing for the fall and winter. *Advances for Nurse Practitioner, 5*(9), 20–27.

Delfico, A. J., Dormans, J. P., Craythorne, C. B., & Templeton, J. J. (1997). Intraoperative anaphylaxis due to allergy to latex in children who have cerebral palsy: A report of six cases. *Developmental Medicine & Child Neurology, 39,* 194–197.

DeStefanol Lewis, K., & Thomson, H. B. (1986). *Manual of school health.* Menlo Park, CA: Addison-Wesley.

Duggan, C. (1996). HIV infection in children. *Pediatric Nursing, 8*(10), 32.

Faust, K., Shrewsbury, C., Zaglaniczny, K., & Jarrett, M. (1999). A comparative analysis of latex allergy in the healthy versus high-risk pediatric population. *ANA Journal, 67,* 461–466.

Fox, J. A. (2002). *Primary health care of infants, children, and adolescents* (2nd ed.). St. Louis, MO: C. V. Mosby.

Gildea, J. H. (1998). Human parvovirus B19: Flushing in face though healthy (fifth disease and more). *Pediatric Nursing, 24,* 325–331.

Graham, M. V., & Uphold, C. R. (1999). *Clinical guidelines in child health.* Gainesville, FL: Barmarrae Books.

Greene, C. (Ed.). (1995). *First aid for children fast: Emergency procedures for all parents and caregivers.* New York: Dorling Kindersley.

Grose, C. (1997). Varicella-zoster virus infection. In K. B. Johnson & F. A. Oski (Eds.), *Oski's essential pediatrics* (pp. 1127–1130). Philadelphia: J. B. Lippincott.

Hale, C. M., & Polder, J. A. (1997). *The ABC's of safe and healthy child care: A handbook for child care providers.* Washington, DC: U.S. Department of Health and Human Services, Public Health Service, Centers for Disease Control and Prevention.

Hoeman, S. P. (2002). *Rehabilitation nursing: Process, application, and outcomes* (3rd ed.). St. Louis, MO: C. V. Mosby.

Jackson, P. L., & Vessey, J. A. (1996). *Primary care of the child with a chronic condition* (2nd ed.). St. Louis, MO: C. V. Mosby.

Kerr, J. R., & Preston, N. M. (2001). Current pharmacotherapy of pertussis. *Expert Opinions in Pharmacotherapy, 2,* 1275–1282.

Kline, M. W. (1997). Otitis media. In K. B. Johnson & F. A. Oski (Eds.), *Oski's essential pediatrics* (pp. 1301–1303). Philadelphia: J. B. Lippincott.

Klippel, J., & Weyand, C. (1997). *Primer on the rheumatic diseases* (11th ed.). Atlanta, GA: Arthritis Foundation.

Kranowitz, C. S. (1998). *The out-of-sync child: Recognizing and coping with sensory integration dysfunction.* New York: Skylight Press.

Lee, M. H., & Kim, K. T. (1998). Latex allergy: A relevant issue in the general pediatric population. *Journal of Pediatric Health Care, 12,* 242–246.

Leung, A. K., & Robson, W. L. (1996). Evaluating the child with chronic diarrhea. *American Family Physician, 53,* 635–643.

Lubkin, I. M., & Larsen, P. D. (2002). *Chronic illness: Impact and interventions* (5th ed.). Boston: Jones & Bartlett.

Matson, D. O. (1994). Viral gastroenteritis in day-care settings: Epidemiology and new developments. *Pediatrics, 94,* 999–1001.

McCarthy, A. M., Williams, J. K., & Eidal, L. (1996). Children with chronic conditions: Educators' views. *Journal of Pediatric Health Care, 10,* 272–279.

Meeropol, E. V. (1998). The RUBBER tool: Screening children for latex allergy. *Journal of Pediatric Health Care, 12,* 320–323.

Mudd, K. M., & Noone, S. A. (1995). Management of severe food allergy in the school setting. *Journal of School Nursing, 11*(3), 30–32.

Nowicki, M., & Balistreri, W. (1992). Hepatitis A to E: Building up the alphabet. *Contemporary Pediatrics, 9*(11), 118–128.

Oski, F. (1994). *Principles and practice of pediatrics.* Philadelphia: J. B. Lippincott.

Petty, S. (1997). *Piercing: A guide to safety.* Waco, TX: Health EDCO.

Pillitteri, A. (1999). Nursing care of the child with an infectious disorder. In A. Pillitteri (Ed.), *Child health nursing* (pp. 667–697). Philadelphia: J. B. Lippincott.

Potts, N., & Mandelco, B. (2002). *Pediatric nursing: Caring for children and their families.* Clifton Park, NY: Delmar.

Sampson, H. A., & Burks, A. W. (1996). Mechanisms of food allergy. *Annual Review of Nutrition, 16,* 161–177.

Santen, S. A., & Altieri, M. F. (2001). Pediatric urinary tract infection. *Emergency Medicine Clinics of North America, 19,* 675–690.

Schmitt, B. D. (1993). When your child has an eye infection with pus. *Contemporary Pediatrics, 10*(3), 117–118.

Silverman, P. R. (2000). *Never too young to know: Death in children's lives.* New York: Oxford University Press.

Stiefel, L. (1995). Erythemia infectiosum (fifth disease). *Pediatrics in Review, 16,* 474–475.

Tipsord-Klinkhammer, B., & Andreoni, C. P. (1998). *Quick reference for emergency nursing.* Philadelphia: W. B. Saunders.

Votroubek, W. L., & Townsend, J. L. (1997). *Pediatric home care* (2nd ed.). Gaithersburg, MD: Aspen.

Waley, L. F., & Wong, D. L. (2000). *Nursing care of infants and children.* St. Louis, MO: C. V. Mosby.

Ward, R. G. (2001). Tourette syndrome. *Nursing Spectrum, 14,* 22–24.

Wilkinson, B. (1998). *Coping with the dangers of tattooing, body piercing, and branding.* New York: Rosen Publishing Group.

Wong, D. L., & Hockenberry-Eaton, M. (2001). *Wong's essentials of pediatric nursing.* St. Louis, MO: C. V. Mosby.

Index

Abrasions, 343
Abscessed teeth, 318-319
Abuse, 16-17, 18, 23
Accidental injury, 5-6
Acquired immunodeficiency syndrome
    (AIDS), 180-182
Acute psychosis, 272-274
ADHD (attention deficit/hyperactivity
    disorder), 70-72
Adjustment disorder, 32-33
Advisory Committee on Immunization
    Practices (ACIP), 357
Affective violence, 16, 19
Aggressive behaviors, 25
Alcohol abuse, 34-36
Allergic rhinitis, 42-43
Allergies, 4
    drug reactions, 37-38
    EpiPen use, 361-364
    food intolerances, 39-41
    hay fever, 42-43
    insect bites/stings, 193-196
    latex allergy, 44-46
    poison oak/ivy/sumac, 254-255
    snake bites, 289-291
    spider bites, 292-293
Anaphylactic shock, 4, 47-49, 361, 362
Anemia, 50-51
Anger, 52-54
    childhood hospitalizations and, 9
    child self-hatred and, 25
    family systems and, 11-12
Animal bites, 55-56
Animal-borne diseases, 355-356
Anorexia, 130-131
Antiviolence interventions, 19
Anxiety disorder:
    fear of strangers/separation
        anxiety, 60-61

generalized anxiety, 57-59
    hospitalization and, 9
Appendicitis, 62-63
Arthritis, 199-201
Aspergers's disorder, 64-66
Asthma, 6-7, 67-69
Astigmatism, 331-332
Athlete's foot, 285-286
Atopic dermatitis (AD), 132-133
Attention deficit/hyperactivity
    disorder (ADHD), 70-72
Autistic disorder, 73-75
    Asperger's disorder, 64-66

Bacterial meningitis, 214-216
Bagging, 191-192
Becker's disease, 221-223
Bed-wetting, 85-86
Behavior disorders, 12
    aggressive actions, 25
    conduct disorder, 76-78
    discrimination and, 21
    impulse control, 25-26
    oppositional defiant disorder, 79-81
    violence, exposure to, 19
Bereavement, 15-16, 154-156
Bipolar disorder, 82-84
Bisexual identity, 27-30
Bites:
    allergic reactions to, 4
    animal bites, 55-56
    human bites, 183-184
    insect bites/stings, 193-195
    snake bites, 289-291
    spider bites, 292-293
Bladder control problems, 85-86
Bladder infection, 329-330
Blended families, 13-14
Body piercing infection/reaction, 87-88

Borrelia burgdorferi infection, 206-208
Bowel control problems, 89-91
Breathing difficulties:
   asthma, 6-7, 67-69
   cystic fibrosis, 9, 114-115
   tracheostomies and, 347-349
Broken bones, 149-151, 345-346
Broken teeth, 322-323
Bronchitis, 92-93
Bullying, 16, 19
Burns, 94-96
   chemical eye splash, 139-140

Cancer, 97-99
Cardiac disease, 166-167
Care procedures. *See* Procedures
Cast care, 345-346
Cavities, 320-321
Centers for Disease Control and
   Prevention (CDC), 4, 5, 19, 357
Cerebral palsy (CP), 102-104
Chicken pox, 105-106
Child abuse, 16-17, 18, 23
Christmas disease, 172-173
Chronic cough, 92-93
Chronic dermatitis, 132-133
Chronic illness, 6-7, 14
Classroom health concerns, 3
  accidental injury, 5-6
  chronic illness, 6-7
  common health problems, 4-5
  disabilities, individualized
    education plans and, 7-9
  hospitalizations and, 9-10
  See also Community issues; Family
    systems; Stigmatization
Clinical depression, 116-118
Cognitive impairment, 124-125
Cold sores, 107-108
Color blindness, 109-111
Common cold, 4, 112-113
Community issues:
  child abuse/neglect, 16-17
  community violence, 18-19
  homelessness, 18
See also Stigmatization
Conduct disorder (CD), 76-78
Congenital heart disease, 166-167
Conjunctivitis, 246-248
Contact dermatitis, 132-133
Cooties, 4, 161-163
Corneal abrasion/laceration, 137-138
Cough, 92-93

CP (cerebral palsy), 102-104
Crohn's disease (CD), 187-188
Curvature of the spine, 275-276
Cuts, 343-344
Cystic fibrosis, 9, 114-115
Cystitis, 329-330

Deafness, 164-165
Death, 15-16
  homicide, 17, 19
  See also Grief
Dental caries, 322-323
Dental emergencies, 316-318
Depression, 15,17, 19, 116-118
Dermatitis, 132-133
Developmental issues:
  child abuse/neglect and, 17
  childhood hospitalizations and, 10
  chronic family illness, 14
  death and, 15-16
  self-esteem, 22-24
  violence, exposure to, 19
Diabetes, 119-121
Diarrhea, 122-123
Dirt ingestion, 244-245
Disabilities, 7-9, 14
Discrimination, 20-21
Divorce, 12-13
Down syndrome, 124-125
Drug abuse, 191-192
Drug reactions, 4, 37-38
Duchenne's disease, 221-223
Dystonia, 126-127

Earache, 128-129
Ear infection, 128-129
Eating disorders, 17, 128-129
EBV (Epstein-Barr virus), 217-218
Eczema, 132-133
Encopresis, 89-91
Enuresis, 85-86
Epilepsy, 9, 134-136
EpiPen use, 4, 362-364
Epistaxis, 224-225
Epstein-Barr virus (EBV), 217-218
Erythema infections, 147-148
Eye injury, 137-138
Eye scratch/trauma, 137-138
Eye splash, 139-140
Eye stye, 141-142

Family systems, 11
  anger/conflict within, 11-12

bi-nuclear family structure, 13
blended families, 13-14
child abuse/neglect, 16-17, 23
chronic illness/disability and, 14
death and, 15-16
divorce, 12-13
same-sex parents in, 28-29
sexual identity issues and, 27-30
See also Community issues
Farsightedness, 331-332
FAS (fetal alcohol syndrome),
    1396-1397
Fear:
    hospitalization and, 9
    stigmatization and, 20-21
Fear of situations/objects, 251-252
Fear of strangers, 9, 60-61, 249-250
Fecal incontinence, 89-91
Feeding procedures, 360-362
Fetal alcohol syndrome
    (FAS), 1396-1397
Fever, 1397-1399
Fever blisters, 108-109
Fifth disease, 147-148
First-aid. *See* Procedures
Flu, 122-123, 189-190
Folliculitis, 304-305
Food intolerance, 39-41
Fractures, 149-151, 345-346
Frostbite, 152-153
Fungal infections, 285-286

Gastric gavage, 350-352
Gastrostomy, 350-352
Gay identity, 27-30
Gender identity, 26-27
Generalized anxiety disorder, 57-59
Geophagia, 243-244
German measles, 209-210
Grief, 15-16, 154-156

Hand washing, 340-342
Hard of hearing, 164-165
Hard measles, 211-213
Hashimoto's thyroiditis, 318-319
Hay fever, 4, 42-43
Hazardous waste cleanup, 341
Headache, 157-158
Head injury, 159-160
Head lice, 4, 161-163
Health problems, 3, 4-5
Hearing loss/impairment, 164-165
Heart disease/defect, 166-167

Heat exhaustion/prostration,
    168-169
Heatstroke, 170-171
Hemophilia, 172-173
Hepatitis A, 174-175
Hepatitis B, 176-177
Hepatitis C, 178-179
Herpes simplex type, 1, 107-108
HIV/AIDS, 180-182
Homelessness, 18
Homesickness, 60-61
Homicide, 17, 19
Hookworms, 335-337
Hospitalization experience, 9-10
Huffing, 191-192
Human bites, 183-184
Human immunodeficiency virus
    (HIV), 180-182
Human parvovirus B19, 147-148
Hyperopia, 331-332

IBD (inflammatory bowel disease),
    187-188
IDDM (insulin-dependent
    diabetes), 119-120
IEP (individualized education
    plan), 7-9
IgE (latex) reaction, 44-46
Immunizations, 357
Impetigo, 185-186, 304-305
Impulse control, 25-26
Inclusive classrooms, 3, 6-7, 8
Individualized education plans
    (IEPs), 7-9
Individuals with Disabilities Education
    Act (IDEA), 7, 125
Infantile eczema, 132-133
Infectious hepatitis, 174-175
Infectious mononucleosis, 217-218
Infectious parotitis, 219-220
Inflammatory bowel disease
    (IBD), 187-188
Influenza, 189-190
Inhalant abuse, 191-192
Injuries:
    accidental injury, 5-6
    broken bones, 149-151
    child abuse and, 16-17
    eye scratch/trauma, 137-138
    head injury, 159-160
    spinal cord injury, 297-301
    tooth injuries, 322-323
Insect stings/bites, 4, 193-195

Insulin-dependent diabetes (IDDM), 119-121
Interventions:
    antiviolence programs, 19
    autism and, 65, 74
    chemotherapy, 98, 99
    clotting factor replacement therapy, 172
    See also Procedures; specific disorders
Intestinal flu, 122-123
Iron deficiency anemia, 50-51
Itch mites, 268-269

Jock itch, 285-286
Juvenile diabetes, 119-121
Juvenile rheumatoid arthritis (JRA), 199-201

Kidney infection, 329-330
Kissing disease, 217-218

Lacerations, 343-344
Latex allergy, 4, 44-46
LCP (Legg-Calvé-Perthes)
LEAP (Learning Experiences, an Alternative Program for Preschoolers and Parents) intervention, 65, 74
Legg-Calvé-Perthes disease (LCP), 203-4
Lesbian identity, 27-30
Leukemia, 97-99
Lice, 4, 161-163
Low energy, 50-51
Lupus, 203-205
Lyme disease, 206-208
Lymphoma, 97-99

Malignancy, 97-99
Manic depressive disorder, 82-84
MD (muscular dystrophy), 221-223
Measles, 209-210
Measles rubeola, 211-213
Media influence, 18
Medical emergencies, 353-354
Meningitis, 214-216
Meningocele, 294-296
Mental retardation, 17, 124-125
Mild autism, 64-66
Mites, 4, 268-269
Mononucleosis, 217-218
Mood disorders:
    bipolar mood disorder, 82-84

suicidal behavior in, 310-311
    unipolar mood disorder, 116-118
Morbid obesity, 228-229
Mourning, 15-16, 154-156
Mumps, 219-220
Muscular dystrophy (MD), 221-223
Mutism, 240-241
Myelomeningocele, 294-296
Myopia, 331-332

Nasogastric gavage, 350-352
Nasopharyngitis, 112-113
National Network for Immunization Information (NNii), 357
Neglect, 16-17
Neural tube defect, 294-296
Night terrors, 287-288
Nosebleed, 224-225
NRL, 44-46
Nystagmus, 331-332

Obesity, 226-227, 228-229
Obsessive compulsive disorder (OCD), 230-232
Oppositional defiant disorder (ODD), 79-81
Oral abscess, 320-321
Organ transplant, 233-234
Otitis externa, 312-313
Otitis media, 128-129
Over anxiety, 57-59, 60-61
Overweight condition, 226-227

PANDAS (pediatric autoimmune neuropsychiatric disorder), 237-239
Panic attacks/disorder, 9, 235-236
Paraplegia, 297-298
Parotitis, 219-220
Parvovirus B19, 147-148
Pediatric autoimmune neuropsychiatric disorder (PANDAS), 237-239
Pediculosis, 4, 161-163
Peer relationships, 24-26
Pertussis, 335-336
Pets in class, 355-356
Pharyngitis, 308-309
Phobia:
    social phobia, 240-241
    specific phobia, 242-243
Pica, 244-245
Pink eye, 246-248
Pinworms, 335-337

Plaster casts, 345-346
Pneumonia, 249-250
Poisoning, 251-253
    lead poisoning, 201-202
    poison oak/ivy/sumac, 254-255
Posttraumatic stress disorder
    (PTSD), 17, 256-257
Prader-Willi syndrome, 228-229
Prejudice, 20-21
Preventative measures. *See* Procedures
Procedures:
    accidental injury, 5-6
    cast care, 345-346
    deep cuts/lacerations, 343-344
    EpiPen use, 362-364
    hand washing, 340-342
    immunizations, 357
    medical emergencies, 353-354
    minor cuts/abrasions, 343
    pets, classroom
        housing/care, 355-356
    spill cleanup, 341
    tracheostomy care, 347-349
    tube feedings, 350-352
Psoriasis, 258-259
Psychosis, 272-274
PTSD (posttraumatic stress
    disorder), 17, 256-257
Pyelonephritis, 329-330
Pyoderma, 304-305
Pyrexia, 145-146

Quadriplegia, 297-298

Red measles, 211-213
Reye's syndrome, 260-261
Rheumatic fever, 262-264
Rheumatoid arthritis, 199-201
Rhinovirus, 4, 112-113
Rickettsia rickettsii, 265-267
Ringworm, 285-286
Rocky Mountain spotted fever
    (RMSV), 265-267
Roundworms, 335-337
Royal disease, 172-173
Rubella, 209-210
Rubeola, 211-213
Runs, 122-123

Scabies, 268-269
Scalded skin syndrome, 304-305
Scarlet fever, 270-271
Schizophrenia, 272-274

Scoliosis, 275-276
Seizure disorders, 9, 134-136
Selective mutism, 240-241
Self-esteem, 22
    child abuse/neglect and, 16-17, 23
    chronic illness and, 7
    components of, 22
    development of, 22-24
    disabilities and, 8-9
    gender identity and, 27
    homelessness and, 18
    hospitalizations and, 10
    negative experiences and, 22-23
    peer relationships and, 25, 26
    See also Stigmatization
Self-mutilation, 17, 310-311
Self-starvation, 130-131
Sensory integration
    dysfunction, 277-279
Separation anxiety, 9, 60-61
Serum hepatitis, 176-177
Seven-day measles, 211-213
Seven-year itch, 268-269
Sex abuse, 17
Sexual acting out, 280-281
Sexual identity, 27-30
Shaming, 23
Shyness, 240-241
SI (sensory integration) dysfunction,
    277-279
Sickle cell anemia, 282-284
Skin infections:
    body piercing, 87-88
    cuts/abrasions, 343-344
    eczema, 132-133
    fungal infections, 285-286
    poison oak/ivy/sumac, 254-255
    psoriasis, 258-259
    staphylococcus aureus, 304-305
    tattooing infection/reaction, 314-315
Slapped cheek disease, 147-148
SLE (systemic lupus erythematosus),
    206-208
Sleep apnea, 287-288
Sleep disorders, 287-288
Sleepwalking, 287-288
Snake bites, 286-288
Sniffing, 191-192
Snorting, 191-192
Socialization process, 26
    anger control, 52
    gender identity roles, 27
Social phobia, 240-241

Specific phobia, 242-243
Spider bites, 292-293
Spill cleanup, 341
Spina bifida, 294-296
Spinal cord injury:
    acute care, 297-298
    long-term care, 9, 299-301
Spinal curvature, 275-276
Spinal meningitis, 214-216
Splinters, 3002-303
Staph infection, 305-305
Staphylococcus aureus, 304-305
Stereotyping, 21
Stigmatization, 20
    aggressive behaviors and, 25
    gender identity issues and, 26-27
    impulse control issues and, 25-26
    peer relationships and, 24-26
    prejudice/discrimination and, 20-21
    self-esteem and, 22-24
    sexual identity and, 27-30
    socialization process and, 26
    stereotyping and, 21
Stings, 4, 193-195
Stomachache, 306-307
Stomach flu, 122-123
Strep throat, 308-309
Stress response:
    adjustment disorder, 32-33
    hospitalizations and, 9-10
Stye, 141-142
Substance abuse, 17
    alcohol abuse, 34-36
    inhalant abuse, 191-192
Sugar diabetes, 119-121
Suicide, 310-311
Summer cold, 42-43
Swimmer's ear, 312-313
Synthetic casting material, 345
Systemic lupus erythematosus
    (SLE), 206-208

Tattooing infection/reaction, 314-315
TB (tuberculosis), 326-328

TEACCH (Treatment and Education of
    Autistic and Related
    Communication-Handicapped
    Children), 65, 74
Three-day measles, 209-210
Thyroid disorder, 316-317
Thyroiditis, 316-317
Tic disorder, 324-325
Tinea capitis, 285-286
Tinea cruris, 285-286
Tinea pedis, 285-286
Tonsillitis, 308-309
Tooth abscess, 318-319
Toothache, 320-321
Tooth injuries, 322-323
Tourette syndrome, 324-325
Tracheobronchitis, 92-93
Tracheostomies, 347-349
Trisomy, 21, 124-125
Tube feedings, 350-352
Tuberculosis (TB), 326-328

Ulcerative colitis (UC), 187-188
Unintentional injuries, 5-6
Unipolar mood disorder, 116-118
Upper respiratory infection
    (URI), 112-114
Urethritis, 329-330
Urinary tract infection (UTI), 329-330

Varicella, 105-106
Victimization:
    child abuse/neglect, 16-17
    community violence and, 18-19
    See also Stigmatization
Violence, 16-19
Viral meningitis, 214-216
Vision problems, 109-111, 331-332

Whipworms, 335-337
Whooping cough, 333-334
Worms, 335-337

**CORWIN
PRESS**

The Corwin Press logo—a raven striding across an open book—represents the happy union of courage and learning. We are a professional-level publisher of books and journals for K-12 educators, and we are committed to creating and providing resources that embody these qualities. Corwin's motto is "Success for All Learners."